JEALOUSY

Third Edition

Edited by

Gordon Clanton
Lynn G. Smith

University Press of America,® Inc.
Lanham • New York • Oxford

Copyright © 1998 by
Gordon Clanton and Lynn G. Smith

University Press of America,® Inc.
4720 Boston Way
Lanham, Maryland 20706

12 Hid's Copse Rd.
Cummor Hill, Oxford OX2 9JJ

Library of Congress Cataloging-in-Publication Data

Jealousy / edited by Gordon Clanton, Lynn G. Smith. —3rd ed.
p.   cm.
Includes bibliographical references.
1. Jealousy. I. Clanton, Gordon. II. Smith, Lynn G.
BF575.J4J4   1997   152.4'8—DC21   97-41213 CIP

ISBN 0-7618-0949-X (pbk: alk. ppr.)

Contents

Preface to the Third Edition   v

Preface to the First Edition   vii

INTRODUCTION:
Keys to an Understanding of Jealousy   1

I. EXPERIENCING JEALOUSY   13

1   *Confessions of a Jealous Wife*, Judith Viorst, 17
2   *Taming the Green-eyed Monster*,
      Norman M. Lobsenz, 26
3   *On Sexual Jealousy*, Karen Durbin, 36

II. JEALOUSY AND THE PERSON   47

4   *Jealousy in Children*, Hermann Vollmer, 53
5   *Jealousy at Summerhill*, A. S. Neill, 66
6   *Jealousy: A Depth-psychological Perspective*,
      Chris Downing, 72
7   *Fidelity and Jealousy*, Robert Seidenberg, 81
8   *The Social Psychology of Jealousy*,
      Elaine Hatfield and G. William Walster, 91
9   *Romantic Love and Sexual Jealousy*,
      Ellen Berscheid and Jack Fei, 101

III. JEALOUSY AND CULTURE   111

10   *Jealousy: Primitive and Civilized*,
      Margaret Mead, 115
11   *Jealousy and Sexual Property*, Kingsley Davis, 129
12   *Jealousy and American Values*,
      Robert N. Whitehurst, 136
13   *Jealousy and Marriage*, Jessie Bernard, 141
14   *Jealousy Among the Swingers*, Brian G. Gilmartin, 152

Contents

IV. MANAGING JEALOUSY   **159**

   15 *Avoiding Destructive Jealousy*, Ben N. Ard, Jr., 166
   16 *Rational and Irrational Jealousy*, Albert Ellis, 170
   17 *Beyond Jealousy and Possessiveness*,
            Ronald Mazur, 181
   18 *Jealousy: Techniques for Intervention*,
            Larry L. Constantine, 190
   19 *Jealousy Workshops*,
            Robert and Margaret Blood, 199

SYNTHESIS:
Jealousy and Intimate Partnership Today   **209**

APPENDIX I:
Frontiers of Jealousy Research   **241**

APPENDIX II:
Jealousy in American Culture, 1945-1985   **258**

APPENDIX III:
Developmental Correlates of Jealousy   **278**

APPENDIX IV:
A Sociology of Jealousy   **297**

Bibliography   **315**

Preface to the Third Edition

This book, first published in 1977 by Prentice-Hall, is an integrated anthology of writings on jealousy that will be useful to researchers, students, and helping professionals — and to individuals and couples seeking a better understanding of their feelings and relationships.

The book includes 19 chapters on various aspects of jealousy by sociologists, psychologists, and three perceptive journalists. As with any interdisciplinary collection, the points of view are diverse, the vocabularies are disparate, and the findings are not all of equal weight.

The 19 chapters, comprising about half of the book, are framed, interpreted, and integrated by means of the Preface, the Introduction, the section introductions, the comments before and after the collected articles, and the Synthesis. Taken together, these connective materials will give the reader the main findings and conclusions of the book.

This third edition includes four additional articles by Gordon Clanton. You may wish to read these first, perhaps beginning with Appendix IV, because they summarize more recent research and express some key issues more clearly.

Appendix I, "Frontiers of Jealousy Research," argues that the jealousy felt by an individual is shaped by relationship issues, by social institutions, by society and culture.

Appendix II, "Jealousy in American Culture, 1945-1985," shows how and why jealousy has changed in recent decades — and it challenges the popular notion that jealousy is caused mostly by low self-esteem.

Appendix III, "Developmental Correlates of Jealousy" challenges the widespread assumption that adult jealousy is associated with early childhood conflicts or mental illness.

Appendix IV, "A Sociology of Jealousy," reveals the hidden usefulness of jealousy and summarizes many of the main points of this book.

Unlike many popular treatments, this book does not assume that jealousy is always bad, that the jealous individual is morally or psychologically defective, or that any particular lifestyle is the "cure" for jealousy.

Jealousy is a protective reaction to a perceived threat to a valued relationship or to its quality.   More specifically, jealousy protects marriage (and relationships leading to marriage) from adultery (and other forms of betrayal).

Although often dismissed as useless, *jealousy is useful* because it helps to preserve marriage, thus contributing to social order.   Although some episodes of jealousy are inappropriate and unconstructive, some jealousy is necessary to protect love and marriage. The frantic search for the "cure" for jealousy often overlooks its protective function and short-circuits the quest for constructive ways of protecting and nurturing love and marriage.

Although neither of the editors are clinicians, we hope that readers will find this book useful for understanding jealousy in themselves and others. We encourage an emphasis on *normal* jealousy, rather than pathological jealousy. We believe that most jealousy is best understood as a *relationship* problem, rather than as a personal problem rooted in the psychological inadequacies of one individual. We do not believe that most jealousy is caused by low self-esteem. Further discussion of the implications of this book for psychotherapy and self-understanding is available on a *Psychology Today* audio cassette from Gordon Clanton.

Gordon Clanton
Department of Sociology
San Diego State University
San Diego, California 92182

Lynn G. Smith
San Anselmo, California

July 1997

Preface

JEALOUSY TODAY: A NEW AMBIVALENCE

Virtually everyone experiences jealousy. Almost everyone agrees that the issue of jealousy is important in marriage and other forms of intimate partnership. And yet relatively little has been written on the subject. Much of the existing literature was published prior to the "sexual revolution" and the women's liberation movement. This book looks at jealousy in the context of these two very important and profoundly interrelated social phenomena of the last decade and a half.

These recent developments in our culture have introduced a new twist to an old problem. Until recently, a certain amount of jealousy was seen by most people as "normal" and as proof of love. Under these circumstances, some experience and expression of jealousy was expected in any intimate relationship. The proper management of jealousy simply involved keeping it under control, that is, making sure jealous feelings did not result in violence, rage, or the destruction of the pair-bond. In other words, the "problem of jealousy" focused on one's own jealousy and, by extension, on the partner's jealousy and its impact on one's life.

But things are no longer so simple. New developments in the understanding of sex, intimacy, and intimate partnership have led many middleclass (and above) persons to question the normalcy of jealousy. Influential psychologists and popular writers on sex and marriage have challenged the notion that jealousy is evidence of love. They have suggested instead that jealousy is evidence of personal insecurity and of lack of faith in the partner and in the relationship. Rather than cementing marriage, these voices declare, jealousy *weakens* it. And so the consumer of these new ideas begins to feel anxious about his/her jealousy. The simple concern about one's jealousy is joined by a new *guilt* about one's jealous feelings. The earlier concern about one's partner's jealousy and its impact on one's life is joined by a new concern about one's manipulations of the partner's guilt about his/her jealousy. And so on.

In recent years, then, a *new ambivalence* has attached itself to the ancient emotion of jealousy. This book has been constructed to address that ambivalence and to speak to the new, expanded "problem of jealousy" which recent developments have generated.

PLAN OF THIS BOOK

In the Introduction, *Keys to the Understanding of Jealousy,* the editors frame several key questions around which to organize inquiry *and* suggest something of the *range* of plausible answers. At the heart of the book stand four clusters of articles and excerpts in which we can find clues and, perhaps, some answers. These materials have been chosen, grouped, edited, introduced and interpreted so that the reader will discover and appreciate connections among them.

Part I, *Experiencing Jealousy,* spotlights three items from the popular media which reveal some of the ways in which jealousy is being felt and understood in the United States in the 1970s. Some tensions in the contemporary understanding of jealousy are introduced.

Part II, *Jealousy and the Person,* begins with an examination of those early experiences of jealousy which influence the feeling and interpretation of that emotion in adulthood. Suggestions are offered of ways in which parents can minimize the pain of jealousy for their children. The internal mechanisms of jealousy are explored from the psychoanalytic and social psychological perspectives.

Part III, *Jealousy and Culture,* presents materials from the sociological and anthropological perspectives and argues that the understanding and management of *one's own* jealousy is impossible without a clear grasp of the *social patternings and institutionalization* of jealousy.

Part IV, *Managing Jealousy*, explores the possibility that jealous feelings and behaviors can be modified by means of education or therapy. The contributors to this section are psychologists and marriage counselors who have worked with persons wishing to become less jealous.

In the Synthesis, *Jealousy and Intimate Partnership Today*, the editors seek to sum up the findings and explanations of the contributors, to suggest some answers to questions posed in the Introduction, and to explore the uses and abuses of jealousy in marriage and other forms of intimate association.

All parts of this book will not be equally interesting to every reader. You should be open to the possibility of skipping or skimming some of the material or of working through it in an order other than that suggested by the organization of this book. But it is a conviction of the editors that *the understanding and management of your own jealousy is unlikely if not impossible without a working knowledge of the psychological mechanisms and the social patternings of jealousy which are common to us all.*

The materials in Parts II and III demand a bit more effort from the reader than the journalistic pieces in Part I, and they contain less concrete advice than the "how to" articles in Part IV. They are, nevertheless, very relevant to the understanding and management of jealousy. We have edited this more challenging material for maximum accessibility.

Most of the contributors to this book are social scientists or "helping professionals." There are, of course, other bodies of literature pertinent to the study of jealousy. A collection of philosophical and/or literary reflections would be a valuable resource; a volume of case studies would almost certainly advance our understanding. This book, however, focuses on the research and reflections of sociologists, psychologists, psychiatrists, marriage counselors, and educators—and the work of three journalists who are sensitive witnesses to recent changes in the public understanding of jealousy.

INTENDED AUDIENCES

This book has been constructed with several overlapping audiences in mind. As an anthology of important social scientific literature on jealousy, the book should be a valuable resource for research scholars and teachers in the several disciplines which study intimate association and interpersonal relationships— especially psychology and sociology. The book is appropriate for use with students in such courses as: social psychology, human sexuality, counselor education, the sociology of the family, and other family studies curricula.

Considerable attention is given to the means by which jealousy is to be understood and managed. Thus, this book should be of value to psychotherapists, marriage counselors, the clergy, and others who work professionally with persons for whom jealousy is a problem. Their clients, too, will find in these pages resources for the analysis and treatment of their own jealousy. Indeed, *Jealousy* is also a self-help-through-understanding book which can be read and digested with profit by large numbers of literate people who simply want to understand themselves better and to manage their intimate partnerships more constructively. Nearly all of the material in this book is comprehensible to the nonprofessional reader.

It is the hope of the editors that these materials will not only illuminate the phenomenon of jealousy but that they will also demonstrate the utility of interdisciplinary social inquiry into complex human affairs. Interdisciplinary, humanistic, problem-oriented social inquiry can help us better understand and thus, better manage our lives. Neither this book nor the approach it advocates claims to have easy answers or universal prescriptions, and we would be suspicious of any "experts" who made such claims. We assert only that, properly marshalled, the literature of social science can help solve personal and interpersonal problems which might otherwise seem quite beyond human control.

Of course, many people—including, recently, a prominent U.S. Senator—believe that we are better off *not* exploring areas such as sexuality, intimacy, and associated issues. And they may be right. Perhaps these are "mysteries" humans should not probe. Perhaps more knowledge of the mechanisms and patterns of love and sex will hinder rather than help in the formation of better intimate partnerships. Social science cannot *prove* that more knowledge of such matters is a good thing. But the editors of this volume have worked from this assumption: The more we know, the better.

PROBLEMS IN THE STUDY OF JEALOUSY

It is not easy to study jealousy. We cannot reliably *observe* jealousy because its expressions take many diverse forms, because it is often displayed only in private, and because individuals often repress or deny it. As one writer (Sokoloff 1947:13f.) has noted:

> ... jealousy is an emotion of which a great majority of us are somewhat ashamed and which we are ready to conceal as completely as possible.

... Not only is it the most common human emotion but the most concealed and disguised. It is present when no one suspects its presence, demonstrating itself in the most bizarre ways.

Neither can we study jealousy by *experimentation.* In recent years the scientific community (and the public) have come to accept the scientific observation of sexual behavior in laboratory settings, but it would probably not be considered acceptable to actually manipulate sexual feelings in an experiment.

Thus, in the case of jealousy, both observation and experimentation—two of the basic strategies of scientific inquiry—are rendered problematic. We must rely, therefore, on our own experience and on what others are willing to disclose about their jealousy. And here we are confronted with another problem: The person who will admit to feeling jealous may in fact be *less* jealous than one who denies feeling jealous.

These methodological and ethical problems are reflected in the selections chosen for this book. We found very little "hard data" research on jealousy. Here are the kinds of materials this book contains: Two articles from the social-psychological perspective utilize experimental data on the nature of emotional experience and on the properties of romantic love. One report is drawn from research with one hundred "swinging" couples and a matched sample of nonswingers. Several of the articles are based on psychological case materials or on observations in workshop and other small-group settings. Somewhat broader in scope are the reflections offered on larger sociocultural issues by several respected sociologists and one anthropologist. We have also included three perceptive journalistic treatments of jealousy in contemporary American society; these accounts, by participants who tried to be observant, add texture and feeling tone to the picture of jealousy we seek to paint.

Seven of the articles were prepared especially for this volume. These fresh contributions add depth, precision, and relevance to the discussion of jealousy now in process. We owe a special debt to the authors of these articles for their patient efforts to "tailor" their contributions to fill some of the gaps we found in the literature.

ACKNOWLEDGEMENTS ... AND A PLEA

This book had its beginnings in a smoky, wine-soaked conversation with friends in Berkeley in October of 1974. Barry Shapiro (co-editor of the book *Psycho-Sources*) said that jealousy was a problem for him and that he had been helped by reading an article on the subject by Ron Mazur (this book, Chapter 17). He asked the others to suggest additional essays he might read with profit. Jay Smith (co-editor of the book *Beyond Monogamy*) named a couple of other articles and wondered out loud if there might not be enough material to make a book. Gordon Clanton said that he'd find out. Lynn Smith, who had done considerable library research on jealousy while a graduate student at Berkeley, offered to devote some energy to the search. As we worked on the book, we received valuable assistance and moral support from colleagues and friends too numerous to thank individually. Colleagues and friends, thank you.

We have tried to be sensitive to the diversity of intimate lifestyles currently being practiced in American society. Sometimes, however, conventions of language and the demand for clarity require that we use expressions or terms that seem to limit the scope of what we say. Thus, much that is said in this volume about *marriage* is also pertinent to the situations of unmarried couples, of gays, and of groups of three or more persons who are intimately associated. We use the term *intimate partnership* to include all these combinations as well as conventional marriage, and we typically use the term *partner* to include legal spouse, partner in cohabitation—heterosexual or homosexual—and even one's steady date. The term *pair-bond* is also employed as an inclusive label for both marriage and nonlegal pairings. Similarly, what we say about "the opposite sex" will often be pertinent to persons of the same sex if they are gay or bisexual. Because many of the articles in this book were written before the advent of the women's liberation movement, they may contain some sexist language. In all these cases we ask that the reader be tolerant and make the extra mental effort without which, these days, almost any material on intimate association can be dismissed as insensitive to the needs and life situations of at least some readers.

Del Mar, California
November, 1976

GORDON CLANTON
LYNN G. SMITH

Introduction: Keys to the Understanding of Jealousy

Americans are reassessing marriage (and other forms of intimate partnership) as never before. They expect a great deal from these most important relationships—much more, typically, than their parents expected—and many persons are seeking resources for the "work" by means of which they hope to improve the quality of life in the intimate sphere. They have replaced the traditional *passive* attitude toward their relationships with an *active* orientation.

The active orientation is for a relationship what therapy is for the individual: a conscious decision to attempt to change it for the better. The emergence of the active orientation is a new development, and its implications are enormous. Betty Yorburg (1973:viii) prefaces her recent study of *The Changing Family* with this analysis of our time:

> We live in an era of unprecedented searching for meaning and guidance. Never before in Western societies has there been so much freedom for so many people to choose varying solutions to the problems of living.

There are as many modes of "tinkering" with marriage as there are sets of assumptions about the nature of sex, love, and commitment. Given the great variety of contemporary attitudes toward intimate partnership, it may be useful to name and differen-

1

tiate three major approaches along a continuum from most conventional to most experimental.

Enriching marriage.   Some couples seek to enrich and enliven quite conventional marriages. They do not seriously challenge traditional understandings of marriage, of sex-role expectations, or of sexual fidelity, but they do want to *improve* their partnerships and they are willing to *work* to that end—at least to the extent of reading an article in *Reader's Digest* or in one of the (so-called) women's magazines and discussing it with their spouse or a sympathetic friend (usually of the same sex). Such persons may enroll in the Total Woman course (Maynard 1975), attend a church-sponsored "marriage encounter," or join a local chapter of the Association of Couples for Marriage Enrichment.

Remodeling marriage.   Other couples believe that they need to do more than "work harder" within the framework of conventional marriage. They feel that some modification of marriage itself is in order. The women's liberation movement has catalyzed reassessment of traditional sex-role expectations in American society and many couples are renegotiating their expectations of each other as a result. The human potential movement in its many manifestations has urged honest expression of feelings, candid communication between partners, and the development of personal autonomy. Consciousness-raising groups (for women and for men), growth centers, and the popular self-help literature (such as the best-selling *Open Marriage*) are among the institutions and resources available to those who seek to remodel marriage.

Revolutionizing intimate partnership.   A few couples go further and seek to redefine their understanding of fidelity so as to allow for sexual and/or emotional relationships outside the pair bond. They seek to incorporate some form of "consensual adultery" into their partnership—hoping that this will strengthen rather than undermine their primary relationship. The "ground rules" for such extramarital involvements vary from couple to couple. Swingers seek extramarital sexual encounters marked by very low levels of emotional involvement; thus they minimize the risk to the primary relationship *and* keep jealousy at a minimum. Other couples desire some sort of emotional connection in their extramarital sexual activities. Some open themselves to "intimate friendships." A few even experiment with communal living and/or "group marriage." In all these cases, ideally, the extramarital involvements are kept subordinate to the primary relationship (although, in practice, experiments with postmonogamous forms of partnership sometimes serve, consciously or unconsciously, as a means of gradual transition from one pair bond to another).

These three strategies differ from one another rather profoundly and yet *all three* are marked by the desire to be more self-conscious about one's most important relationship and to *improve* that relationship. And for the great majority of these people—for the relatively conventional as well as for the relatively radical—*jealousy* is an important issue. Persons seeking to *enrich* conventional marriages may wish to minimize the suspicion and conflict which often accompany jealousy. Even those who believe that a certain amount of jealousy is evidence of love want to keep the emotion "under control". Couples committed to very traditional definitions of marriage and fidelity will experience jealousy in the form of "innocent flirtations" and petty misunderstandings—and so will need tools for understanding, working with, and working *through* their jealousies.

Couples who seek to *remodel* marriage often encounter problems with jealousy. The husband may become jealous of the new friends his wife meets on the job. The commitment to candid communication may bring a couple to confront the interest either partner may have in developing friendships—sexual or platonic—outside the marriage. Spending time with a friend may be an important symbol of the sense of personal autonomy many married people seek today. And all these situations have jealousy potential.

It goes without saying that a postmonogamous life-style—whether it is swinging, group marriage, or any variant in between—is virtually impossible unless the persons involved discover new ways of understanding and dealing with jealousy. For this reason, the experiences of those who confront jealousy in the context of a posttraditional life-style may contain some clues for the understanding of jealousy in general.

Jealousy, then, is an issue for all persons who seek to understand and improve their intimate partnerships, regardless of the assumptions from which they move, regardless of the strategies they employ.

In the preparation of this book we talked with a lot of people representing a wide range of life-style possibilities. Here are the questions we were asked most often: What is jealousy? What causes jealousy? Is jealousy "natural" or learned? Is it good or bad to be jealous? Are women (or men) more jealous than men (or women)? Is *my* jealousy normal or abnormal? Does it enhance my most important relationship or undermine it? Am I more or less jealous than other people? Does my behavior unnecessarily provoke jealous feelings in others? Can I modify or manage my own jealousy—and that of my partner?

Note that some of these questions are general in nature while others are personal. This book cannot directly answer personal questions—although it may *equip* the reader to begin to answer such questions for himself/herself. We shall begin our inquiry by framing several general questions about jealousy. These same questions have long perplexed those who have worried, thought, and written about jealousy; they are also important for contemporary persons who, by whatever strategy, wish to better understand and manage their own jealousy. The articles in Parts I through IV will suggest some answers to these questions, and the Synthesis at the end of this volume will seek to knit those answers into a statement about the nature and meaning of sexual jealousy and the place of jealousy in intimate partnership today.

WHAT IS JEALOUSY?

Jealousy is a Rorschach word: It evokes a rich variety of images and associations. It means different things to different people. Each of us begins the search for the understanding of jealousy with our own experiences. Only gradually, if at all, do we move to an awareness of the similar experiences of others, and, beyond that, to a generalized understanding of jealousy.

To define jealousy in advance of our inquiry into its nature may prejudice the inquiry. Yet to assume from the outset that "everybody knows what jealousy means" will not do because of the wide range of associations evoked by the word. Perhaps the following working definition will serve to focus our attention so that discovery is made possible without, at the same time, presuming to supply an easy answer for a tough question prior to our careful investigation:

> Jealousy may be defined as a feeling of displeasure which expresses itself either as fear of loss of the partner or as discomfort over a real or imagined experience the partner has with a third party (Adapted from Bohm, 1967:567).

The negative feelings can be directed toward the partner, the third party, or both.

There are, to be sure, other types of jealousy. There is jealousy of the spouse's work when it takes time and energy that might have been invested at home. There is jealousy of sports, hobbies, and other outside interests which seem to rob us of the attention of a loved one. But it is sexual jealousy which seems to bother most people most. *Sexual* jealousy is perhaps the hardest jealousy to endure because more is at stake, because we often measure our self-worth and the health of our relationships in terms of sexual fidelity.

The words *jealousy* and *zeal* stem from the same Greek root. This suggests that jealousy reflects a concern about something viewed as precious and that it involves watchfulness with regard to a valued possession. We are *zealous* when we are diligent in our efforts to maintain control over inanimate and abstract possessions such as land, money, material goods, official positions, public reputation, and the like. We are *jealous* when we seek to maintain control over *human beings* who are important to us. Jealousy is the negative feeling that accompanies the fear that one will lose the affection, the support, and the services of another person. That person and those services are a kind of "possession," typically a very *valuable* possession. As we shall see, your understanding of the extent to which you *possess* (and are possessed by) your partner has a profound impact on your experience and understanding of jealousy.

Jealousy is also marked by hostility toward a real or imagined rival, the person who threatens to take away your partner and thus to deprive you of all the benefits of your present relationship. This hostility is often repressed and denied. Sometimes it is expressed verbally. Occasionally it explodes in anger and even in violence.

HOW DOES JEALOUSY DIFFER FROM ENVY?

The words *jealousy* and *envy* are sometimes used as synonyms—and, indeed, they do name related emotions and behaviors. For our purposes, however, the *difference* between the two phenomena is more important than the similarities. Put simply:

Envy stems from the desire to acquire something possessed by another, while jealousy is rooted in the fear of losing something already possessed (Foster 1972:168).

Jealousy, then, is more "conservative" than envy, more concerned with the *maintenance* of a relationship in the face of an apparent challenge to its continuation. It was this quality of jealousy which led the French moralist La Rochefoucauld to suggest that

> Jealousy is somehow right and rational, since it aims at keeping something that belongs to us, whereas envy is a rage that cannot tolerate possession by someone else (In Foster 1972:189).

Of course, it is possible to be both envious and jealous of the same person; the two emotions, though conceptually distinct, are often mixed together in real life.[1]

IS JEALOUSY INSTINCTIVE OR IS IT LEARNED?

This is a key issue in the history of the study of jealousy and a central question for all who seek to understand and manage their own jealousy. If jealousy is *instinctive,* a function of our animal *nature,* then it must be very resistant to conscious efforts toward its modification and control. At best, we might hope to hold our jealous impulses in check so as to prevent violent outbursts. If, on the other hand, jealousy is *learned,* if it is a function of our *nurture* in human society, then we might be more optimistic about the possibility of *re*learning or changing the behaviors and even the feelings which flow from jealousy. Of course, firmly established cultural patterns and personal tendencies learned in childhood are themselves quite resistant to change. In general, however, an understanding of jealousy as rooted in *nurture* encourages and invites educational and/or therapeutic intervention in a way that an understanding of jealousy as rooted in *nature* does not.

On this pivotal issue, "expert opinion" appears to be badly divided. William James (1952:735) insisted, without elaboration, that "jealousy is unquestionably instinctive." John B. Watson (1924:186ff.), a father of behaviorist psychology, saw jealousy as learned . . . and as destructive. Havelock Ellis (1936:563ff.) described jealousy as an instinct which is incompatible with civilization. Alfred Adler (1928:221-223) saw jealousy arising from

---

[1] A detailed discussion of envy is beyond the scope of this book. For useful treatments of the phenomenon see George M. Foster, "The Anatomy of Envy: A Study in Symbolic Behavior," and Helmut Schoeck, *Envy: A Theory of Social Behavior.* Both writers point to the pervasiveness of envy, its importance in social life, the near-universal tendency to repress and deny envy, and the social and economic importance of the fear of being envied. Both writers are politically conservative and both are critical of attempts to minimize envy by means of more egalitarian distribution of material goods, political power, and opportunity.

the striving for power which is part of the experience of every person from infancy on. (This suggests that jealousy, if it is not inborn, is, nevertheless, inescapably a product of every person's life experience, an inevitable outcome of life in society.)

Popular opinion is also divided on this question. Some people believe that jealousy is "natural" and, therefore, ineradicable. Others insist that jealousy, like racial prejudice, is "taught" to us by our parents, our peers, and the human institutions in which we live and move and have our being. Generally speaking, persons who view jealousy as "good" or "normal" emphasize its natural roots. Persons who view it as "bad" or "pathological" stress the cultural patterning of jealousy and the possibility of unlearning or relearning some of what we have been taught about it. Constructive conversation about jealousy often breaks down because one party views jealousy as instinctive and the other views it as learned.

Several of the articles in this book address this question, and the reader will be guided toward his/her own formulation of the extent to which jealousy is instinctive and the extent to which it is learned. For now, the editors wish only to introduce the possibility that, in this debate, *both sides may be right.* Perhaps jealousy is *both* instinctive *and* learned—and perhaps every attempt to argue for one or the other interpretation of the phenomenon ought to be viewed as an *emphasis* rather than as an adequate description. In both scholarly and nonscholarly contexts the word *jealousy* is used to name *both* the instinctive biological *impulse* one feels when access to or control over one's partner is threatened *and* the culturally patterned feelings and behaviors which issue from that impulse. Thus, the debate over whether jealousy is instinctive *or* learned may be a misplaced debate. An adequate understanding of jealousy must include consideration of *both* elements . . . *and* of the dialectical relationship between the two (See Kardiner 1939:200-205).

IS JEALOUSY NORMAL OR ABNORMAL, HEALTHY OR PATHOLOGICAL?

Here again we have a problem with semantics and with the "or." Definitions of "normal" or "healthy" psychological states are hard to come by. And, here again, both scholarly and popular opinion seem to be divided. Some insist that jealousy is normal. Others insist that it is pathological. Again we suspect that both are right. There is a normal jealousy, the negative feeling that comes when a valued relationship appears to be threatened.

There are numerous nonpathological means by which these feelings can be discharged. The "pathologically jealous person" is one who cannot find a nondestructive outlet for these feelings. He/she begins to damage himself/herself, or the partner, or their relationship.

What we have called the jealous *impulse,* the natural kernel of jealousy, would appear to be quite normal. If a person claims never to feel this jealous "flash," we cannot help but wonder if he or she really cares about the partner and the maintenance of the relationship. And, with Freud (1922:232), we may suspect that jealousy is being repressed and/or denied. It is what we do with that "flash" which determines whether our jealousy is "normal" or "abnormal," "healthy" or "pathological."

Of course, a great deal of felt jealousy is repressed (hidden from oneself) and/or denied (hidden from others). This is a "normal" (socially sanctioned) response in our society. It is functional in that it minimizes conflict. It may or may not be functional for the individual.

Sometimes felt jealousy is expressed, perhaps in the form of a demand that one's partner break off a developing relationship with a third party. This often results in the "negotiation" of a new equilibrium within the pair-bond. In one way or another the expression of jealousy alters the situation so that felt jealousy is reduced. This too would appear to be a "normal" pattern, one that is approved in our society.

Some jealous feelings are expressed less constructively: with a blow, with verbal cruelty, with flight, with long seiges of paranoic suspicion. Clearly, some responses to and expressions of the jealous "flash" are pathological, that is, obviously detrimental to the well-being of the individual and to his relationships with others. The clinical psychological literature reveals cases of pathological jealousy marked by behaviors that nearly all observers would judge self-destructive. Newspaper accounts of "crimes of passion" (usually meaning murder committed in a fit of jealousy) further attest to the existence of pathological jealousy. But note well: The plea of "not guilty by virtue of temporary insanity" is a relatively recent legal category which reflects the traditional tendency of juries to judge even violence as the "normal" (socially approved) response when the fidelity of one's spouse (especially of a wife) is undercut by her involvement (especially sexually) with another.[2]

[2]For a psychiatric study of 110 persons who committed or attempted murder under the influence of jealousy see Ronald Rae Mowat, *Morbid Jealousy and Murder.*

We suggest, then, that some jealousy is normal/healthy and that some is abnormal/pathological. The jealous impulse is normal, an instinctive reaction of self-protection. Many expressions of jealous feelings are "normal," at least in the sense that they are socially acceptable and somewhat functional to the individual who must cope with jealous feelings. Some expressions of jealous feelings are pathological. Few persons, we suspect, would hesitate to label as pathological the behavior of a jealous husband who was preoccupied with the fear that his allegedly unfaithful wife was trying to poison him and who later killed the wife in a fit of rage. But even in this extreme case, many would soften their judgment if it came to light that the woman was, in fact, involved with another; and many more would vote to acquit the murderer if he killed his wife upon discovering her in bed with her lover.

We note, then, considerable confusion and ambivalence regarding this issue. While almost everyone would agree that *some* expressions of jealousy are pathological, there are many other expressions of jealousy which would be viewed as "normal" by some and "pathological" by others. Indeed, we shall suggest that it is precisely the ongoing *redefinition of normal and pathological jealousy*—within the individual, the couple, and the culture—that is the key to understanding jealousy in contemporary North American society. We must, therefore, use the terms *normal/abnormal* and *healthy/pathological* with caution, if at all. These terms are of limited usefulness in light of the lack of consensus which we have noted. Such terms are especially unsuited for use in a time of transition with regard to the meanings of sex, love, fidelity, and the like.

WHAT IS THE RELATIONSHIP
BETWEEN JEALOUSY AND LOVE?

Is jealousy evidence of *love* or of *self-love?* This question has perplexed philosophers for centuries and "authoritative" testimony can be found for both positions. Generally speaking, however, it seems that *religious* authorities (and those strongly influenced by organized religion) are most likely to see jealousy as evidence of love. For example, St. Augustine: "He that is not jealous is not in love." *Secular* thinkers seem more apt to take the opposite point of view. For example, La Rochefoucauld: "Jealousy springs more from love of self than from love of another." An additional polarization on this question may be noted: The notion that jealousy is evidence of love (and, thus, a virtue) is part of the conventional wisdom subscribed to by very large numbers of people. The view that jealousy is an expression of self-love (and, thus, a defect) is endorsed by numerous "experts": psychologists, sociologists, and moral philosophers.

We have already noted that the word *jealousy* means different things to different people. Surely this is also true of the word *love.* Perhaps discussion of the relationship between jealousy and love can be sharpened if we use Abraham Maslow's (1968: 42f.) distinction between the love which seeks the best interest of the other (Being-love or B-love) and the love which is an expression of dependence upon the other (Deficiency-love or D-love). In conventional usage, the single word "love" is used to mean *both* "being able to love" and "being hungry for love." When we say, "She loves him," we may mean, "She cares about him and seeks his happiness," *or* we may mean, "She is very dependent upon him and cannot be happy without him." Typically, we mean some of both; love is a mixture of *attachment* and *caring.*

Until we make the distinction between these "two faces of love," discussion of the relationship between jealousy and love will bog down. On the other hand, if we appreciate this distinction we can see that, once again, the two positions in an age-old debate about jealousy are both right—as far as they go. *Jealousy is evidence of one kind of love,* Maslow's D-love, love rooted in dependency upon the partner. The relationship between jealousy and Being-love is less clear. We would not want to invert the equation and baldly state that jealousy is incompatible with the love that seeks the happiness of the partner. Since the two kinds of love are always present together, such a statement would be of limited usefulness and it might easily be appropriated for polemical purposes. Example: "You're jealous, Howard. That means you are dependent on me but don't really seek the best for me." That, obviously, would be an unconstructive use of the insight with which we are working here.

For now, then, let us be content to say that D-love, the love which is dependency on the partner, reinforces jealousy and that B-love, the love that seeks the good for the partner, reduces jealousy. In other words, given the jealous "flash," the natural kernel of jealousy experienced by virtually everyone who is intimately associated with another, Being-love resists the drift toward anger and distrust while Deficiency-love accelerates it. We do not wish to suggest that some people are perfect B-lovers and that they feel no jealousy, but we would endorse Otto Fenichel's (1955) assessment that, "The most jealous persons are those who are not able to love, but who need the feeling of being loved."

ARE THERE DIFFERENCES IN THE WAYS MEN
AND WOMEN EXPERIENCE AND EXPRESS JEALOUSY?

Because of the women's movement and its impact on our society, there is more interest than before in the question of male/female differences generally. Unfortunately, there is very little hard data on which to base answers. If such data were available, there would likely still be considerable disagreement as to whether measured differences reflected innate differences between the genders or differences in socialization. And, it might be argued, things are changing so rapidly that research results may soon be out of date.

The pertinent literature (Gottschalk in Bohm, 1967:570ff.; Reik, 1949:438-442; and Corzine, 1974) is based on studies of small samples and on observations in clinical settings. From these sources we derive, tentatively, the following male/female differences. Men are more apt to *deny* jealous feelings; women are more apt to *acknowledge* them. Men are more likely than women to express jealous feelings through rage and even violence, but such outbursts are often followed by despondency. Jealous men are more apt to focus on the outside *sexual* activity of the partner and they often demand a recital of the intimate details; jealous women are more likely to focus on the *emotional* involvement between her partner and the third party. Men are more likely to *externalize* the cause of the jealousy, more likely to blame the partner, or the third party, or "circumstances." Women often *internalize* the cause of jealousy; they blame themselves. Similarly, a jealous man is more likely to display *competitive* behavior toward the third party while a jealous woman is more likely to display *possessive* behavior. She clings to her partner rather than confronting the third party.

In general, we may say that male and female experiences and expressions of jealousy reflect male and female role expectations which are general and well established in society. Very little may be said with confidence about innate or intrinsic male/female differences. Further, in a time marked by a reassessment and by some redefinition of sex-role expectations, generalizations about such differences become increasingly problematic.

With these initial reflections on several key questions about jealousy, we have set the stage for a fuller, deeper exploration of these important issues. The questions with which we have begun will recur, explicitly and implicitly, in the readings and interpretations which follow. We shall continue our inquiry with a consideration of the contemporary experience of jealousy as reflected in the popular media.

I

Experiencing Jealousy

I didn't know that anybody could hurt so much and live. I suppose it's jealousy. I didn't know it was like this. I thought jealousy was an idea. It isn't. It's a pain. But I don't feel as they do in Broadway melodrama. I don't want to kill anybody. I just want to die.

—A man in Floyd Dell's novel of reminiscences
Love in Greenwich Village, p. 231.

The experience of jealousy varies considerably from person to person. We cannot plot its graph with precision. At best we can discover some regularities in the chaos of jealousy, some patterns amid the flux.

The popular media of a society can serve as an imprecise but useful barometer of the interests and concerns of the population—or, at least, of those portions of the population served by the media in question. For clues to the way in which persons in our society have experienced, expressed, and interpreted jealousy, we scanned the *Reader's Guide to Periodic Literature* since World War II. We found a steady trickle of articles on sexual jealousy—on the average, about one article a year from 1953 through 1966. Perhaps significantly, most of these appeared in the so-called women's magazines; one searches in vain for a substantive discussion of jealousy in *Playboy* and *Penthouse.*

From World War II until the late 1960s, most of the articles in the popular magazines said that a certain amount of jealousy was a natural by-product of love. The reader (typically, a woman) was advised, simply, to keep her jealous feelings "under control" and to avoid the "unreasonable" jealousy that is marked by suspicion, hostility, accusations, and threats. The woman was told to avoid situations which might make her husband jealous *but* to interpret his small expressions of jealousy as evidence of his love. If jealousy threatened the stability of the marriage, professional help was advised.

Representative of the best of these articles was a short piece in *McCall's* (May 1962) by David R. Mace, a well-known marriage counselor and author. The article, entitled "Two Faces of Jealousy," hinged on the distinction between normal and abnormal (or pathological) jealousy and moved from the assumption that the differences between the two were self-evident and nonproblematic. Normal jealousy, according to Mace,

> is the instinct that flashes a warning when the exclusiveness of marriage is threatened. . . . Normal jealousy is a protective instinct that has saved many a marriage. Abnormal jealousy is a destructive obsession and often requires professional treatment.

In this article, little or no attention was given to the possibility that definitions of "normal" and "abnormal" jealousy might vary from time to time, from place to place, and from couple to couple.

Toward the end of the 1960s, the trickle of articles on sexual jealousy was interrupted. The magazines were relatively silent on the subject from 1966 to 1973. It is as though writers, editors, and publishers sensed that jealousy was changing somehow, that jealousy was becoming problematic in a way which worked against a continued dispensing of the conventional wisdom. After this lull, articles on jealousy typically took account of a new concern: They began to question the appropriateness of jealous feelings in marriage. It was no longer assumed that jealousy was evidence of love. For the first time *guilt* about jealousy became an issue for large numbers of people.

The three articles in this section reflect the emergence and development of this new concern. They are personal and experiential, not analytical. We have included them in order to help the reader get in touch with his/her *own* jealousy—and to provide glimpses of some of the ways *others* experience the emotion. Also, these materials informally present issues which will be discussed in depth in later sections.

Our first selection, "Confessions of a Jealous Wife," was apparently the only article on sexual jealousy written by a professional writer for a popular magazine between 1966 and 1973. Like most earlier articles, this one presents jealousy as a normal accompaniment of love. Judith Viorst describes typical jealousy-provoking situations and suggests that "everyday jealousy has less to do with a fear of overt sexual betrayal than with a fear of intimacy that excludes us." Some conventional strategies for coping with jealousy are discussed, among them: sarcasm, violence, and trying to make the spouse jealous. The "open marriage" approach is ruled out. The author concludes that nothing really works. Jealousy is inevitable: "A man who wasn't attractive to other women, a man who wasn't alive enough to enjoy other women, a man who was incapable of making me jealous, would never be the kind of man I'd love."

This article offers no prescription for eradicating jealousy, and so it can serve as a kind of popular media base line against which to plot the recent wave of advice on how to modify or eliminate jealousy. A comparison with our second selection, "Taming the Green-Eyed Monster," by Normal M. Lobsenz, is very revealing in this connection.

Confessions of a Jealous Wife

Judith Viorst

Over on the other side of the room there is a 19-year-old girl with long hair parted down the middle, a clingy dress about an inch shorter than her hair and the clear-eyed, fresh-faced look of someone who is not awakened by babies at six in the morning. She is hanging on to my husband's every word as if he were Warren Beatty, only smarter, and he is hanging on to her every word as if she were Simone de Beauvoir, only better-looking, and I am beginning to feel like Othello in *Othello*.

I am, in a word, jealous, which I know is considered an unwholesome, unattractive and immature emotion. My only consolation for having such an unwholesome, unattractive and immature emotion is the suspicion—no, the certainty!—that every wife from time to time feels jealous too.

And why not? Jealousy isn't reserved for those cataclysmic moments when a husband packs his electric toothbrush and runs off with the lady next door. It is ready to spring at far, far less provocation—a lingering glance at a bell-bottomed bottom, an extended conversation with that long-haired 19-year-old or even an undue enthusiasm for the lady next door's views on water pollution. In fact, we can become jealous of our

Judith Viorst is a regular contributor to *Redbook* magazine. "Confessions of a Jealous Wife" appeared in *Redbook*, March 1970, and was reprinted in *Readers Digest*, June 1970. Reprinted with permission of author. Copyright © 1970 by Judith Viorst.

husband's family, his business partner, his best friend, his psychiatrist or his entire bowling team if we feel he is seeking or finding in them something that he isn't getting from us.

Other women, however, tend to make us more jealous than bowling teams. What many of us brood about, I suppose, after we've been married for a few years, is that we no longer constantly thrill, dazzle, charm and delight the man we've married. He's seen us at breakfast wearing the terry-cloth robe with the torn sleeve, a smudge of last night's mascara under the eyes. He's seen us with bellyaches and without the padded bra, shaving our legs and wearing rollers and screaming at the plumber.

He may guess that other women also snore, snarl and sometimes forget to rinse out their stockings, but when he looks at his lawfully wedded wife he doesn't have to guess—he knows. He knows, we know he knows, and so if an attractive, *unknown* woman smiles at him (or he at her) across a crowded room and they eventually wind up on the same couch nibbling on the same hors d'oeuvre, we feel a twinge of jealousy.

We wives worry about the appeal of another woman, not only because she is unknown to our husband in that special, married sense of torn terry-cloth robes, but also because he is unknown to her. Which means that when he talks about his business trip to Denver (he's told you about it three times) she glows with interest, and when he complains about his bad back (you warned him not to pick up that heavy box) she pouts with sympathy, and when he tells her that hilarious story about the poker game (he lost $50 and you really don't see what's so funny) she roars with appreciative laughter.

Is she putting him on? Does she mean it? Can she actually want to know why he is thinking of buying a Ford instead of a Chevy—or is it the other way around—next year?

Yes, she probably does want to know. She hasn't heard it all before, and if this nice-looking man wants to confide to her his innermost thoughts on automotive design, she'll be happy to listen. Wives listen too—of course they do—but rarely with the flattering concentration (and glows and pouts and roars of laughter) that other women muster without effort. Watching a husband's ego expand under this treatment, watching the obvious pleasure he derives from this brief (we hope) encounter, we very well may be stabbed by jealousy.

Another distressing effect of the other woman is her talent for evoking in our thoroughly familiar mates new aspects, hidden depths and secret yearnings. A married lady can pick up some astounding items of information about her husband simply by observing him tête-à-tête with another female. For instance . . .

Husband to philosophy major home from fashionable women's college for the holidays: "Yes, I've often thought that Nietzsche had a profound grasp of the human condition." Is that what he's often thought? How come he never mentioned it to me?

Husband to dazzlingly chic career woman: "There's no question that a life without children can be freer, more exciting." This is the man who has been trying to talk me into a fourth baby for the last two years? . . .

Many of my friends have discovered for the first time, thanks to a little discreet surveillance, that their husbands can quote entire verses of Catullus, or yearn to chuck their jobs and become veterinarians, or wish they had gone to Harvard, or wish they hadn't gone to Harvard, or are thinking seriously of converting to Zen. They've also discovered that, spurred onward by an unwifely smile, a husband can suddenly master the art of lighting a lady's cigarette and finding her pocketbook and even listening to every word *she* says. And while he is feeling charmed, charming, soulful, profound, witty, gallant and titillated . . . we are feeling jealous.

Other women, alas, are to be encountered not only at parties, where a wife can at least study the competition in action, spill a drink on her dress, interrupt prolonged chats, develop a headache so she can demand to be taken home, and once at home, attempt to bring a husband to his senses by saying, "Since when have you been reading Nietzsche?"

Unfortunately there is an endless supply of other women out there in the big world—secretaries and dental assistants and waitresses and women executives and even in our case a very pretty lady eye doctor. And wives with traveling husbands have an even wider selection of potential temptations to get aggravated over—TWA stewardesses, San Francisco topless go-go dancers, old flames in Minneapolis, new models in Detroit.

I don't mean to say that we wives spend all our waking moments fearing that our husbands may fall into the arms of another woman. But there are many circumstances—external and internal, real and imagined, ultimately innocent or ultimately leading to disaster—that can give a wife a first-class case of jealousy.

I remember the time my husband received a bill for two from a hotel in Pennsylvania and I had never been there.

I remember the time I found the key to a local motel tucked into a corner of his dresser drawer.

I remember the time I was visiting in New York and phoned home at eight in the morning to say hi ("Just tell him his wife is calling," I said to the operator) and a sweet female voice answered the phone. ("Should I *still* say his wife is calling?" the operator asked me.)

I needn't bother explaining what passed through my mind before I learned, incontrovertibly, that the hotel was where he had taken our oldest boy skiing, the motel key had been left behind by a visiting friend and the lady on the other end of the phone was a baby sitter brought in to get the kids off to school so my husband could attend an early meeting.

Family fights always seem to leave me particularly vulnerable to jealousy. Last month, for instance, after one of our little battles about child rearing ("Don't you ever tell that kid no?" . . . "*You* tell him no; you're the sadist in the family") we went to a PTA meeting where we met our boy's first-grade teacher. I think my husband said the weather was turning cold and the teacher said yes, it sure was, but that was enough for me. I could see that they understood each other, had total rapport, would never disagree about how to raise a child or about anything else, obviously could have a rich, full life together if only I weren't standing in their way . . . and on I went, stopping just short of where they were weeping quietly over my grave.

Whenever we're feeling low on self-esteem, the chances are we wives can reach new heights of jealousy without much effort. If I'm feeling dowdy, I become extremely uneasy about my husband's young, gorgeous research assistants. (My husband never had old, ugly research assistants.) If I'm feeling stupid, I don't like to see him in the vicinity of a lady Ph.D. in political science. If I'm feeling very stick-in-the-mud unadventurous about life, I hate having him spend any time with one of those daring, spunky females who are always doing things like going around the world on freighters.

There are lots of wives—and I confess I'm among them—who have jealousy problems because they are persuaded that they have married a superior male, a man so marvelous that every woman must surely covet him. Thus anyone who laughs at his jokes, dances with him, asks for a lift home or wants to discuss something personal with him at lunch becomes a potential home wrecker.

The point is, we don't have to be married to a certified love object like Paul Newman the actor to be troubled by the possible encroachment of another woman. Our husband can be Paul Newman the optometrist, but if we find him irresistible, chances are we will assume that everyone else does too.

Then there are women who are jealous of their husband not because hey think he's so marvelous but because they think he's unduly susceptible to feminine wiles. To put it bluntly, they consider their man a pushover, an easy mark for any woman who so much as sits next to him on the bus. Still other wives regard their husband as a pushover for certain types, for women with special characteristics they know their man really digs. I, for example, don't like Milton getting cozy with ladies who look like Leslie Caron. My friend Elizabeth worries about women with a brilliant grasp of the urban crisis.

Well, what is it, exactly, that we are jealous about? Do we really think that within minutes after our man meets another woman they will be locked in a passionate embrace in someone's executive suite and the next day we'll get a call from the lawyer offering us a generous settlement and we keep the children? Do we think they are going to go to bed and maybe begin a serious affair? Do we think they are going to go to bed and begin a casual affair—whatever *that* is?

I suspect that many of us, at some time, have every one of those dismal thoughts, but I also suspect that these thoughts are not what common, everyday jealousy is all about. I think the everyday kind of jealousy has less to do with a fear of overt sexual betrayal than it does with a fear of intimacy that excludes us.

If a good marriage means sharing most of life's experiences together and finding most of our satisfactions in each other—and I believe it does—then a wife may very well feel threatened when her husband seems to be sharing experiences and finding satisfaction elsewhere. Although we're not unrealistic enough to believe that we are our husband's entire universe, and, I hope, not foolish enough to want to be, we sometimes see his pursuit of outside satisfactions as a rejection, an abandonment, a betrayal, of us.

I imagine that's why we can be jealous of phone calls to his mother or hikes with his best friend. (What is he telling her that he doesn't tell me? What is he discussing with him that he doesn't think I'm smart enough to understand?) And if his intimacy with these other people can make us jealous, then how very, very jealous we can become when we believe that another woman, however briefly, is making him feel something—something sweet or romantic or exciting or tender—that maybe we haven't made him feel in a long time!

In any case, it often doesn't seem to matter whether our husbands are having assignations with other women or merely soliciting their opinion on hoof-and-mouth disease. When we are jealous, reason flees, and we do all the mean, nasty, scared, desperate and sometimes funny things that people tend to do when they are feeling angry and hurt.

The stony-silence technique is a great favorite among jealous wives because it succeeds in punishing the man while maintaining the dignity of the woman.

Maybe while he was out of town some lady called the house a couple of times, or a letter, pale violet and smelling of Arpege, arrived in the mail. Now, you're certainly not going to humiliate yourself by asking who these women are. No, indeed. You wouldn't think of demeaning yourself by bringing up the subject. In fact, you don't particularly feel like bringing up any subject right now. So you walk around the house with your lips sealed, except for occasional monosyllabic replies.

For those who don't have the self-restraint to maintain stony silences (I don't; I have never been stonily silent for more than 30 seconds) there is always the verbal assault, which may range from rational discussion to sarcasm to outright denunciation, often accompanied by tears.

The rational discussion, unfortunately, is rarely as rational as it pretends to be. My friend Connie, for instance, says that whenever jealousy strikes she sits down with her husband and urges him to tell all, on the grounds that she is a sensible, realistic woman who can deal intelligently with the truth, whatever it is. "And if he ever tells me that he's having an affair," Connie adds, "I'm going to grab a butcher knife and stab him right through the heart."

Sarcasm as a device for handling jealousy has the advantage of allowing a woman to simultaneously let off steam and demonstrate her devastating wit. "All right, Fred Astaire, time to go home," you may say to a husband who has been twirling around the dance floor with everyone but you. (You may say that, but there *must* be something cleverer to say.) I like sarcasm a lot, but when I'm jealous I'm usually too outraged to practice it. I do much better with direct denunciation, like, Lecher! Sex maniac! Humbert Humbert!

For the jealous wife it is sometimes only a short step from violent denunciation to physical violence, and I'll have to admit that I do, on occasion, cross that line. Like a lot of women I began with indirect action—telephone slamming, door banging—and later moved on to the real thing. To date I have thrown two avocado-green earthenware plates, one avocado, many books and shoes and once—and this is direct proof of the evils of watching old movies on TV—a custard pie. I don't personally know any wives who, in a jealous rage, have stabbed or shot or poisoned their possibly faithless husbands, but I am acquainted with several scratchers and one ankle-kicker.

Some women, rather than resort to wordlessness, words or even a good kick in the ankle, express their jealousy by a relentless supervision of their husband's activities. These are the ladies who try to make sure his dentist appointments are on Thursdays, when the cuddly, redheaded nurse is off duty and the graying-grandmother nurse is on. These are the ladies who, often with admirable skill and discretion, obtain from him a minute-by-minute report of what happened between 5:30, when he left the office, and 7:05, when he arrived home. These also are the ladies who haven't a qualm in the world about breaking up a lifelong friendship if the particular lifelong friend happens to be a footloose bachelor or an unnecessarily attractive divorcee.

It's true that I too have dropped a couple of young lovelies from our guest list, but I really don't have the time to play private eye to my husband. I prefer occupying my spare moments with self-improvement projects, on the theory that an excellent way to deal with jealousy is to attempt to become intriguingly attractive and versatile. Since we've been married I have tried isometric exercises and Canadian Air Force exercises, piano lessons, guitar lessons and French lessons, abstract painting, an English literature course and—Lord help me—skiing. Unfortunately, Milton threatened to move to a hotel if I continued with the piano, and he finished my painting career two years ago when he hung one of my masterpieces in the basement next to the boiler. Most of my other projects, I fear, are destined to meet a similar fate.

Anyway, whatever success we may achieve at becoming a whole new person, or even several different new people, I'm afraid we are still instantly recognizable to our mate as that same old wife in the torn terry-cloth robe. Our sad conclusion must be that we can be another woman only to another man, which is the kind of reasoning that can lead to the most dangerous and frustrating game a jealous married lady can play—trying to make her husband jealous too.

One good friend of mine, married to an intense Mediterranean type, grew unhappy about the amount of overtime he was putting in at the office assisted by a very sexy secretary. "Oh, Michael," she told him one evening in her most unconvincingly casual voice, "I met this actor while I was out walking the dog and I think he's going to come over Wednesday afternoon to discuss Saint Bernards. You don't mind, dear, do you?" Michael, she told me, didn't bother to answer. Instead, he walked straight over to where she stood and gave her a resounding smack on the face, a smack that has permanently discouraged her from trying this particular gambit again.

The problem with trying to make a husband jealous is that he may wind up far angrier than we've ever bargained for. An even bigger problem, however, is that he will probably refuse—despite our determined provocation—to show the remotest signs of jealousy.

I'm afraid I've failed at the get-him-jealous game. Whenever I've played it by making comments like, "If you don't want to see that movie tonight, maybe I'll go with Dave," or, "Paul says I'd look terrific if I cut my hair short," I inevitably draw a most unsatisfying reply. "Do whatever you want," my husband always tells me. Which always leaves me doing nothing at all.

For the most part, women appear more prone to jealousy than men, and I've been trying to figure out why. Maybe it's because it is almost impossible for wives to contemplate squeezing in a rendezvous between the school play and the grocery shopping, and our husbands know this very well. Maybe it's because women find it easier to satisfy their physical and emotional needs with one man than it is for men to vice-versa. Or maybe my friend from the Women's Liberation Movement has the answer. "Women are more jealous," she told me scornfully, "because they're convinced of their own inferiority. They think that men do them a tremendous favor merely by staying married."

There's probably truth in that somewhere, but I'm not about to liberate my marriage. I'm going to continue standing around at cocktail parties fretting over miniskirted 19-year-olds, and I'm planning to make a terrible scene if I ever find pink lipstick (mine is beige) on my husband's collar. But on those days when I happen to be feeling mature and secure I'm also going to admit that a man who wasn't attractive to other women, a man who wasn't alive enough to enjoy other women, a man who was incapable of making me jealous, would never be the kind of man I'd love.

Like Judith Viorst's "Confessions," the next selection also appeared in *Redbook*—exactly five years later. The title suggests that jealousy is *not* inevitable, that we can *do something* constructive with jealous feelings.

Norman Lobsenz cites psychologists and sociologists who suggest that jealousy is becoming outdated as we move into an era of "liberated relationships" between men and women. He recounts the experiences of several young couples who have tried to minimize jealousy in their marriage. The "liberated," it seems, are sometimes troubled by *unexpected* jealous feelings which are all the more painful because these young people have convinced themselves that they *ought not* to feel jealous.

Lobsenz finds the roots of jealousy in self-doubt and lack of self-esteem. He seems confident that we can learn from our experiences of jealousy and that we can constructively redirect jealous energy. This article provides an optimistic, rational, and very masculine counterpoint to the preceding selection.

2

Taming the
Green-Eyed Monster

Norman M. Lobsenz

According to the apostles of liberated relationships between men and women, jealousy is becoming outdated. In his book *The New Intimacy*, Ronald Mazur says jealousy will "diminish as it ceases to serve a useful function."[1] George and Nena O'Neill, authors of *Open Marriage,* writing that sex outside marriage "can enhance the marital relationship," declare that jealousy is "never a constructive feeling." And sociologist Dr. Jessie Bernard, in *The Future of Marriage*, concludes that as alternatives to monogamy are increasingly accepted, "jealousy in the traditional sense . . . is hardly salient at all today."[2]

If these experts are correct, it is hard to explain the sort of thing that happened at a recent conference of the National Council on Family Re-

Norman Lobsenz, M. S., is a free-lance journalist whose specialty is the area of marriage and the family. He has written several hundred articles for major national magazines and a number of books, including *No-Fault Marriage* (Garden City, N. Y.: Doubleday & Co., 1976). He is a former member of the Board of Directors of the National Council of Family Relations. "Taming the Green-Eyed Monster" is reprinted from *Redbook*, March 1975, with permission of the author. Copyright © 1975 by Normal Lobsenz.

[1]*Editors' note:* For Ron Mazur's suggestions for moving "Beyond Jealousy and Possessiveness," see Chapter 17.
[2]*Editors' note:* Jessie Bernard's analysis of jealousy and marriage is Chapter 13.

lations. There one of the best-attended lectures was given by the well-known family sociologist Robert Blood and his wife Margaret. Their topic: How to Design a Workshop on Jealousy.[3] Scores of counselors and therapists crowded into a stuffy Midwestern hotel meeting room to find out, in the words of the program, how to help "couples, individuals and whole triangles to work through some of their jealous feelings and to decide how they wish to prevent, minimize or manage jealousy-provoking situations."

Strange that jealousy should continue to arouse such interest and concern. It has been denounced by Biblical prophets, by poets, by psychiatrists. Moreover, though once excusable as a side effect of romantic passion, jealousy is supposed to be a dying conceit in these non-possessive times when excessive emotional demands in the name of love are considered unfashionable.

Yet, as Blood explains it: "The popularity of the concept of open marriage has *increased* the number of persons coping with the experience of jealousy." Indeed, while researching an article for Redbook last year on couples who choose to live together rather than to marry (*June, 1974*), I found much the same paradox. Men and women who freely gave each other the right to have other sexual partners were deeply troubled by their unexpected jealous reactions.

In recent weeks I've had many conversations about jealousy (not just of the sexual variety but also jealousy of a loved one's time, interests, friends, family, work) with dozens of young married couples. Many were at first reluctant to talk about it at all, as if the mere admission that jealousy might exist could somehow awaken the green-eyed monster. A few defended a "reasonable" amount of jealousy as a sign of continuing love. Sherry, a New York City schoolteacher, 25 years old and married for three years, summed up the attitude.

"I'd be disappointed if my husband didn't act a little jealous occasionally," she said. "It's a compliment to show you think your partner is still attractive to other people. It means you aren't just taking him or her for granted. And it's certainly good for morale!" Of course, the key word in Sherry's comment is "act." Playing at sexual jealousy may be harmless, even stimulating, as long as both persons know that it is a game—and as long as neither sets out deliberately to provoke it in the other.

Actual jealousy proves to be quite another matter. The couples I spoke with were for the most part clearly distressed by the disillusioning

---

[3]*Editors' note:* The Bloods describe their jealousy workshops in Chapter 19.

realization that although they believed jealousy "should not" occur, it did. When it did, they said, they tended to deny or repress it. If they yielded to jealousy, they felt guilty or demeaned.

A few people, however, did not accept the cliché concept of jealousy as an inevitably negative reaction to an emotional conflict. "I try to examine my jealous feelings in a realistic way," one young woman said thoughtfully. "Then sometimes I can find out what the feelings are trying to tell me."

It makes sense, I submit, to take a new look at jealousy from this perspective. For it is quite possible that jealousy can be helpful if it is put to intelligent analysis and use. After all, several other traditionally negative emotions have come to be seen—and to be used—in a positive way over the past few years. For example, to vent anger or to admit fear or to be reasonably selfish about one's emotional needs—all these are now increasingly accepted as potentially constructive ways to cope with life's stresses.

"Feelings can never be categorized simply as 'good' or 'bad,'" Dr. Beatrice Harris, a psychologist, told me, "Feelings are signals, symptoms of complex reactions. Just as pain alerts us to a physical problem and spurs us to do something about it, so jealousy may be one way of calling our attention to an emotional problem we might not otherwise be aware of, or not want to face. What matters is not that we *are* jealous, but whether we can find out *why*—and then how we deal with the jealousy, what we learn about ourselves as a result, what we do about the situation."

An experience that a 23-year-old Boston secretary I'll call Linda Thomas went through is a good example of how this approach can work. Linda grew jealous of her husband Paul, a lawyer, when, about eight months after they were married, he made increasingly frequent references to Kathy, an unmarried colleague in his firm. "It was never one of those 'Hey-let-me-tell-you-about-this-dish-in-the-office' things," Linda said. "In fact, I don't think Paul ever mentioned what she looked like, and that's what first made me suspicious. All he ever talked about was Kathy's grasp of the law, her skill at preparing briefs. But I wanted to think Paul's emphasis on her ability was a way of trying to cover up what really interested him in Kathy. I used to wallow in mental images of the two of them nuzzling in the law library."

When Linda finally met Kathy at the firm's Christmas party she was confounded. "The moment I saw her I knew she wasn't the kind of woman Paul found physically attractive," Linda said. "But he was mesmerized by her. They talked and laughed together all evening. Every once in a while Paul would ask if he could get me something, but otherwise he ignored me.

"When we got home I exploded. Paul apologized for neglecting me but he said he couldn't understand why I was so upset. 'Because you're so damned involved with Kathy!' I said. 'Kathy? She's smart and interesting and I learn a lot from her,' Paul answered. But surely I didn't think he was in love with her? No, I said. 'Then what in heaven's name are you jealous *about*?' he asked. And I couldn't answer."

But the question stuck in Linda's mind. Instead of brooding about her suspicions, she began to probe for the hidden wellspring of her jealousy. As she explored she discovered—and eventually was able to face up to—insecurities in herself. "I'd always worried that I wasn't clever enough or informed enough to be interesting to Paul," she said, "and I guess I never tried to be. I realized that the reason I had to think Kathy attracted him physically was that then I could compete; if it was her mind, I was licked."

With this much insight into the real reasons for her jealous feelings, Linda was able to do something positive about the situation. First she took an adult-education course on "Law for the Layman." "It may sound silly," Linda said, "But just being able to talk to Paul in some of his own language—to know something about his work even in a small way—gave me some of the confidence I needed. What I did surprised Paul, but I could see he was touched, pleased." As a result Linda was able to confide in Paul, telling him of her feelings of insecurity and inadequacy, and to enlist his help in overcoming them.

In a world where we are so at the mercy of rapid change and capricious chance, it is little wonder that we seek stability and certainty in intimate relationships, especially with the one we love most. Anything that seems likely to upset or interfere with that becomes a threat. Jealousy, most psychologists agree, is one understandable response to this situation. (Some definitions are needed here. Originally jealousy meant vigilance, a zealous watchfulness, with perhaps a hint of potential wrath, as in Jehovah's promise and warning, *I the Lord thy God am a jealous God.* In current usage, jealousy is perhaps best defined as suspicion or resentment of someone you consider to be a rival, someone or something you fear threatens a relationship you value.)

If jealousy is used in a negative way—to punish, to get attention, to excuse self-pity, to provoke, to fuel arguments—then it probably will live up to its reputation and corrode matters further. But if it is channeled into a positive approach, it can lead to constructive ends: at best, to clarify a conflict or resolve a problem; at least, to provide enough insight and self-awareness to help you deal with difficult situations.

Examining your jealous feelings also can lead to an awareness of how jealousy can be provoked purposely in a relationship, what that says about the relationship and about yourself. The experience that Marci Anderson, a 27-yearold biologist, went through recently is a good example.

For nearly a year, Marci said, she was in love with a man who seemed to be everything she'd hoped for. They lived together, planned to get married. "But once Bill was sure of *my* feelings, he began to change," Marci said. "He'd call at the last minute to say he wasn't coming home that night, and give me a patently phony excuse. He'd tell me how he had to brush off the adoring women in his office. He'd make a pass at a woman at a party and then look over at me and shrug, as if to say, 'What can I do? She likes me.' I never was the jealous type, but Bill had me acting like a first-class bitch.

"One night we fought about it," Marci continued, "and in the midst of the argument I suddenly realized Bill was *enjoying* himself. He *wanted* me to be jealous. That shook me. *What kind of man needs a woman to be jealous of him?* I thought. A weak one, I realized. *What kind of man would do that to a woman he said he loved?* Not one you could trust. *And what was wrong with me, going along with it?* Clearly I was mixed up; certainly I wasn't ready to commit myself to anyone, much less to Bill. Once I was sure of my answers, I walked out on him. But if I hadn't got jealous in the first place, I might never have asked myself those questions."

One reason jealousy is so painful, psychotherapist Leah Schaefer points out, is the feeling that you can't do anything to change the situation that's causing it. "But you can take your jealousy and ask questions of it—what or whom am I really jealous of? Am I being melodramatic or realistic? Do I enjoy the pain? Can I do something to stop it?"

It works. I tried it myself recently at a party where my wife (who enjoys flirting) spent most of the evening in animated conversation with a good-looking man. Normally she is not that animated when *we* talk together. Jealousy stirred, mild but undeniable.

I asked myself some questions. For example, why is she animated? Obviously she's having a good talk. Perhaps I don't discuss things that interest her much—maybe I should work a bit harder, be less conversationally predictable. Do I love her? Yes. (If I didn't, why would it matter *how* animatedly she talked to someone else?) Since I do love her, why shouldn't I be pleased that she is enjoying herself? Don't I want her to have a good time at the party? Or do I think because she is enjoying a conversation she is arranging a tryst with Good-looking Fellow? Obviously not.

Once I realized that my wife's conversation with someone else took nothing away from me—in fact, it pointed to a way I could improve our relationship—I also realized that there was no reason for jealousy.

Many of the couples I spoke with raised the question of jealousy of a spouse's time. This was especially true of the more recently married couples, some of whom seemed to feel that any time spent away from the spouse was an emotional affront. "You think marriage means you will be together all the time, and you want to be," one young woman, wed five months, said to me. "Then look at what happens. You have half an hour together at breakfast, when you aren't coherent anyway; you don't see each other until dinner; then it's time for Jerry to study and both of us to share the household chores; and then we go to bed. I'm shocked at how little time we *do* have together, and that's why I'm jealous of the time Jerry spends with anything or anybody else!"

This wife is resentful (i.e., jealous) because Jerry has refused to give up the Sunday-afternoon two-hour tennis matches he has been in the habit of playing with his bachelor friends. "I don't want to ask Jerry to give up his tennis," she says, "but it's accepted that once you're married, you spend Sundays with your wife." Jerry replies: "I work all week and I go to business college and study every night. Is it also accepted that you give up the one thing that's fun and relaxation just because you're married? How can she be jealous of two little hours?"

Well, another young husband is jealous of *one* little hour. An engineer who also has night classes and homework, David has arranged a schedule for himself and his wife so that every night from 8 to 9 P.M. they are free to be with each other. "Once a week," he said, "my wife has lunch with a friend, Mike. He has an hour of her time on that day—the hour we have at night *he* has at lunch. We each have the same time with *my* wife!"

Unrealistic? Of course. But real enough to the men and women caught in this situation. "Dealing with this kind of jealousy by holding a stop watch on each other is obviously pointless," one marriage counselor said. "If jealousy could motivate these people to examine their ideas about what marriage is and requires, what they can realistically expect from it, it would be useful in helping them get rid of the stereotypes."

Ann Watkins, 26, tells how jealousy of her husband's work almost broke up their marriage. Bill Watkins, a chemical engineer in a plastics factory, was put in charge of a special experimental project only a few weeks after he and his wife had moved into a new home in a rural New Jersey community. Soon he was working late several nights a week, and many Saturdays as well.

"I worried about his health at first," Ann recalls, "but he thrived on the schedule. The only one who suffered, I felt, was me. There I was, stuck in a country town with nothing to do, and as I saw it, Bill didn't even want to come home to spend the evenings with me. I was jealous—he had something interesting in his life and I didn't."

Ann expressed her jealousy in small, resentful gestures—she stopped bothering to keep dinner warm; she took no pains to look nice; she either went to bed before Bill came home or sat up only to argue with him. "Things reached the point where it was either break up or get help," she said, "and we weren't prepared to break up."

They went to a marriage counselor, who after two sessions challenged Ann with some sharp questions: Did she make an honest effort to understand the job pressures on her husband? Had she ever really believed that he worked late because he had to? Did she try to develop any interests or resources of her own, rather than expecting her husband to provide the stimulation in her life?

"The answers—when I was able to face them—were unpleasantly revealing," Ann admits. It turned out that Bill's special project—running a series of several hundred complicated tests on synthetic compounds—was not all that fascinating to him. "It's donkeywork," Bill said. "It was given to me because I'm the junior man on the staff. But if I finish it on schedule and come up with some useful findings, I'll probably get a raise and a promotion. I know Ann would like that." And Ann came to see that part of her jealousy of Bill's work involvement was actually discontent with herself and her emotional dependency on others: "If I were doing more myself, and therefore were more interesting, I wouldn't be concerned that he'd find his job more fascinating."

These days, jealousy of a spouse's job can reflect a man's insecurities too. "My husband was all sweetness and light when I told him I was going to work in an interior-design firm," said a 29-year-old New York woman. "I knew he didn't really want me to take a job, but he didn't openly object to my decision. A year later I was offered double my salary with a competing company. That meant I was earning more than Larry—enough to support myself if I had to.

"Right away he became controlling about money. He wanted me to deposit my pay check in our joint account. He badgered me about things I bought. 'Look,' I finally said, 'I earn the money and I know how to spend it.' Larry just glared at me and turned away. I suppose he never really wanted me to make anything of myself—it was too threatening to him. But he had managed to disguise or control his feelings until I outearned him. He couldn't take that.

"I left Larry a year later. It took that long for me to know that I couldn't love a man I didn't respect—and I couldn't respect a man who would be jealous of me for being successful."

For many young married couples, jealousy can be particularly distressing when it involves their own children. It is always a shock to recognize and admit the feeling. "What kind of monster am I," a new father asks, "to feel jealous of the attention my wife gives my own baby?" "How can I possibly feel hurt because my little daughter always runs to her daddy instead of to me?" asks a young mother.

Both reactions, however, are essentially natural. Indeed, they might almost be called "existential jealousy"—a sensation that is simply *there*, which will not yield to reason or wisdom or even shame. To deal with this jealousy—indeed, to convert it into a positive force for growth—requires an understanding of what it represents.

"Every time we move from one major stage in the life cycle to another a sense of loss is involved," says family therapist Sanford Sherman, executive director of New York's Jewish Family Service. "For example, as a child grows more independent he must give up some of the satisfactions of dependency. Maturity develops at the expense of youthfulness. The rewards of marriage mean some loss of freedoms. We always feel 'jealous' of what we must give up at the crisis points of growth. Unless we can understand that, such jealousy can become an obstacle to that growth."

Sherman cites a father's jealousy—especially of his first child—as an example of this process. It is understandable, he explains, for a man to be jealous of a baby who he feels displaces him as the main object of his wife's affection and concern; who makes enormous demands on her time and energy; who invades the intimacy and privacy of a marriage.

"But repressing jealousy may serve only to implant it more firmly and keep a father in childish competition with his child for a much longer time," says Sherman. "If a man can admit to his feelings of loss and if his wife can share these feelings sympathetically, something more realistic takes place. A father begins to see the child as a person who needs him rather than as a rival. He joins his wife in nurturing the child; the emotional balance of the marriage is gradually restored. Jealousy and the sense of loss are transmitted into emotional growth."

Sherman cites jealousy of a spouse's parents as another case in point. "A man resents it that his wife calls her mother every day or asks her advice instead of his; or a woman resents what she feels is her husband's excessive concern for his parents or his overinvolvement with relatives. If they allow those jealousies to go unquestioned," Sherman observes, "they'll fight about them, and each will cling even more closely to the parents for emotional support. But if they recognize and deal with the jealousy as part of maturation, it can help them to advance to the next stage of their life cycle—one of mutual interdependence as adults rather than as children.''

In all its manifestations, jealousy springs essentially from self-doubt, a lack of self-esteem, feelings of inadequacy—all the things psychotherapists lump under the heading "low self-image." For example, I asked each of the men and women I talked with what one thing their partner might do that would make them most jealous. Only a few mentioned philandering or sexual infidelity. Most mentioned situations that threatened their self-esteem: *If he talked with old friends about things I didn't know and I felt left out . . . When she tells me about all the good times she had before she met me, all her old boy friends . . . When he talks about his work and I don't understand it . . . When everybody clusters around her at a party and ignores me . . .*

To confront such jealousy—to convert it from a negative to a potentially positive reaction—requires that we stop concentrating on what the other person is doing. "It requires," says psychoanalyst Dr. Rollo May, "turning one's attention to one's self and asking: 'Why is my self-esteem so low in the first place?' I quite understand that this question may be difficult to answer. But at least it turns your concern to an area you can do something about."

All too often most of us permit jealousy to deteriorate into feelings of guilt or self-pity or helplessness. What jealousy says then is, "Poor me!" But jealousy can be used to motivate us to constructive action: to examine our emotional needs more intelligently; to do something positive about shortcomings; to work harder at a relationship; even to voice an honest cry for help—to say, "I love you . . . I want you . . . I'm afraid of what's happening and I need you to help me stop it." When allowed to go unquestioned, jealousy remains malevolent. Examined in the light of reason, it can be a stimulus for growth.

Like Norman Lobsenz, Karen Durbin notes that jealousy is "well on the way to becoming the New Sin of the liberated generation." But, she argues, the elimination of jealousy is very difficult and its suppression may be dangerous. She knows because she *tried* to be liberated. Her counter-cultural milieu—heavy on radical politics and women's liberation—demanded that of her and she made the effort. But for her and for others she knew, "The energy required for all that coping was too much, and I fled." All jealousy, she concludes, is a cry of pain. It "will probably be with us as long as sex remains an expression of love and as long as love remains the most effective means (apart from religion) of assuaging our essential isolation."

Durbin's article and her TV talk-show appearances were much discussed in New York City. Many of the would-be liberated were relieved to hear a voice "from the left" saying that it was all right to feel jealous.

3

On Sexual Jealousy

Karen Durbin

There is a house in Greenwich Village that lacks the bathroom door-knob and has a hole in the front bedroom wall. Actually, by now, privacy has probably been restored to the bathroom by the current tenant and the wall re-plastered as well. It's also likely that the upstairs phone, which was ripped out of the wall, has been re-connected.

I know about the lock and the hole and the telephone because I caused the damage. The doorknob and lock went when I shut myself into the bathroom and threatened to commit suicide. I didn't threaten, actually. I just locked myself in and took enough Seconal to make me look weird and hid the rest of the pills in the cabinet, leaving the empty bottle lying significantly in the basin. Then I waited, hoping to create an ominous silence for the person shouting at me from the other side. It worked; he smashed the lock, and the doorknob sympathetically fell out. He also pulled the telephone out of the wall, but that was my fault, too, in a way, since I was pretending to make a phone call he didn't want me to make. The hole in the wall was my own. I threw a nice, heavy Olafdaughters clog, and he ducked.

Karen Durbin (1944 -   ) is senior editor of *The Village Voice*. "On Sexual Jealousy" appeared on October 18, 1973 and is reprinted by permission of the author and *The Village Voice*. Copyright © *The Village Voice,* Inc., 1973.

What was the cause of all this senseless violence? Jealousy. Sexual jealousy, in fact. You remember jealousy. It's what made Othello strangle Desdemona. It's the thing that's responsible for a large proportion of what the police call crimes of passion: husbands shooting wives, wives shooting husbands, husbands shooting wives' lovers, and so on.

It's also the thing that makes calm, sensible people like me act crazy. Admittedly, I grew up in a household where people tended to express themselves emphatically. One of the more riveting things my mother ever said to my father was at 5 a.m. one morning (they didn't believe in fighting in front of the kids; they also assumed we were sound sleepers). It went something like this: "You break those dishes, and I'll take a sledge hammer to your Cadillac." Daddy, it seems, had piled up all the good dinner plates and was preparing to drop them on the kitchen floor. My parents deal in fairly overt sexual symbols. For all that early combat training, I am not moved to violence except by jealousy. I think, apart from sex itself, it's probably one of the strongest human passions going. And the kind that really stings is sexual jealousy.

Which makes it all the odder that sexual jealousy should be well on the way to becoming the New Sin of the liberated generation. But that's what seems to be happening. The sexual revolution that began in the early 1960s with the Pill and which then took on fresh impetus and a new direction with the rise of the women's movement a few years later is still going on.

A new sexual morality is forming as the old one crumbles. The old one, with its categories of Good Girls (they got married and then fucked) and Bad Girls (they just got fucked), rated fidelity and monogamy very high. Sex was a symbol of total commitment and couldn't be justified without proof of that commitment—the marriage contract. Adultery was a sin.

Things started softening up about 10 years ago, when Episcopal bishops made headlines with something called situational ethics, and premarital sex was okay with someone you loved but better if you were engaged. The line between Good Girls and Bad Girls began to dissolve; in some cases—say, the sweetly promiscuous hippie chicks in their granny dresses—it washed out altogether. Nevertheless, transitional morality, like the sexual revolution, left the basic ideals of marriage and fidelity intact.

The women's movement changed all that. Marriage and, for that matter, monogamy itself (pair-bonding, as Ti-Grace and the anthropologists call it) came under attack; it was argued that a woman who committed herself to one man was collaborating in her own oppression. And while that argument remains unsettled among feminists, it pulled the last prop out from under an already badly shaken system of sexual ethics. An attack on monogamy is implicitly an attack on sexual fidelity, and that, in turn, makes jealousy an indefensible state.

From the politico's point of view, to be jealous is to be a kind of capitalist pig of the heart: you're being possessive, treating your lover like a piece of property with No Trespassing signs posted along the fence. You are, in other words, being politically incorrect. Shame on you.

I first encountered some aspects of this kind of thinking a couple of years ago, not, interestingly enough, in the women's movement but in conversation with a guy I knew in the peace movement. He's very much a committed freak (as opposed to straight) who earns a little money doing record reviews, spends the rest of his time in radical politics, and lives in a storefront on the Lower East Side. We were talking one night about monogamous relationships. He thought they were bad. "It's selfish and lazy," he said. "Two people lean all over each other and never bother to get close to anyone else." I .ook exception to this, saying that the one really long affair I'd had with someone had been an amazingly vigorous experience, forcing both of us to reveal outselves and to take emotional risks we would never have bothered to take otherwise and, as far as I could tell, still leaving us free to enjoy deep friendships with other people. I admitted, however, that we agreed not to sleep with other people while we were together, that in fact, I got jealous when a man I was really involved with slept with other women.

"But," he said, "doesn't that just *add* to your relationship?" He pointed out that he actually introduces his girl friend to men he thinks she'd like to sleep with. I managed to fight off the conviction that he was some kind of pervert, but it was immediately replaced by the conviction that I was a mean prig. Finally, I said I felt rather guilty if I got involved with a married man, since I was doing something that hurt another woman. He really blew up at that one. "That's none of your business," he said emphatically. "You're interfering with the relationship between that man and his wife when you start feeling guilty about her! That's just pure emotional imperialism."

Emotional imperialism? I left the conversation feeling guilty because I'd felt guilty. And trying to figure out why it's not interference when I sleep with someone else's husband, but it is interference when I feel guilty about it. This new morality was obviously going to be even trickier than the old one.

Shortly afterward, I had an opportunity to put these new revolutionary ideals to the test (it is a boon, after all, for a single woman to be told she should sleep with other women's mates and not feel guilty about it). A woman I know and like, who has the mixed fortune to be married to one of the more attractive men alive and well in the universe today, happened to remark that she didn't think fidelity was important, and neither did he.

"Fidelity?" she asked me, in the same incredulous tone my movement buddy had used. "Oh, we're much too close for that to matter." "Wowee," I said, full of amazement and lust. Lust outed, after a decent interval, and was that ever a miserable mess. It shouldn't have been, rationally speaking. That is, I didn't want to get involved with him to any degree that would threaten the marriage, and he didn't seem inclined in that direction either. So what was the problem? Well, she was jealous, low-down, on-the-ground, what-are-they-doing-now jealous. I saw her at a party at one point, and she looked haggard and in pain. I wasn't the sole source of that pain; it turned out they were going through a difficult time in any case. But I was contributing to it. We both knew that and could barely manage to say hello. We stayed on different sides of the room. At one pointed, I sprawled out on the rug while I was talking with some people, and I saw her eyes travel the length of my body, tracing every curve, like a tongue exploring a sore in the mouth. She was, of course, feeling nothing I wouldn't have felt in her place. Except for one thing—she also felt guilty for feeling jealous.

My part in that situation came to an end, finally, and left me wondering where my common sense had been when I got into it. I might not have given it a lot more thought if it hadn't begun to be clear over the past year or so that attitudes that were once confined to the fairly arcane thought processes of New York movement folk have started spreading like the plague through the popular media.

Without the political framework, political error transmutes into emotional immaturity. We don't have sins any more, just ideological failure or mental illness. In the small flood of how-to-have-a-liberated-relationship literature that has been pouring out during the last year or so, I keep encountering the pretense that jealousy doesn't exist—much like the Victorian pretense that sexual passion didn't exist—at least for mature, free-spirited people. The O'Neills' book *Open Marriage* is a case in point. I think the book, which is boring and puffy and insubstantial, has been such a smash best-seller for two reasons: First, people don't take marriage for granted as a good thing any more and yet they don't know quite what to do instead; second, the ads, as well as that rather clever title, suggest that the book is going to say it's okay for married people to fuck around. Any book that promises to tell people how to have their cake and eat it, too, is likely to sell well. The book does say that, but with the pious caveat that if your relationship isn't "mature" enough to permit such flexibility, then don't try it. Jealousy, these New Moralists imply, is not only unliberated, it's childish. Sort of rude and unnecessary, like chewing with your mouth open. Take that, Othello.

Similar thinking has cropped up in a number of unlikely places, in *Newsweek's* cover story on divorce, for example, and in *New York* magazine's special issue on couples. Even the good, gray *Times* ran an article, somewhat wistfully entitled "Fidelity: Is It Just an Old-Fashioned Concept?", in which a representative collection of recent college graduates allowed as how fidelity *was* just an old-fashioned concept and said they would each do their best not to impose such a ridiculous burden on their future mates. Some of the women interviewed were more hesitant about this than the men, but they were apologetic about their hesitation. Everybody seemed to feel that jealousy was wrong.

This same apologetic air cropped up in a new marriage contract printed in a recent issue of *Ms.* The couple who'd drawn up the contract emphasized, as these new contracts do, not only equality and mutual respect but also freedom and independence. Then they blew it. Starting with a phrase like "Freely recognizing our insecurity in these matters. . .." they swore, to the best of their ability, to be sexually faithful to each other. Ha! Political fuck-ups! Emotional midgets! And there it is on paper for everyone to see! What brass, as my mother used to say.

Have we all gone thoroughly mad? What sort of liberation is it that leaves us apologizing for our passions? Freely recognizing my insecurity in these matters, I'd still argue that in the recent welter of theorizing about how we ought to live, we seem to have lost sight of simple human reality. It is as if we've dipped back into the 18th century, back to the view that people are perfectible and that social relations can be made to function like a well-oiled machine. The trick is to get the grit out of the cogs, and the machine will run the way it rationally, perfectly should.

According to the latest blueprint for happiness, jealousy is grit, mere sludge in the engine of the culturally revolutionary, non-possessive relationship. It's a hangover from the bad old days of capitalist, property-minded closed marriage, and a little consciousness raising ought to be enough to get it out of the way.

The only trouble with the blueprint is that very few people seem to be able to follow it with any success. Take the O'Neills, for example. They have said when interviewed that an open marriage doesn't have to be sexually open; theirs, as it happens, isn't. Well, that, as it happens, is the hard part. I don't need a book to tell me how not to get jealous if my boy friend goes bowling twice a week with his pals. And I know a lot of people who are managing pretty well these days to avoid the cloying, clinging, world-excluding togetherness that traditional marriage was once supposed to mean and who nevertheless find it fairly rattling if one partner slopes off to somebody else's bed.

It's true that the superficial logic of the jealousy-equals-possession-equals-immaturity argument is seductive, and it's also true that the old morality left too little room for human complexity. If your lover sleeps with someone else, it doesn't have to mean he or she is a hopeless moral slob, or doesn't love you any more, or that the world and your romance are coming to an end. But this burgeoning new morality, whether wrapped up in political or psychiatric rhetoric, is no more realistic. It is as if, having discarded a lot of dumb old rules, we're loading right up again on dumb new ones. New guilts for old.

To begin with, a couple of weeks at the library and on the phone to anthropologists is enough to blow the popular notion that somewhere out there in sexy Polynesia or up in Greenland with the wife-proffering Eskimos, jealousy doesn't exist. Serious anthropologists and sociologists reiterate that, however various and liberal the sexual attitudes of different peoples, sexual jealousy appears to be a constant. It occurs in sexist societies and relatively non-sexist ones, in sexually restrictive societies and in societies where sex is frequent and easy. Innate or not (and no one has come up with a firm answer to that one), it plagues societies which have far less use for it than ours. In one polygynous African tribe, the term for fellow wives is "people who roast each other."

Further, it's simple-minded on the face of it to say that jealousy is mere possessiveness. It's like saying that love is mere possession. I don't feel I own a man simply because I love him, but if I love him and I think I'm faced with the threat of losing him, I may well feel jealous.

Why jealousy and not just grief? Perhaps because jealousy is a state of protest, a response to a situation that hasn't reached resolution. Grief is an acceptance of loss. He's gone, I feel terrible, and that's that. Given time and human resilience, one of these days I'll be over it. But jealousy is a refusal to accept. The initial response to the loss of love may be jealousy, but it eventually gives way to grief. Grief is the acknowledgment of a fact, jealousy a response to a threat. He isn't gone; he's still here, at least when he's not there with Her; I may or may not lose him. Jealousy is a state of tension, unresolved and tormenting, which is no doubt why it provokes people to do things like kill each other and, with us milder types, throw shoes at the wall.

Freud defined ordinary, garden-variety jealousy as a cluster of emotions "compounded of grief . . . and of the narcissistic wound . . . feelings of enmity against the successful rival, and of . . . self-criticism which tries to hold the jealous person's own ego accountable for his loss." Freud and other psychiatrists have been at some pains to make the distinction between "normal" and pathological jealousy. Normal jealousy has its basis in a real situation in which a relationship is plausibly perceived as threatened. Pathological jealousy, in contrast, persists despite the absence of any real or even probable threat. It's at once a disguise for and a symptom of a disorder or anxiety in the jealous person, and its solution lies not in the adjustment of the relationship but in identification and treatment of the disorder.

In its most common form, pathological jealousy is a reflex of insecurity. I know a woman who has become so jealous that she can't bear for her husband to spend time with other people, women or men. They're unable to meet new friends and see less and less of the old ones; he's exhausted and frustrated by their increasing isolation. It's no accident that her jealousy coincides with the increasing success of her husband's career (he's a writer) and her anxiety over her own lack of one, particularly now that her children are grown. She's tormented by a sense that her own life is empty, that she's empty, but for the moment she's unable to bring herself to start a career since she's convinced she's incapable of doing anything well. The demands she's placing on her husband threaten to become intolerable and are ultimately pointless: her "jealousy" won't abate until she's able independently to recover her sense of self-worth. To describe this woman as jealous is like describing someone who's shrieking with pain as noisy. She's not jealous, she's crippled.

The distinction between ordinary and pathological jealousy is important, because it's constantly being obliterated in the kind of new social thinking I've been describing. The result is a common assumption—in the O'Neills' book, for example—that jealousy is a sign of inherent insecurity on the part of the jealous person. This makes way for the notion that "healthy" people can "outgrow" jealousy altogether, conjuring up visions of some emotional Land of Cockaigne where everybody is constantly, smilingly secure, infinitely generous, and infinitely undemanding. If there is such a state, it's called Nirvana. It takes Buddist monks years, even lifetimes, to reach, and it calls for some pretty thorough transcending not just of the bad passions—like sexual jealousy—but also of the good ones—like sexual love.

What seems to be going by the boards in the kind of thinking that attributes jealousy to personal insecurity, or emotional immaturity, or nursery-school possessiveness, is the perception that love itself creates the conditions for anxiety. If a man loves a woman (or a woman loves a woman or if any X loves any Y), and that woman seems to be getting seriously interested in another man, then her first lover isn't being insecure if he feels threatened. The relationship itself has become insecure, at least for the moment. Say, then, that the woman turns to first lover and says, "Don't worry, darling, I don't love you any less just because I'm spending half my time with Harold, whom I also love." What if it's true? What if she really does love them both and has no plans to leave first lover for second, and first lover is a busy fellow with lots of interests to take up the time she's spending with second lover?

Well, a number of things might happen. A friend of mine in that situation seemed to retreat emotionally and sexually, from his wife and from other women as well. He is at once very calm and very, very busy; he works almost all the time now. Another friend just seems to have swallowed hard and accepted the situation. She's been married for several years to a man who usually has an outside affair going. *She* doesn't usually have an outside affair going; she says she's just less inclined than her husband to get sexually involved with people. He assures her that he won't leave her, is crazy about her, in fact. She believes him. I asked her once if she would prefer that he not sleep with other women. She said yes. Why? "Well, because then I wouldn't have to be always *coping*."

Coping. I know what that's about. I once found myself on the short end of a triangle and had a go at being big about it. It seemed clear that his feeling for this other lady didn't spring from dissatisfaction with me, that he wasn't going to leave me, and that, presumably, he needed to see the lady or otherwise he wouldn't be doing it. Okay. Part of loving someone is respecting their needs. I kept it up for about a month, and it didn't work awfully well. My peace of mind shattered on little things, like the time a terrific concert came up, and tickets were impossible to get, and he got some and then took her instead of me. Little, right? Petty. Small. Mean. Yep, but I hated him for weeks. Or the time I had my first article rejected and was feeling very low and wanted him to come and comfort me. But he wasn't there. He was off spending time with his friend. Having fun while I suffered. The bastard.

The question, finally, that refused to go away was, "Why is he doing this to me?" Making me cope, in a way I wasn't making him cope. Then I began to contemplate the power he had to hurt me, and I writhed under it, and the need I had for his reassurance, and I cursed myself for it, and I found myself plotting what to do to get away from him, back to my safe, inviolate autonomy. Grief. . .enmity. . .the narcissistic wound. . .self-blame. Around and around it went. If I managed to keep the jealous hydra at bay, it came back, and the struggle started all over again, always with the thought, "I wouldn't do this to you. I wouldn't do this to you." At some point, the energy required for all that coping was too much, and I fled.

Love creates need and power; that's why loving is dangerous, why some people don't do it at all. I need my lover if I'm to be entirely happy; it is only he who knows me, finally. I have the power to hurt him, as he does me, by seeming to love him less, by leaving him. One doesn't seek this power. It's a gift, growing out of the intensity of one lover's feelings for the other. I understand that at some point he chose to make himself vulnerable to me, as I've chosen to make myself vulnerable to him. If there is trust in love instead of terror, it comes from the understanding that neither lover will take advantage of the power the other has granted. We strive for balance in this: to be equally powerful, equally at risk (knowing, of course, that the balance shifts constantly back and forth). Finally, how does one recognize love except by the way one loves? "I wouldn't do this to you," I said and knew that I meant it. It wasn't blame, simply the perception of a difference between us that I found, as the divorce courts say, irreconcilable.

Not that it would have been for everyone. There is my friend who finds it tolerable to "cope," even though she wishes she didn't have to. There are other couples around who are moving more or less spontaneously into communal or group marriages. And I've met one couple, at least, who both sleep with other people regularly without feeling jealous—provided the relationships outside the marriage remain clearly secondary.

Different strokes for different folks. It seems reasonable to assume that sexual jealousy in some form will probably be with us as long as sex remains an expression of love and as long as love remains the most effective means (apart from religion) of assuaging our essential isolation. This sort of jealousy is a kind of intelligence: a perception of one's needs, not necessarily the need to control, or to possess, but the singular emotional needs which are for each of us a corollary of love. Love is as various as lovers are, and so our needs are various. Loving and all that has to do with loving will never be a well-oiled machine. Its parts are too mutable and too distinct from one another.

There's always an impulse when old rules break down to set up new ones in their place. "Thou shalt not commit adultery" to be replaced by "Thou shalt not be jealous." It makes life so much simpler; it saves a lot of thought. You know just where you are at any given moment. There's no existential terror for folks with a master plan for living.

But the point of liberation, of course, whether sexual, political, or personal, is to live with as few rules as possible, and that means making as much room as we can afford for human variety. The only guidelines, in the end, are experience and necessity. For some of us, that may well mean an end to fidelity or the need for it. But not for everyone. All jealousy, finally, is a cry of pain. To ignore, suppress, or condemn it is at best unhelpful, at worst cruel. One must heed the cry and look to its cause. The causes will be as various as people are various; so will the solutions.

Myself, I sing the Song of Solomon and will stop only when I find that, for me, it no longer rings true:

'Set me as a seal upon thine heart, as a seal upon thine arm; for love is strong as death, jealousy is cruel as the grave.''

Taken together, these three articles reflect the emergence of some new attitudes toward the basic emotion of jealousy. Judith Viorst's "Confessions" is similar to so many discussions of jealousy from the 1950s and 1960s. A certain amount of jealousy is seen as a natural by-product of love—and even as *evidence* of love. The reader is advised to "contain" this normal jealousy, to bear it stoically. Only "pathological" jealousy—defined in terms of excessive abuse of the self and/or others—is viewed as worthy of concern or as requiring conscious intervention. Norman Lobsenz—writing for the same audience five years later—introduces an alternative understanding of jealousy. Now, for some, *all* jealousy—not merely the "pathological"—is negatively valued. "Little jealousies" are seen not as proof of love but rather as evidences of insecurity and mistrust—and, therefore, as "opportunities for growth." *And*, although he knows that all the data are not yet in, Lobsenz is hopeful that the green-eyed monster can be tamed. Like Lobsenz, Karen Durbin has considered the possibility that jealousy can be reduced and perhaps eliminated. She and some of her friends tried to eliminate it, but couldn't. If Greenwich Village is seen as one of our sociocultural laboratories, this experiment in the eradication of jealousy failed.

These articles—and the testimony of the popular media in general—do not *prove* anything. The Lobsenz article does not prove that jealousy is an obsolete emotion; Durbin's experiences do not prove that every attempt to reduce jealousy is doomed to failure. Items from the media are *clues* which must be interpreted with care. *These* articles—and they are representative of others—seem to suggest that, for some people today, the meaning of jealousy is in flux. The media remind us that a substantial number of people want to be more self-conscious about jealousy, to understand it better, and to manage it more constructively.

While many individuals have adopted or experimented with this more active orientation toward jealousy, many others have not. Alternatives to the traditional understanding of jealousy never *displaced* the older view; they merely *joined* it. Where once there was only one widely held view of jealousy and marriage, now there are two—or more. Dialogue has begun where, till now, there was silence. This book is part of that dialogue. But before we can directly address the question of jealousy management (in Part IV), we must look carefully at the psychodynamics (Part II) and the cultural patternings (Part III) of jealousy. Before we look at ways of working with jealousy, we must learn something of how jealousy works—in ourselves and in our society.

II

Jealousy and the Person

My husband was so jealous of the baby he wouldn't let me nurse it.

—Young wife, Chicago area

We turn now from the personal experiences of jealousy described in Part I to a more general consideration of the ways in which jealousy is experienced and understood by the individual. We seek in Part II to explore the *psychology of jealousy*. Although some attention will be given to "pathological" jealousy, our primary focus is the inner workings of "normal" jealousy common to us all.

Contemporary psychology is not all of one piece. The articles in this section represent three distinct-but-overlapping psychological points of view. Hermann Vollmer and A. S. Neill focus on the developmental process, on the ways in which jealousy is experienced and expressed in infancy and childhood—and the imprint of those experiences on adulthood. Chris Downing and Robert Seidenberg work out of the psychoanalytic tradition; they seek to uncover the hidden causes and meanings of jealousy and to offer insights which rob it of some of its power to disrupt. The articles by the Walsters and by Ellen Berscheid and Jack Fei are rooted in the social psychological perspective; they explore the relationship between the individual and the surrounding social context. The first article of each pair offers an overview of a way of looking at jealousy; the second applies or extends the basic paradigm.

The separation of this section from the one which follows is in many ways artificial. Jealousy in the individual cannot be divorced from sociocultural considerations, as Seidenberg points out in Chapter 7. But jealousy is a complex emotion; in order to understand it we must look at the parts as well as the whole. It is individuals, after all, who together create the cultures in which we live.

In our search for material on jealousy in the popular magazines, we found roughly twice as many articles on jealousy in children as on sexual jealousy among adults. Many of these were "how to" articles designed to help parents cope with sibling rivalry. We found a *few* references in both kinds of articles to the relationship between the child's and the adult's experience of jealousy, but we found *no* popular article which presented both concerns as deeply interrelated. In many articles the child's jealousy is treated primarily as a problem for the *parents*: It disrupts the household, makes demands on the mother, thwarts her plans, and so forth. (Fathers are seldom mentioned.) These media suggest that jealousy is a problem in childhood and again in adult relationships, but little is said about the connection between the two.

We see the jealousies oɪ childhood and adulthood as deeply interrelated. Although there is no firm consensus among social scientists as to the precise measure, it seems safe to conclude that the parents' handling of the child's inevitable jealous feelings affects the extent to which jealousy will disrupt his/her life in adulthood. Therefore, in order to better understand our adult experiences of jealousy, let us look in more detail at the developmental process through which each of us has passed and by which each of us has been marked.

Jealousy appears to be almost universal in children. And how could it be otherwise? To the infant, the mother is the principal love object and, indeed, the center of the world.[1] He comes to see her as *his* ʰe takes her attention for granted. Only gradually does he learn to let the mother out of sight without undue anxiety or rage. Erik Erikson (1963:247) calls this "the infant's first social achievement."

Because the newborn makes such heavy demands of the mother, the father often feels neglected and ma; come to feel jealous of the child. The new arrival, after all, requires more time and energy from the mother than would a lover. The father may feel that he is deprived not only of sex and affection but also of innumerable *services* previously performed by his wife—including things as simple as her availability for small talk. Some fathers handle these tensions adequately, but others develop strong—although usually unconscious—hostilities toward the child. An angry response is perhaps most likely from a man who is very dependent on his wife and on the services and support she provides. But even fathers who can prepare their own meals and enjoy extra time alone often feel jealous of their children. *And* they feel *guilty* about this jealousy. One jealous father asked disgustedly: "What kind of a monster am I to feel jealous of my own baby?".

The child, typically, is largely unaware of the rivalry with the father but he is *very* conscious of a younger sister or brother as one with whom he must share the attentions of the mother which previously were his alone. As Simpson (1966:257) has written:

> The erstwhile only child on whose tender psyche is suddenly thrust a a new baby feels that he has lost his mother. For some days he does not even see his mother during her hospital confinement. When the baby comes home [the older child] is exiled from his mother.

[1] For the sake of clarity we shall use *he/him/his* to refer to the child and *she/her* to refer to the mother. Our general account of jealousy in childhood is pertinent to both genders.

The mother is also faced with a new challenge: She must "divide herself" so that the needs of both children are met and so that neither of them feels neglected or rejected. *She* knows that she loves the first child no less than before, but the child cannot understand this: He views the younger sibling as an interloper, a competitor for a scarce commodity, the mother's love.[2]

As for the adult, so also for the child, jealousy creates a double bind. Bettelheim (1969:114) tells of kibbutz children who must watch their peers being put to bed by their parents when their own parents have not come. Those of whom they were jealous were also those on whom the jealous ones had to rely for comfort, stimulation, and company—so a lot of jealousy had to be repressed. This same condition obtains among siblings in a nuclear family and among playmates in a neighborhood.

The normal jealousy of competition is not literally inborn but it is part of the life of every person born into a family. It is necessarily exacerbated by the long dependency required by the nature of the human organism (and made still longer by the educational demands of industrial society). Parents cannot eliminate this experience for their children, but they can work to prevent its transformation into paranoia or delusions of persecution. In general, this is done by making sure the older child feels that he is loved. "The more confident a child is that his parents love and approve of him as he is, the less he needs to struggle against real or imagined rivals." (Quoted in Simpson, 1966:259).[3]

The next selection explores the causes of jealousy in children and some of the common reactions to or expressions of jealous feelings, including aggression, identification, withdrawal, repression, and masochism. Hermann Vollmer suggests that jealousy can be managed by means of detachment, sublimation,

[2] The sibling rivalry may be intensified by conditions of material scarcity. Anthropologist George M. Foster (1972:174) reports that in Mexico and Guatemala the post-weaning physical decline that afflicts many children—a function of the protein-calorie deficiencies resulting from withdrawal of the breast—"is popularly explained as due to the envy [jealousy] of the child toward the new foetus in his mother's womb which, when born, will replace him in his mother's affection."

[3] Future empirical research on jealousy might profitably devote considerable attention to number of siblings and birth-order. A key question in these days of concern for zero population growth is the jealousy potential of the only child. Will he be *less* jealous as an adult (because he never had to share the affection of his parents with another and so was always sure of their love) or *more* jealous (because, having never learned to share, he is now possessive and dependent in the extreme)?

and creative competition. But, he warns, the constructive use of jealousy is rare before puberty. Thus, parents should seek to minimize jealousy-provoking situations in the home. Also, the child should be encouraged to express his jealousy rather than being forced to repress and conceal it. Because early experiences of jealousy contribute to adult expectations and patterns, this article can be of value to adults exploring their own jealousies as well as to parents who wish to help minimize destructive experiences of jealousy for their children.

4

Jealousy in Children

Hermann Vollmer

A relation of mutualism exists between mother and infant: the mother needs her baby as much for the satisfaction of her maternal instincts as the infant needs his mother for the satisfaction of his instinctual drives. As soon as the child grows beyond infancy this archaic mutualism is disturbed, to his disadvantage. While the child still remains dependent, he no longer satisfies her maternal instincts as fully as he did as an infant. To him, his mother remains unique and irreplaceable, while he can be replaced by others. Usually beginning in the second year of life, this causes an emotional conflict for the child which is manifested by jealousy.

Jealousy is a normal response to actual, supposed, or threatened loss of affection. It is based on the child's possessive love for his mother, which lacks the sense of reality and calls for exclusive and unlimited possession of the beloved person and her affection. Though the child's first experience of jealousy invariably centers around his relationship to his mother, other relationships in later life may be similarly affected. Their psychological pattern is usually determined by this first experience of jealousy.

Herman Vollmer, M. D., (1896-1959) was a psychiatrist in a private practice in New York City. "Jealousy in Children" originally appeared in the *American Journal of Orthopsychiatry*, 16 (1946): 660-671. Copyright © 1946 the American Orthopsychiatric Association, Inc. Reproduced by permission.

In general, jealousy springs from an affection for a person who actually or supposedly diverts his love to others. Jealousy remains in continuous connection with the underlying affection, depends on and is nourished by it. Its intensity usually varies with the degree and actuality of the basic affection. In turn, jealousy is superimposed upon and overshadows the basic affection. It may merely accompany this affection as a secondary emotion. More often jealousy modifies the basic love into jealous love, an amalgamation of love and jealousy. With increased intensity, jealousy may penetrate and corrode the underlying affection. As a result, love may lose its original character and be more or less replaced by jealousy. In its extreme forms jealousy may assume pathologic proportions and a paranoid character: it severs its connection with the affection from which it springs and asphyxiates it. Jealousy thus becomes an isolated hostile emotion, exists without love, and as such is unreasonable.

Those are the possible correlations between jealousy and underlying affection. Jealousy itself is evidently an uneasiness of the ego through fear that the affection of a beloved person has been or may be diverted to someone else. The emotional security previously derived from the exclusive and unlimited affection of the beloved person is shattered or threatened by an actual or supposed rival. The less independence an individual has achieved, the more significant and painful is the loss of emotional security. In the case of a child, it touches the sole lifeline since he is entirely dependent on his mother. Jealousy may therefore mean central emotional disaster to him. In later life this extreme degree of jealousy is to be expected only if maturity is not accomplished and infantile trends, persist, such as possessiveness of love and the determination of unmodified emotional reactions by the pattern of childhood experiences.

Jealousy is charged with tension, and usually discharges into a variety of reactions.

AGGRESSION

Hostility is the most primitive and common reaction of the jealous individual. Primitive man destroyed his rival. As a remnant of this archaic form of reaction, there still persists in civilized man a psychosomatic state of anger—pallor and tachycardia—possibly due to the outpouring of adrenalin which prepares him for physical aggression. Yet individual physical aggression is no longer feasible in our civilization. Repressing this aggression only prolongs the suffering from jealousy, and necessitates more refined reaction forms in order to relieve emotional tension.

Aggression and hostility are forced into hiding. This "underground" hostility may then manifest itself as a false, exaggerated affection for the rival. The subconscious, however, continuously watches for the weak spot and for the right moment, with a minimum of obvious aggression, to do maximal harm.

This type of behavior is frequently seen in children and usually misinterpreted by their mothers. An older girl may tip over her baby brother in his bassinet while playing with him. The mother rationalizes that it was an accident, that the girl is very fond of her brother, and just wanted to cuddle him. Most such "accidents" are the result of subconscious hostility disguised by great affection. A girl under my observation showed distinct signs of mental depression following the death of her younger brother from tuberculous meningitis. "She was always very fond of him, and took it too much to heart," explained the mother. The truth was that this girl was always very jealous of her preferred brother, and saw in his death the result of her concealed death wishes. It was the guilt which brought on the depression.

Hostility and aggression may assume more refined forms, such as devaluation of the rival. Many parents, more or less intentionally, take advantage of this mechanism to decrease jealousy in a child. One has no need to be jealous of a baby "who cannot walk nor talk."

The aggression of a jealous individual may be directed against more than one rival, such as all siblings, or against any one with whom the beloved person is in contact. In an extreme form of jealousy, aggression is directed against everyone. A child may see every other child as a potential rival, and show habitual aggressiveness in kindergarten, school, or on the playground.

The aggression may be directed not only against rivals, but also against the person whose exclusive attention and affection are wanted. This person is thought to be responsible for the situation which creates the jealousy. Hostility against the mother for having another baby is an example. This hostility can rarely be relieved by frank acts of aggression. A conflict between dependency and affection on the one side, and hostility on the other, usually results in anxiety which bars open aggression. Instead, a child may withdraw all "favors"; e.g., all results of training. After having been clean for a long time, this child may begin to wet and soil his bed again, or become a poor eater. Since another mechanism (to be discussed later) acts in the same direction, such symptoms are rather frequent.

Finally, hostility can be reflexively directed against the jealous individual himself. A child may feel that if he had been a "good child" and pleased his mother she would not have permitted an interloper to intrude. This self-accusation and self-aggression is not checked by any conflicting fear. It may seem to the child the least dangerous channel for reactive hostility. Having a free course, it may create a severe sense of inferiority and tendencies to self-destruction. On the other hand, secondary gains from these self-punitive elements may compensate for the suffering.

IDENTIFICATION

The jealous individual is compelled to compare himself with the rival. Subconscious tendencies toward identification result. Attempts at being like the rival may lead to regression if the rival is a baby, or progression if the rival is an older sibling. The former situation is a more common source for regressive tendencies. In such children a normal maturing process is suddenly interrupted and a relapse into infantile behavior occurs. They refuse solid foods, take milk only from the bottle, want to sleep in a crib, and lose bladder and bowel control. Speech progress is arrested, or an attained level relapses into a more infantile state. Speech defects such as stuttering may even develop, as the following case illustrates.

> Case 1: A four year old girl had developed normally and did not present any problems until a little sister was born. She was obviously jealous and hit the baby repeatedly. Scolded for her aggressive acts, she became increasingly nervous, slept poorly, started excessive masturbation, refused to eat unless she was fed, and showed great fear of being abandoned by her parents and nurse. At this time she started to stutter, especially at home. In spite of all efforts, the speech defect disappeared only a year and a half later when the baby sister needed and received less attention, and she herself had developed into a brilliant "young lady" who became the center of interest and attention.

Jealous children, in a state of regression, appear very stubborn, negativistic, and even malicious. Loss of patience only aggravates the situation. It should be remembered that these children do not intend to make difficulties and to sabotage the family peace. They are rather the unhappy victims of emotional turmoil.

If the rival is an older sibling, who rightly or wrongly is considered by the child to be the parents' favorite by virtue of outstanding ability, talent, or other qualities, progressive tendencies may develop which are manifested in various ways. Imitation of the rival is one possibility, ambitious self-development another. A third way is a perfectionistic tendency which looks neither at the rival nor at the self, but at the image of an ideal having all lovable qualities. The following is an example of such progressive tendencies.

> Case 2: The older of two brothers, age 4½, was very attached to his mother and conspicuously preferred by her. He was jealous of his younger brother, was very egoistic and negativistic, had temper tantrums, and showed signs of an anxiety neurosis. In his attitude to his brother he manifested frank hostility, kicked him, and took his toys away. The younger boy, age 2½, was unwanted and neglected by his mother. While his father was in the Army, the older boy slept in the same room with his mother and spent a good deal of the day with her alone. The younger boy was kept in the background, lived in a remote room with his elderly nurse, and was kicked away by his brother whenever he tried to get near his mother. He took this unbearable situation with admirable poise and courage; he was kind, cooperative, and tidy. He even tried to be-little his brother's bad behavior, and was not resentful toward his mother. His speech was developed beyond his age to almost the level of his brother's. He did not appear unhappy. That he was profoundly so was only manifested in symptoms such as daily vomiting and spastic constipation for which no physical basis could be found, and had to be regarded as psychosomatic.

Identification with a parent may lead to progression, as the following example illustrates.

> Case 3: A 5½ year old girl suffered from severe anorexia [loss of appetite] for about a year. Her first disappointment was the arrival of a sister. However, the anorexia coincided with the birth of a baby brother. Her mother, a psychologist, understood the situation, and encouraged the elder girl to share with her the responsibility of taking care of the younger children. She taught her to change diapers, prepare the formula, and feed the children. Since the mother worked as a teacher, this child had to take over a good deal of the home responsibilities. For hours she watched the children, gave them their meals, answered the telephone, and behaved like an adult, as earnest, conscientious, and composed as her mother. There was no frank manifestation of jealousy. The identification with her mother was obvious.

Boys in a similar situation of jealousy may identify with the mother as well as with the father. In the first instance, feminine features may develop as one of the possible causes of later homosexuality. Identification with the father usually manifests itself in superficial imitation rather than in real progressive tendencies. Such boys are seen going around with a stick and father's hat and pipe and being "bossy." They "play father" rather than being mature beyond their age.

Whenever progressive tendencies lead to the imitation of a rival or parent or to the realization of an image, the fundamental drive of

unfolding self-creation is interfered with and severe personality disturbances may develop. On the other hand, when progression is directed to
the self, the unfolding self-creation is stimulated and may become a source
of creativeness.

WITHDRAWAL

Jealousy is a painful and disturbing experience. Both aggression and
identification may be unfeasible or unsuccessful. In an attempt to
overcome emotional distress and tension, the jealous individual may
withdraw from the beloved person. If he loves less he will suffer less. Yet
detachment is difficult. Unlike aggression and identification, withdrawal
is a mental process which requires maturity and will power. Younger
children may temporarily turn away from the object of their affection but
are unable to maintain this attitude. They are too dependent. Soon they
find that they suffer less from jealousy than they do from detachment. As
maturity progresses, withdrawal becomes possible. It remains not always
restricted to the person from whom detachment was originally sought, but
tends to develop into retreat from a group and, finally, from the world. An
attitude of resignation with narrowed interests and restrained actions
results which in extreme cases resemble schizophrenic withdrawal.

Case 4: An example of this attitude was a 14 year old boy, a diabetic since his
second year of life. His parents were unhappy in their married life, and
separated when he was 13 years old. He was very attached to his overpowering
mother. She worried about his diabetes, and concentrated more and more on
this boy and the treatment of his disease. She gave the insulin injections herself, watched his diet, and kept careful records.
The boy was very jealous of his 16 year old sister, a brilliant and attractive girl
who was generally admired and lived a rather independent life. He showed open
hostility toward her, and resented his mother's strict supervision of him. On
rare occasions when he was alone with his mother he continued to show great
affection, yet in general, he became negativistic, uncooperative, sullen, and
taciturn. He sabotaged his diabetic regime, repelled his mother, and avoided
her whenever he could. He did not want to see a doctor, was inattentive at
school, and indifferent toward his teachers. He made poor progress in school
and in social adjustments. He was shy, withdrawn, obstinate, and did not seem
to like anyone or anything. Athletics was his only interest. His excellence in
this field seemed to satisfy his repressed aggressive trends. He occasionally
mixed with a few much younger boys whom he tried to impress and whose
admiration he accepted and needed.

Withdrawal does not diminish suffering. It may therefore be substituted by a more positive and satisfactory attitude, such as turning the affection toward another person. Withdrawal from the mother may make its appearance as attachment to the father, an attachment which seems entirely natural. Yet whenever a boy is affectionately attached to his father and emotionally indifferent toward his mother, withdrawal from the mother is to be suspected as the underlying psychological act. Every critical event will reveal that the over-attachment to the father is not entirely genuine, and that the indifference toward the mother is in reality a withdrawal from an ambivalent emotional relation.

Detachment may be the final aim and achievement in the escape from the calamity of jealousy. It may, on the other hand, be the first step to real independence. Withdrawal may be followed by concentration on the self, by unfolding self-creation, and real creativeness.

REPRESSION

Some children as well as adults are said not to be jealous. They do not appear jealous, and they themselves are convinced they are not. Jealousy, however, probably develops without exception whenever sufficient reason for it exists. Certain defense mechanisms may prevent full cognizance and frank manifestation of this emotion. Yet it appears doubtful whether jealousy can ever be completely shut out of awareness at the moment of or after its appearance. Young children, particularly, act and react spontaneously to specific situations, and are unable to repress an emotion. With the development of social adjustment and psychic economy such an ability is gradually acquired. It seems, however, that awareness of jealousy persists even while repressive acts are operative. Acute jealousy may, for instance, be counteracted by an "I don't care" attitude. This does not result in complete elimination but only in the displacement of jealousy from the center into the periphery of psychic life and awareness. Removed from the spotlight of consciousness, jealousy affects and hurts less, but does not necessarily become unconsciousness.

In this way actual jealousy and repressive acts interfere with each other. Continuous repressive efforts may finally succeed in banishing jealousy into the remote periphery of emotional life and awareness; cognizance of jealousy no longer exists. Nevertheless, jealousy continues to manifest itself in changed forms such as indifference, false friendliness toward the rival, submission, or vague aggressiveness and irritability. Some of these manifestations have been described previously. The following cases offer additional illustrations.

Case 5: A girl, the third of four children (an older brother and sister, and a younger brother), enjoyed none of the advantages of being the eldest or the youngest. In addition, she suffered from her mother's preference for boys. In spite of this precarious situation, she never showed signs of jealousy or aggression. She was quiet, modest, kind, helpful, almost angelic, and complied entirely with her mother's autocratic ideas of what a child ought to be. The mother always contrasted this "good child" with the others who displeased her by going their own ways. Evidently this girl had repressed her jealousy and achieved through submission what she could hardly have attained by aggression or in any other way. However, she was permanently harmed by her way of coping with the given jealousy situation. Out of this temporary expediency of submission grew an habitual servility and submissiveness with a weak drive toward self-development.

Case 6: A 4 year old girl had been well prepared for the arrival of a new baby. The newcomer, a boy, was taken care of by a motherly, overprotective nurse. The little girl was allowed to be present when her mother nursed the baby. The mother showed full understanding of the situation and tried to prevent jealousy by concentrating her attention on the little sister. The baby was left to the nurse. The sister showed great affection for her baby brother and was never aggressive toward him. She was curious about his sex organs and asked repeatedly whether her father also had such a "nipple."
For the first three months after the baby's arrival, the girl lost bladder control. This was sensibly and successfully handled. She was treated like a big girl, permitted to eat at the table with her parents, and ostensibly preferred to the baby. She continued not to show jealousy, but became nervous, irritable, and occasionally very naughty. Though she manifested love for the baby at every occasion, she said she did not want another baby brother, and that this one must later do everything she said. She showed unreasonable aggresiveness toward younger playmates in surprising contrast to her genuinely kind nature. In this case we observe repression of jealousy change in the direction of hostility from the baby to other children, and discharge of psychic tension into general irritability.

MASOCHISM

In case 5 are exhibited clearly masochistic features. This girl coped with a jealousy situation by complete submission. By submerging her own individuality, she gained a certain reassurance and security. In an old German proverb, jealousy is characterized as being closely associated with masochism: *Eifersucht ist eine Leidenschaft, die mit Eifersucht, was Leiden schafft* (Jealousy is a passion which seeks with zeal that which causes suffering). It appears doubtful that jealousy is merely a manifestation of masochistic trends, as defined in this proverb. The "zeal" which is the root of the word "jealousy" is obviously not directed toward suffering primarily, but toward maintaining a love relation, and against rivals who may disturb this relation. However, a masochistic individual may react to jealousy with masochistic manifestations, and masochism may make its first appearance in any individual during the experience of jealousy.

The definition of masochism is beyond the scope of this paper. Freud defined it as the turning of sadistic impulses from the outside toward the self; Horney, as a tendency toward self-deflation. Even such authoritative explanations leave much room for further speculation. It seems that non-aggressive natures, or individuals who in a given situation cannot dare open aggression, find a satisfactory compensation in an opposite trend; namely, in suffering and self-degradation. The ecstatic suffering of a martyr is a well-known phenomenon of this kind.

To take suffering as a source of lust, and thus to utilize an adverse situation to one's advantage and satisfaction is a spiritual process. Therefore the gratification occurs on a higher human level than that derived from sadistic aggression. Suffering, humiliation, and defeat are turned into a subtle victory and feeling of superiority.

Aggression, identification, detachment, and repression do not solve the emotional problem of jealousy. They relieve suffering to a certain extent, but maintain fear, or distort the personality, thus becoming sources of new suffering. The masochistic coping with the situation brings a more satisfactory solution: fear is banished by renouncing aggression; self-degradation regains attention and affection; misery and suffering themselves are changed into delightful sources of satisfaction.

Such a masochistic response to a jealousy situation is less frequently observed in younger than in older children, particularly those around the age of puberty. Yet some masochistic elements appear in many of the examples shown. Whether a jealous child represses hostility and turns his aggressive trends against himself, whether he withdraws, regresses into a state of helplessness, or submits completely—we recognize the masochistic strategy of geting something by a display of helplessness, self-denial, and misery. Only exceptional cases show a fully developed masochistic pattern as illustrated by the following example.

Case 7: A boy of seven had always been in a situation where his mother obviously preferred his older brother to him. She took the older boy on shopping trips or outings, and made the younger one feel that he could not live up to the achievements of his brother. Most of the time he was left with a nurse who loved him, but she was also very severe with him. At the slightest misbehavior she would take his pants off and whip him. He developed into a child who could never stand up for himself in any group situation, always provoked fights with other boys who consequently beat him up severely. When in the company of adults whom he trusted and liked, after a short while he would beg them to hit him. He became very unhappy when they refused. Without proper treatment this child would probably have grown up to be a typical masochist who finds pleasure only when he is hurt by his love object.

SUBLIMATION, CREATIVE COMPETITION

In the cases described, the jealous individual remained in a dependent position. He maintained his claim for exclusive and unlimited affection and for unselfish love, and tried to regain it whenever it appeared endangered. By and large, his attempts failed, mainly for two reasons. So long as he continued dependent, his security remained actually or potentially in danger. His claim for affection was based merely on his possessiveness or on archaic rights, such as the child's right to his mother's love, and not on individual merits or achievements which would justify it.

First, steps were observed to decrease dependency by withdrawal, and to retain affection by conforming with outside wishes and ideals, or by self-degradation. These attempts proved more helpful but remained in the realm of emotional life, and did not bring a satisfactory solution. To be sure, there is no final solution. So long as individuals love and need affection, there will be jealousy and suffering; and there will be dependency. Moreover, the affection claimed and needed is unconditional. Children want to be loved for their mere existence, and not for special merits or achievements.

Nevertheless, in the course of normal maturation, a way of release can be found from emotional entanglement, from victimizing dependency, and from fear. It is the way of detachment and sublimation. To abandon possessiveness, to depend more on one's self, and to denounce hostility in favor of creative competition are the means. The situation remains essentially the same, but is transferred from a purely emotional to a more rational level. Instead of possessiveness which is emotional insistence on affection, affection is sought with a sense of reality. Dependency is shifted from the love object to the self. An actual or potential rival is taken as stimulus, less for destructive aggression than for creative competition. In this state of mind the jealous individual turns to himself. He directs previously wasted energy into unfolding self-creation which is the fundamental drive of man, and into creative work.

Jealousy is a possible source of creativeness. It rarely assumes this role before puberty, the period of sublimation. The following case shows jealousy as a source of creativeness.

Case 8: A boy, the youngest of four siblings, had for years been unfavorably compared by his mother with his sisters and brother, and with other children. Disappointed in his mother's love, he turned against her. In essence, his hatred was merely the negative expression of continued love. Temporarily, this boy found a substitute satisfaction in autoerotic acts, and later in a close attachment to his older sister. He withdrew more and more from members of his family, appeared only at meals, and spent much of his time alone outdoors or behind the locked doors of his room.

Around the age of puberty he took up poetry and painting. His achievements in these fields were not extraordinary but certainly beyond the cultural level of his environment. Definite narcissistic features became apparent. He needed admiration; he was very sensitive to criticism and lack of affection, and preferred solitude to the risk of such exposure. During adolescence he began to excel in writing and philosophic contributions which secured him a privileged position in school and uncontested admiration in his family. His mother was proud of him, but he maintained his rejecting attitude toward her.

By the age of twenty he had become a calm, intensive worker and a successful scientist. His narcissism became less conspicuous. For a long time he avoided any association with the opposite sex. When he finally became attached to a girl, he demanded from her the same unselfish and exclusive love which he had sought from his mother. In the beginning he zealously watched that nothing and no one but he entered her mind. His creative accomplishments served well to maintain the uncontested central position which he needed. For a time creative periods coincided conspicuously with the wavering of this secure position, and alternated with episodes of complacent inactivity. Gradually he derived more security and self-confidence from his work, and depended less on the reassuring affection of his partner. By this development, both his creative work and his love relation were benefited and stabilized.

REVIEW AND OUTLOOK

Though this enumeration is not complete, it contains the most essential reactions to jealousy. They rarely occur in the distinct and separated patterns here discussed, rather are they interwoven with each other, forming a variety of reaction patterns. Which of them will develop depends on individuality, age, and specific jealousy situation. Certain patterns are particularly common and represent well-known types such as the selfish-aggressive, the negativistic-withdrawn, or the infantile-regressive type.

Jealousy appears to be almost universal in children. It gives rise to a variety of symptoms and disturbances of basic functions which are frequently misunderstood and misinterpreted. Correct interpretation is the prerequisite of dealing with these phenomena. If they are correctly under stood, the question of dealing with them is of a philosophical as well as of a pedagogic and psychotherapeutic nature. Can and should jealousy be prevented? If it occurs, should jealousy be suppressed? These are only a few of the questions which call for an answer.

Extreme degrees of jealousy in a child certainly can be prevented by proper planning. A child should be prepared for the arrival of a new baby. If changes in his routine become necessary, they should never coincide with the arrival of the new child. Unavoidable changes of the room or the bed, or being sent to kindergarten are easily taken as displacement and punishment unless they are properly timed. Too much attention to the new baby in the presence of the older child should be avoided in favor of demonstration of continued attention and reassuring affection to the older child. Such and similar well-known precautions, even if carefully observed, do not entirely prevent jealousy. This is an empiric fact as well as the necessary result of the specific relationship between child and mother. This relation is intimately linked with and is the root of jealousy. Consequently both must be equally acknowledged as essentials of life, or equally abolished.

A child regards his mother as an indispensable possession, as a source of life, love, and security. He cannot be expected to share this unique possession easily with someone else. If he must, he will be jealous. It seems apparent that this jealousy cannot be prevented, and should not be suppressed. Suppresion only leads to a distortion of the personality and does not abolish jealousy.

Jealousy is a formative factor as essential as the child-mother relationship itself. It profoundly influences psychic development, character structure, and social adjustment. Its constructive elements should be utilized to the child's benefit and advantage.

The jealous child needs sympathetic understanding, help, and guidance. He should be encouraged to express his jealousy instead of being compelled to hide and repress it. In this way he experiences catharsis and relief from emotional distress, tension and fear. He simultaneously learns to express himself freely in words and play as well as in transformed acts of simple creation. This self-expression makes the child aware of himself.

The jealous child should be guided to know his values as well as his limitations. During an actual experience of jealousy, his world picture is disfigured by emotional evaluations. Gradually he can be led to replace these emotional evaluations by rational and realistic ones. Through guidance and experience he learns his own real values and those of the rival, as well as the specific role of each member of the family. Likewise, the child can be led to comprehend the limitations of what he has to offer, and to what he is entitled and also the limitations of others. He gradually understands, without resentment, that resignation and relinquishment are as inevitable for himself as for others, and do not mean deprivation of love. The cognizance of his limitations saves the child from two dangers: first, from boundless demands which would result in disappointment and frustration; and second, from overstraining his potentiality (as by imitation of older siblings or parents) which would lead to spurious development. Once the child understands his limitations, he is ready to retreat to what remains within these limits—his rights, his values, and his potentialities.

How does a child come to an adequate self-evaluation? During the early period of mutualism, the baby merely senses his value from his mother's love. He feels loved and therefore worthy of being loved. As he sees his evolving expressions and performances acclaimed and acknowledged, he becomes conscious of his value. With his ever-growing achievements and creative evolution, the child gains a proper self-evaluation and self-confidence. In this state of development the experience of jealousy is no longer detrimental. The partial deprivation of love is compensated by the appreciation of his values. Consciousness of his own value keeps him from emotional misinterpretation and overestimation of the dangers which the rival threatens. The jealousy situation is therefore not likely to activate the destructive and negative reaction patterns, but rather to stimulate constructive reactions, unfolding self-creation, and creative competition.

The next selection, a short chapter from A. S. Neill's very influential book *Summerhill,* serves as terse and colorful counterpoint to Vollmer's more detailed account of jealousy in children. These anecdotes and impressions touch on sibling rivalry, competition among children, parents' unwitting contributions to the jealous outbursts of their children, and adults' jealousy of youth. Neill withholds judgment on the question of whether or not jealousy is a permanent trait in human nature, but he clearly believes that parents and teachers can and do unnecessarily exacerbate children's jealousies.

5

Jealousy at Summerhill

A.S. Neill

Jealousy arises from the sense of possession. If sexual love were a genuine transcendence of self, a man would rejoice when he saw his girl kiss another man, because he would rejoice to see her happy. But sexual love is possessive. It is the man with a strong sense of possession who commits a crime of jealousy.

The absence of any visible sexual jealousy among the Trobriand Islanders suggests that jealousy may be a by-product of our more complicated civilization. Jealousy arises from the combination of love with possessiveness about the loved object. It has been often said that a jealous man does not usually shoot the rival who runs away with his wife—he shoots the wife. Probably he kills the woman to put his possession beyond the reach of touch, just as a mother rabbit will eat her young if people handle them too much. The infant ego will have all or nothing: It cannot share.

Jealousy has more to do with power than it has to do with sex. Jealousy is the reaction following an injured ego. "I am not first. I am not the

A. S. Neill (1883-1973) was headmaster of Summerhill, an experimental English school in which students were given maximum freedom to pursue their own interests and to develop their capacity for self-direction. This article is reprinted from his book *Summerhill: A Radical Approach to Child Rearing* (New York: Hart, 1960), pp. 317-322, with permission of the publisher.

favored one. I am placed in a position of inferiority.'' This certainly is the psychology of jealousy that we find among, say, professional singers and comedians. In my student days, I used to make friends with stage comedians by the simple method of saying that the other comedian in the cast was rotten.

In jealousy, there is always a definite fear of loss. The opera singer hates another prima donna, dreading that her own applause will suffer in volume and intensity. Indeed by comparison, it is possible that fear of loss of esteem accounts for more jealousy than all the love rivals in the world.

In the family, much depends, therefore, on the elder child's feeling of being appreciated. If self-regulation has given him so much independence that he does not need to be constantly seeking his parent's approval, then his jealousy of the newcomer in the family will be less than if he were an unfree child, one tied forever to his mother's apron strings, and therefore never quite independent. This does not mean that parents of siblings should stand aside and merely observe how the elder child reacts to the younger. From the start, any action that might aggravate jealousy should be avoided, such as a too obvious showing off of the baby to visitors. Children of all ages have a keen sense of justice—or rather of injustice—and wise parents will try to see that the younger child is not in any way favored or given preference over the elder, although this is almost impossible to avoid to some extent.

That baby gets mother's breast may seem an injustice to his older brother. But it may not be so, if the older one feels that he has been allowed to live out naturally his breast-feeding stage. In drawing sound conclusions about this aspect, we need much more evidence. I have had no experience of the self-regulated child's reaction to the arrival of a new baby. Whether jealousy is a permanent trait in human nature, I do not know.

In my long experience with children, I have found that in later life many persons retain with angry emotion some memory of what they considered an injustice they suffered in their kindergarten days. This is especially so with the memory of an incident in which the older child was punished for something that the younger one did. "I always got the blame" is the cry of many an older sibling. In any quarrel where the baby cries, the busy mother's automatic reaction is to storm at the older child.

Jim, aged eight, had a habit of kissing everyone he met. His kisses were more like sucking than kissing. I concluded that Jim had never got over his infantile interest in sucking. I went out and bought him a feeding bottle. Jim had his bottle every night when he went to bed. The other boys, who at first went into screams of derisive laughter (thus hiding their interest in bottles), soon became jealous of Jim. Two of them demanded bottles. Jim suddenly became the little brother who long ago got the monopoly of mother's breast. I bought bottles for all of them. The fact that they wanted bottles proved that these boys still retained their interest in sucking.

Jealousy is something to be particularly guarded against in the dining room. Even some of the staff are jealous when visitors receive any special dish; and if the cook gives one senior pupil asparagus, the others will wax eloquent about kitchen favorites.

Some years ago, the arrival of a tool chest brought trouble into the school. The children whose fathers could not afford to buy them good tools became jealous, and for three weeks they were antisocial. One boy who knew all about handling tools borrowed a plane. He took the iron out of the plane by hammering the cutting edge; and of course, he spoiled the plane. He told me that he had forgotten just how to take an iron out. Whether conscious or unconscious, the destructive act was one of jealousy.

It may be impossible to give each child a room to himself, but each child should have a corner with which he can do what he likes. In Summerhill schoolrooms, each pupil has a table and his own area, and he decorates his corner with joy.

Jealousy sometimes arose out of P.Ls. ["Private Lessons," therapy sessions with Neill himself.] "Why should Mary get P.Ls. and not me?" Sometimes a girl deliberately and consciously behaved as a problem child merely to be included in the P.L. list. Once, one girl smashed some windows; and when asked what her idea was, she replied, "I want Neill to give me P.Ls." A girl who behaves in this way is usually a girl whose father has not, in her estimation, paid sufficient attention to her.

Since children bring their home problems and jealousies to school with them, what I fear most in my work with them are the letters parents write their children. I once had to write to a father, "Please do not write to your son. Every time a letter comes from you, he goes bad." The father did not answer me but he ceased to write to his son. Then about two months later, I saw the boy receive a letter from his father. I was annoyed but said nothing. That night about twelve, I heard awful screams from the boy's bedroom. I rushed into his room just in time to save our kitten from strangulation. Next day, I went to his room to look for the letter. I found it. "You will be glad to hear," ran a sentence, "that Tom [the younger brother] had his birthday last Monday, and Auntie Lizzie gave him a kitten." The fantasies that arise from jealousy know no bounds in criminality. The jealous child kills off his rivals in fantasy. Two brothers had to travel home from Summerhill for the holidays. The elder got into a state of fear. "I'm frightened I will lose Fred on the way," he kept saying. He was afraid his daydream would come true.

"No," said a boy of eleven to me, referring to his younger brother, 'no, I wouldn't exactly like him to die; but if he went away on a long, long journey to India or somewhere and came back when he was a man, I'd like that."

Every pupil new to Summerhill has to endure three months of unconscious hate from the other pupils. For a child's first reaction to a new arrival in the family is a hate reaction. The older child usually believes that mother has eyes only for the newcomer, for the baby sleeps with mother and takes up all mother's attention. The child's repressed hate of his mother is often compensated for by an excess of tenderness to her. It is the older child in a family who hates most. The younger child has never known what it is to be king in the house. When I come to think of it, I see that my worst cases of neurosis are either only children or eldest sons and daughters.

Parents unwittingly feed the hate of an older child. "Why, Tom, your young brother wouldn't make such a fuss about a cut finger."

I remember when I was a boy, another boy was always held up as an example to me. He was a marvelous scholar, was never known to be anywhere but at the top of the class, took all the prizes in a canter. He died. I recall his funeral as being rather a pleasant affair.

Teachers often encounter the jealousy of parents. I have lost pupils more than once because the parents were jealous of the child's affection for Summerhill and for me. It is understandable. In a free school, the children are allowed to do exactly what they like as long as they do not break the social laws which are made by staff and pupils at General School Meetings. Often, a child does not even want to go home for the holidays, for to go home is to be encompassed by restrictive home laws. The parents who do not become jealous of the school or its teachers are those who treat their children at home just the same as we treat their children in Summerhill. They believe in their children and give them the freedom to be themselves. These children delight in going home.

There need be no rivalry between parent and teacher. If the parent turns the child's love into hate by arbitrary orders and rules, he must expect a child to seek love elsewhere. A teacher is merely a father or a mother surrogate. It is the thwarted love for parents that is showered on the teacher only because the teacher is easier to love than the father is.

I couldn't count the number of fathers I have known who hated their sons because of jealousy. These were the Peter Pan fathers who wanted mother love from their wives, hating the young rival and often beating him cruelly. You, Mr. Father, will find your situation complicated by the family triangle. Once your baby is born you are, in some measure, odd man out. Some women lose all desire for a sex life after having a baby. In any case, divided love will characterize the home. You should be conscious of what is happening; otherwise you will find yourself being jealous of your own child. At Summerhill, we have had scores of children who suffered from either maternal or paternal jealousy, mostly cases in which the father's jealousy had made him stern and even brutal to the son. If a father vies with his children for the love of Mother, his children will be more or less neurotic.

A helpful resource for understanding and working with a child's jealousy is *Sometimes I'm Jealous* by Jane Werner Watson et al. (New York: Golden Press, 1972). This "read-together book" for parents and children is part of a series on the problems of childhood created in cooperation with the Menninger Foundation.

The articles by Vollmer and Neill help us better understand the *origins* of our jealous feelings. The next selection invites us to explore the "inner workings"—the psychological mechanisms of jealousy and provides us with a Freudian roadmap for our journey.

The psychoanalytic tradition seeks to discover the uses or *functions* of jealousy in the psyche (self). Perhaps jealousy affords one a socially-approved outlet for feelings and behaviors which others typically condemn. For example, jealous behavior is tolerated in our society; sadistic behavior is mostly condemned and the masochist is pitied. This might lead to the expression of sadism by means of a violent "jealous" outburst, or of masochism by long and sorrowful recitals of one's partner's infidelities. An unmarried businesswoman of 28 told an interviewer: "I think one of the pleasures of jealousy is that it gives one the right to be cruel" (Ankles 1939:50). Jealousy also gives one the right to be cruel *to oneself* by demanding full details of a confessed infidelity or presenting oneself to friends as a martyr.

If jealousy can be used to legitimize behaviors which otherwise would be condemned, perhaps it can also be employed as a *defense* against feelings we prefer to deny. Freud believed that jealousy could function as a defense against (1) the impulse to be unfaithful and (2) the impulse to engage in homosexual behaviors. If a person's moral values require that she hide from herself the desire to be sexually involved with someone other than her husband, she may instead accuse *him* of the desire to be unfaithful which is deep within her—or she may come to feel that her best woman friend is "being seductive" toward her husband. If a man's self-image requires that he repress and deny all interest in having sexual contact with another man, he may come to suspect his *wife* of sexual interest in that man and behave in a "jealous" fashion.

Much of the literature on jealousy comes from the psychoanalytic tradition. (See, in the bibliography, Freud 1922; Jones 1929; Riviere 1932; Bohm 1967; Seidenberg 1967.) The next selection presents a summary and integrative critique of the very influential understandings of jealousy found in the writings of Freud and Jung. Because this body of thought is complex and subtle, this article is demanding; but it does *not* presuppose a familiarity with Freudian concepts and language, and so may serve as an introduction to the psychoanalytic perspective as a distinctive way of viewing human affairs.

6

Jealousy: A Depth-psychological Perspective

Chris Downing

The phrase "depth psychology" refers to that way of understanding human existence introduced in Sigmund Freud's *Interpretation of Dreams* (published in the first year of this century) and elaborated by him and others, both followers and dissidents, who find the notion of the "unconscious" necessary to their description of human behavior and experience. There are, they believe, "depths" to human beings' wishes and fears and memories of which they are not immediately or easily self-aware. Every conscious feeling is likely to be accompanied by its unconscious opposite. We tend to be ambivalent: to hate those we love, to desire what we fear. In every present, and in ways likely to be surprising, our whole past is active and influential; and perhaps not only our own literal lived past but in some strange way the accumulated past of countless human generations. Such a psychology is inevitably a *deep* one also in the more obvious sense of the word: It is subtle, complex, and easily misunderstood.

Chris Downing, Ph. D., (1931 -) is Chairperson and Associate Professor in the Department of Religious Studies at San Diego State University. She is on the core faculty of the California School of Professional Psychology and is past president of the American Academy of Religion. Currently she is working on a book exploring the role of myth in the work of Freud and Jung. "Jealousy: A Depth-psychological Perspective" was written especially for this volume.

The psychologies that derive from Freud are sometimes also called "insight therapies." This designation suggests that they focus more on extending insight than on cure. Psychoanalysis represents a different way of looking at our experience. With respect to jealousy, for example, it would hope to be able to extend our understanding of the *meaning* of human jealousy, by showing what *intentionalities* are expressed in it, rather than to teach us how to eliminate it. The assumption is that jealousy is not a self-evident phenomenon, that it calls for interpretation. Psycho-analytic interpretation claims to offer us a self-understanding which uncovers some common self-deceptions. It calls upon us to recognize our finitude—that is, our mortality, our limitation by the needs and desires of others, and the impossibility of the fulfillment of some of our deepest longings.

Jealousy is a pervasive theme in the psychoanalytic explorations of man because it refers to this central human dilemma: the necessity of coming to terms with "reality" in all the aspects just named *and* the inevitability of our resistance to such limits, denials, and frustrations.

Indeed, jealousy is so central to Freud's image of man that it hardly occurs to him to focus on it explicitly, except in one disappointingly con-densed essay written in 1922. Thus, to discover his understanding of jealousy, we must pay careful attention to the many allusions and, occasionally to the more extended discussions scattered throughout his work. It soon becomes apparent that we can not disentangle what he has to say about jealousy from the other most important, typically Freudian, themes: the Oedipus complex, bisexuality, ambivalence, repression, regression, displacement, and narcissism.

Jealousy is, from this perspective, not innate, and yet it is inevitable. It has its origins for each of us in our earliest familial experiences.[1] Freud calls the whole complex of events and feelings associated with the child's relations to his parents "the oedipal situation." He means thereby to denote not only the character of the child's desire for his mother and his resentment toward his father, but the universality of these feelings. This universality, and the intensity of the emotions, suggests to Freud that something more than the imprint of actual childhood experiences is at work here. Somehow my memory also has an ancestral or "racial"

---

[1]Freud's discussions of jealousy are in the first instance discussions of jealousy as it is experienced by *males*. Because his understanding of what distinguishes female from male sexuality changes significantly during the course of his work and would lead us into an enormously complicated issue, I am deliberately, throughout this essay, using masculine pronouns as a way of indicating that some of it would need to be modified if applied to women. For a useful study, see Juliet Mitchell, *Psychoanalysis and Feminism* (New York: Pantheon, 1974).

dimension; my jealousy is in some way the re-enactment of the jealousy felt by human beings since the beginning of time.

"Normal" jealousy is competitive; it arises first in relation to rivalry with the father (and probably siblings) for the exclusive love of the mother, and it is felt again whenever the fear of losing the object of our love is aroused. The childhood experiences do not "cause" the later ones; but they are re-evoked and they help to shape how and how intensely we respond to the tensions of adult life. "There is not," Freud (1922:232) says in his typically offhand way, "much to be said from the analytic point of view about normal jealousy." But then he goes on to suggest that perhaps there is no wholly "normal" jealousy, no jealousy that is "completely rational, that is, derived from the actual situation, proportionate to the real circumstances and under the complete control of the conscious ego."

We can understand jealousy better from its pathological manifestations because in all of us jealousy assumes some pathological characteristics. Freud does not want to eliminate the distinction between "normal" (by which he means rational and congruent with "reality") and pathological, but rather to suggest that most of us who are "normal" in our conscious orientation also harbor pathological tendencies.

In its root sense, which Freud wants to return us to, pathology means woundedness. He hopes to bring us back in touch with that in each of us which has been wounded, hurt, and abandoned, that which still cries and rages. We have all been deprived of the mother's breast, we all have had to give up our claim for exclusive possession of her. Mostly, we have forgotten these childhood longings and losses, and especially how much feeling was attached to them. We have little sense of the strength of these jealousy impulses, of the tenacity with which they persist, and of the magnitude of their influence on later life.

Jealousy is "regresssive," immature; but at some level every one of us *is* still a child, as well as the adult we pride ourselves on having become. The memories and the overintense feelings persist. We continue to respond emotionally in ways that are exaggerated, are not appropriate to a rational response to situations, and are perhaps not even based on a realistic assessment of them. In us, too, there is something that wants to "kill" the one who has usurped our place (as in childhood we dreamt of murdering a father or younger brother), or the one who has proven "faithless" (as the mother was when we were infants). In all of us there still lives the child's unregarding possessiveness—the longing for an absolute, certain, and exclusive love. Each of us still experiences the child's greedy passivity, his conviction that *love* means *receiving* love. The child is "narcissistic," is unquestioningly its own preferred love-object, and so are all of us.

It is these claims, these expectations, which manifest themselves anew in the jealousy which takes our adult selves by surprise. Thus jealousy is not, for Freud, in the first instance, *sexual* jealousy except in the extended metaphorical sense of sexuality peculiar to psychoanalysis. It relates more to the affectionate, personal, possessive side of a love relation than to its strictly sensual or sexual side. But Freud has been concerned to help us see how easily sexuality is invested with over-meanings, so that my failures or successes in this realm become paradigmatic, representative of how I most basically feel about myself. Thus sexual infidelity almost inevitably becomes a symbol for the most threatening loss we might suffer.

Psychoanalysis seeks to open us to the continued power of these old desires and hurts. Analysis of a jealousy that may, on the surface, seem only a distorted, ineffective, and perhaps destructive response to a present situation may reveal that jealousy as the way to a recovery of neglected and repressed, denied but still alive, aspects of ourselves. It encourages me to look upon my jealousy as something by which I may be taught, through which I may be made whole.

The tendency in psychoanalytical interpretations is to bypass consideration of the reality factors which may have prompted the immediate jealousy and to assume that *all* jealousy is to some degree *delusional* jealousy. Little attention is paid to the factor of literal infidelity, except sometimes to show how I provoked, in some sense desired, the very betrayal that arouses my anger and anxiety. Psychoanalysis tends to ignore what my jealousy suggests about anyone other than me. The assumption is that all jealousy is a kind of fantasy activity that both expresses and disguises some of my deepest wishes and fears. Because psychoanalysts are persuaded that jealousy has more to do with self-love than with love of others, it seems appropriate to them to view it as primarily an intrapsychic problem.

The explanations of jealousy that emerge from such an exploration are intended firstly to help me to recognize how much in my present feeling is "displaced" from earlier, never accepted experiences of loss, and particularly from a deeply ingrained sense that if I *was* betrayed by my mother's infidelity I somehow *deserved* it, that I am not worthy of love, and so am destined to be betrayed over and over again. The further interpretations are equally subtle, deliberately farfetched, and consciously upsetting to our self-esteem. They provoke reflection and call for honest self-probing: "Can this possibly be part of what's going on here?" Freud never suggests that all of these meanings may attach to any one experience of jealousy; rather, he suggests that jealousy is not a single thing—that it may have a variety of meanings, express various intentionalities. Often, he believes, jealousy represents the disguised, transferred fulfillment of a tabooed wish. I may "project" my own longings for extramarital experience onto my spouse, and accuse him of living out what I wish to live myself but fear to, or perhaps can live because I believe he does also.. Or I may be expressing my wish that he were *more* sexually free—with me. Or my projection of infidelity might mean anger at not being loved as completely as in my childish dreams I still imagine being loved—or it might mean a resentment of being loved in too containing or smothering a way. Sometimes jealousy may be a way of bolstering my self-esteem: "My wife is worthy of *his* attention!"

Freud also believed that delusional jealousy may sometimes be a disguised expression of an "acidulated homosexuality": "I don't love him; *she* loves him." Freud believed that we are all to some degree bisexual; that in all of us there are "masculine" and "feminine" dispositions—a longing to play the active, aggressive role and a longing to be passive, receptive. But because our acculturation often makes it difficult for us to accept this, it may be only in unacknowledged (and thus distorted) fantasies that a man can take on the feminine role. He projects onto his wife the desires he must repudiate in himself.

Another method Freud uses to get at the "meaning" of jealousy is to look at what he calls the "secondary gain." What wish is fulfilled by my jealous behavior itself? Do I gain solicitous attention that I have been craving? Or a reaffirmation of *my* innocence, my victimization? Or the pleasure of indulgence in elaborate sexual fantasies? Or a self-punishment I somehow deserve?

What these various proposed explanations have in common is that they all involve the uncovering of *hidden* meanings—forgotten memories, unadmitted wishes, denied fears, a hurt that has its primary locus *within* (a wounding to my self-esteem) rather than in an outward relationship. They are strange explanations in that they can't be verified, except by our assent. There is no way of *proving* the pertinence of these invisible factors. What psychoanalysis does is to provide a perspective, a way of looking at jealousy—a way of understanding it that we may find provides us with a sense of how jealousy fits in with a whole way of being in the world. As I see how *my* jealousy is congruent with *my* history, it no longer seems an isolated "symptom." This perspective may appeal because it is more interesting, more subtle, more capable of unifying some particular experience with others; it doesn't in any way invalidate other perspectives. Jealousy is what Freud called "overdetermined"; that is, it may be interpreted in several equally valid ways.

Freud sees jealousy as normal, inevitable, and universal; but he also sees that jealousness and particular familial and cultural forms are correlated. Jealousy is aggravated in a culture which worships a jealous monotheistic god, which holds up an ideal of monogamous marriage and of a monocentric, rational, and repressed self. Such a culture seems to encourage an expectation of exclusiveness in loving which makes it very difficult for us to come to terms with our own or another's infidelities, real or imagined. Freud understands, too, how the illusions connected with romantic love both make jealousy reprehensible and create it. Different social patterns may undoubtedly mitigate the pains of jealousy; nevertheless Freud cannot imagine a civilization in which men would be wholly freed from this "discontent."

Because all societies demand the renunciation of the child's boundless impulses toward self-gratification, we can no more completely overcome jealousy than we can entirely extinguish our childhood. The recognition of the persistence of feelings and longings which are inconsistent with "reality," "rationality," and "maturity" is what makes this a *depth* psychology. Yet Freud gives us some hints as to what an unrepressed and therefore nonregressive jealousy might be. Psychoanalysis may free us to accept the "pathological," the exaggerated, emotional, tied-to-childish-illusions, aspect of our jealousy as dangerous only if it is not met by a normal, reality-oriented, aspect. It may free us to recognize that in all of us love of others arises out of and remains deeply entwined with love of self. It may open us to living our jealousy with less guilt and less repression, and with more awareness of it as something that may move us forward rather than back. Depth-psychological insight stimulates a kind of jealousy of my own integrity. As Robert Seidenberg (1967:37) puts it:

> The turning away from one's origins, from one's history, the denial of impulses and relationships, are attitudes of deception about one's own being. They are the greatest infidelities of which we are capable.[2]

To live my jealousy as rage against another is to betray, to hide from, its most central meaning. Thus psychoanalysis itself becomes a substitute for acting-out jealousy: The suspicion is redirected towards oneself, one's own duplicity. This duplicity, this doubleness, is something *all* of us participate in; for we are all conscious *and* unconscious, mature *and* infantile, masculine *and* feminine, loving *and* hating, self-loving *and* other-loving, rational *and* emotional.

[2]*Editors' note*: An abridgement of Seidenberg's article, "Fidelity and Jealousy," is the next selection.

It is the oedipal *triangle*, the discovery that I cannot have my mother to myself, that moves me out of my self-absorption into a recognition of the otherness of others, to what Freud called *object*-love. Sibling jealousy, Freud says in *Group Psychology and the Analysis of the Ego*, is the impetus to group feeling, to communal identification, to a concern for social justice. To learn that I cannot have any other wholly to myself is to be educated to reality and finitude; to know that the longing nevertheless persists is what energizes all my imaginative activity.

Loss initially issues in mourning; but then leads to an awakening of my capacity to love elsewhere, to love this same one differently, or to turn my love energies in a new direction, be it toward another individual or toward a cultural task. Loss means education to reality *and* to creativity. To know that there is, in me, a child whose longing for love is unappeasable can mean the discovery that I can love rather than punish that child without letting it become the central actor in my adult relationships. It makes no sense to expect another to satisfy that primal longing; that only devalues and perhaps destroys what we *can* be to one another. But the longing itself, utopian and romantic as it is, is to be cherished as the source of the wishes and hopes that underlie all my activity. The capacity to overinvest is but the other side of the capacity for creativity, substitution, symbolization, "sublimation."

Such an affirmation of jealousy, which is only hinted at in Freud, is more explicitly elaborated by Carl Jung in *his* depth psychology. The perspective here is even more radically intrapsychic than in Freud. The focus is less on how jealousy inevitably arises in the interpersonal context of the family than on what my jealousy reveals about my incompleteness, about my tendency to depend on another for a wholeness only really to be achieved within.

The "other" in me to whom my jealousy introduces me is, in Jung, not the child but what he calls the "shadow." The shadow is my dark other self, that part I tend to disvalue and disown, or to use as a scapegoat. Indeed, so blind am I to his role in my own psyche that I tend to "project" him, to see my shadow qualities not directly in myself but in others towards whom I have exaggeratedly negative feelings. Infidelity, anger, and vulnerability are all more easily seen in another than in myself. But the upsurge of a feeling like jealousy forces upon me the recognition of the presence in me of a hitherto unsuspected person-like entity—one who has memories, desires, and fears as complexly organized as those of my familiar ego-self and yet radically different. The shadow is not a child so much as it is a person who has grown up without real nurture and care, and so he is a strangely misshapen figure. He is first experienced as ugly, disruptive, and fearsome, like the toad whom the princess must (in the unexpurgated version of Grimms' fairytale) take to bed. Yet Jung believes that if we can bring ourselves to acknowledge, "this too is me," we can transform him into a new brother who continually provides me with new energies, new perspectives. The shadow provides access to the unconscious, and thus to sources for renewal and transformation.

Freud saw in the unconscious primarily unrecognized *motives.* Jung sees it in terms of mythical *motifs*, patterns operative in my life which connect me to the experiences recounted in age-old, apparently universal myths. The confrontation with the shadow is not simply the confrontation with my peculiar denied experiences and feelings but with an "archetypal" figure: the dark "other" of countless tales and legends. The discovery of this *transpersonal* quality is what seems most important to Jung. It is through my "pathology," my shadow, my jealousy, that I am introduced into the mythic dimension of my own life. Through my jealousy I am being pulled to live anew primordial transformative experiences, the stuff out of which the myths and literature that most deeply affect us are composed.

Jung suggests that instead of struggling to overcome my jealousy, I should let it teach me how to move from "single vision" to an imagination that is attuned to symbolic repetitions. I can learn to proceed from a focus on the literal situation that provoked my jealousy to a recognition of how, through it, I participate in Aphrodite's jealousy of Psyche, or that of Psyche's uglier sisters, or perhaps in Hera's jealousy of Zeus. Jung then wants us to learn how consciously to exploit what Freud called the *delusional* aspect of jealousy: its capability of stimulating our propensity to fantasy. Jealousy releases *daemonic* energies which can be creative as well as destructive.

It may even be possible to enter this transpersonal imaginal realm *with* the others who are part of the jealousy-provoking situation, so that we can celebrate together the archetypal as well as the personal dimensions of our mutual involvement. To be released from the illusion that this is just *our* problem, and to see it as a perennial human experience, may open us to see, by means of jealousy, what otherwise we were blind to. Jealousy is thus an initiation into the *depths* of our psychology.

The next selection offers some amplification and modification of Freud's position on jealousy in the light of sociocultural considerations. Thus, it invites link-up with the essays in the next section, "Jealousy and Culture." In Seidenberg's view, Freud's early formulations did not give adequate stress to the forces of male-dominant society and the inordinate faithfulness demanded of women. "Jealousy and possessiveness are as much derived from societal demands as from childhood." Jealousy, Seidenberg concludes, is exacerbated by the double standard. "The best safeguard for mutual fidelity may be a healthy balance of power."

7

Fidelity and Jealousy

Robert Seidenberg

The vocabulary of infidelity is almost exclusively sexual. The only type of unfaithfulness that can be reasonably communicated to others is a mate's extramarital sexual experience. Adultery is something that everyone understands and generally condemns. The wife who complains that her husband appears more interested in his work than in her may find sympathetic ears, but this is generally never thought a good reason for drastic action. Such an abstract complaint never moves the listener, but the concrete accusation of sexual infidelity is a worldshaker. Whatever the provocation or internal marital circumstance, the mate with such a complaint is clearly the righteous victim, recognized as such by the courts and society.

For these reasons, many kinds of unfaithfulness in marriage have no voice, whereas sexual infidelity often assumes an exaggerated importance. As a matter of image, unfaithfulness and infidelity have suffered the pejoration of meaning "sexual" exclusively. Yet other acts of unfaithful-

Robert Seidenberg, M. D., (1920-   ), is a practicing psychoanalyst and psychiatrist in Syracuse. He is Clinical Professor of Psychiatry, Upstate Medical Center, State University of New York at Syracuse, and is the author of *Mind and Destiny, Marriage Between Equals,* and *Corporate Wives—Corporate Casualties?*. This article is abridged by the editors from *The Psychoanalytic Review,* 54 (Winter 1967), 583-608, through the courtesy of the Editors and the Publisher, National Psychological Association for Psychoanalysis, New York, N.Y.

ness among human beings eclipse the sexual by far. The playwrights and poets know all about this.

Jean Giraudoux (1938) wrote in *Amphitryon 38,* "You know, Mercury, most faithful wives are unfaithful to their husbands with everything except men—with jewels, with perfumes, with reading, with religion and the contemplation of Spring, with everything in fact, except a man." . . .

The issue of fidelity can become quite abstract. Is infidelity always immoral? Can one be immoral by being faithful to another yet unfair or unjust to oneself? Chekhov's (1964) Voynitsky in "Uncle Vanya" observed of Professor Serebryakov's docile young wife: "Her fidelity is false from beginning to end. There is plenty of fine sentiment in it, but no logic. To deceive an old husband whom one can't stand is immoral; but to try and stifle one's youth, one's vitality, one's vitality to feel—that's not immoral." The distinction made here is between fidelity as sentiment and as logic. In the former instance, the principle is followed more or less blindly for its own sake, whereas in the latter fidelity is a principle in the service of exigency.

The problem of sharing a mate with others or with other interests is probably the chief source of feelings of infidelity and often pathological jealousy. This inability to share may extend to the children. An intense feeling of infidelity can result when a husband feels left out or alienated by a wife's exuberant turn toward a child. Yet the husband and also father would lose his self-respect if he verbalized or even felt such a resentment. The jealousy is displaced to other more "tolerable" areas, usually the sexual one. It is more respectable for an adult to resent the intrusion of another man than to become petulant over his wife's attention to his own child. Only the well integrated can consciously feel and express the agony of rivalry with one's own child; for others, the shame is unbearable or the intensity of disappointment too great, so that the obsession, or often delusion, of sexual infidelity is established.

What about actual sexual infidelity? Do we live in such a pristine world that adultery is a delusion? It often is the cause of marital breakup, but not as often as one might suppose, and it is not the cause of the agonies that are usually attributed to it. First of all, the cuckold is very much like the cancer victim; he is the last to know, not because he is stupid, but because he chooses to deny what he perceives. He would perhaps rather be quite gullible and a laughingstock than confront his wife with an issue that might jeopardize what he does get from her. If he "knew" that his wife were sexually unfaithful, his pride and conventional mores would dictate that he take "some action," usually both punitive and destructive, even if he did not want to. . . .

An extramarital affair is usually a result of dependency needs as much as sexual needs. Prostitutes report that their chief business problem, a production bottleneck if you will, is the men who want to stay and talk. One married male patient carried on an affair that was the scandal of the small town in which he lived. He provided an expensive apartment, furs, automobile, and the other accoutrements required for a conventional, respectable affair. No one in that town knew, nor would they ever believe, that all that transpired between them was a discussion of books and the reading of poetry. His infidelity to his wife was a verbal one; he chose to talk to another woman. His need for this was great, yet he would suffer humiliation if it were revealed to the community that it were just that and not the expected somatic orgy. . . .

Jealousy is an expected affect of living. Who would want to live a life in which one cared so little about another, or the other was of so little value that nothing he did, or who he went with, mattered. Who in the world would like to be fully trusted, fully taken for granted in every situation? If someone is precious to us, we must have a modicum of jealousy as basic cement.

Jealousy is often a part of the titillation, the foreplay, between partners. Each mate takes turns in accusing the other of infidelity when they are quite sure of their devotion. In fact, it is only when they are quite sure of each other that they can indulge in this playfulness. "How come the butcher gives you the best cuts of meat?" he asks. Later she might say, "No wonder you're so tired at night with that new blonde secretary at the office." However, when trust is lacking in one or the other, there is no laughter but instead the serious, "Just what did you mean by that remark?" The remarks are innocent to those able to love well, but are no joke to those whose hold on reality and to an object are tenuous at best. It is a sign of loyalty when people can share their illicit suspicion fantasies, and a sign of mistrust when everything must be concrete—no playful accusations allowed. . . .

Freud (1922) stated that analytic work had shown that instances of jealousy revealed themselves in three classes: *competitive* or oedipal, *projected,* and *delusional.*

Normal or *competitive* jealousy is thought of as being compounded of the grief of losing the loved object and the pain because of the personal wound. To lose out to another reopens the old wound of the oedipal situation, where the child endures the humiliation and despair of being outdone in the struggle with his father for the mother's love.

Tied to the above mechanism is *projected* jealousy, derived from actual unfaithfulness in adult life or intense repressed thoughts of unfaithfulness on the part of the subject. The subject, then, battling with his own unacceptable drives of infidelity, salves his own conscience by self-righteously "giving" them to the object. This type of jealousy has its origins in the human, albeit infantile, need to maintain an air of personal innocence.

The third and most malignant type is *delusional* jealousy. This, associated with paranoia and the paranoid psychoses, as illustrated by Freud in his analysis of the Schreber case, is a construction to hide dreaded homosexuality. Here the "loved" object is really the purported intruder.

Freud's early formulations today appear oversimplified. He did not stress the forces of the male-dominant society which have demanded inordinate faithfulness on the part of women in the roles they are forced to play. Jealousy and possessiveness, then, are as much derived from societal demands as from childhood. . . .

Our dreams regularly show extensive sexual infidelity even if we try to deny its existence in waking thoughts and daydreams. It has been observed by Freud and others that sexual dreams are rarely if ever with one's mate. Some people become disturbed by these nocturnal lapses and would like to feel that their dreams come not from themselves but from some capricious god who imposes this phantasmagoria to plague or test them. The dream allows for fanciful indulgences and excursions into immorality and transgression that generally go against one's wakeful integrity. To some observers, this has been an indication that our morality is but skindeep and is subject to strong pressures from an inner life which would overthrow those values we consciously prize dearly.

Psychoanalysis, along with poets and dramatists, has uncovered the conflictual nature of man in regard to the opposing forces of orderliness and disintegrative chaos. The great struggle, as Freud defined it, is between the pleasure principle, which would seek gratification without much thought about consequences, and the reality principle, which would measure gratification of an impulse in terms of present and future variables. Under the reality principle one would take into account both self-preservation and altruistic considerations. In dreams, the pleasure principle often prevails. Dreams help keep us goal directed in our waking hours by draining off in harmless nocturnal fantasy those asocial and wanton acts of sexuality and aggression, so that in our waking hours we may act and play properly. But dreams reveal what we hate to admit in our conscious state, that the past is very much with us and may haunt us in ways not usually clear to us. Dreams regularly reveal intense sexual desires toward members of one's own family.

For instance, fathers, in dreams, see themselves in sexual situations with young daughters. Mothers find their sons or brothers as lovers. These family romances are almost "organic" in their persistence and power in the lives of all of us. Fortunately, in most instances, they are relegated to, and perhaps partially handled by, the dream drain, and this allows us to live rationally the rest of the time. In many instances they are not "contained" by dreams and spill over into the day where they are apt to be most disruptive of important object relations and personal aims. These errant sexual thoughts from infantile life may interfere with conjugal sexual behavior. Because sexuality has become tainted by its association with "unnatural" objects, i.e., family members, etc., it becomes a forbidden act even where normally and legally permitted. Some, then, act as if sex with a mate is incest, with all the revulsion and disgust that such violation of basic social rules would entail. Thereupon, there can ensue a search for objects outside the home or the social group, where the taint of family sexuality can be obliterated.

Freud's discovery that the oedipal complex is a dominant, overwhelming force in the development of every individual, has brought the realization of the long history of sexuality in each of us. Because of this long history, those who design simple explanations and even solutions to sexual problems, as if they are solely current and contemporary "problems of living," are most unrealistic. It is for this reason that efforts at marriage counseling, mental health advice, punitive legal measures, by professionals and do-it-yourself devices, such as trial marriages, affairs, switchings, polygamy, etc., have offered very little to distressed people. There are no panaceas and no substitutes for the work and agony involved in the confrontation of one's history. In seeking these ersatz and makeshift solutions, an individual most often commits his greatest infidelity; he becomes faithless to himself. With all our science, we must not be above the wisdom of certain aphorisms of our heritage. In this instance, we can profitably quote Polonius in his farewell speech to Laertes, "This above all, to thine own self be true." The turning away from one's origins, from one's history, the denial of impulses and relationships, are attitudes of deception about one's own being. They are the greatest infidelities of which we are capable. . . .

Clinically, the jealous person resists reassurance. On the contrary, he comes to therapy for substantiation of his fantasy. He will not easily give up the gratification inherent in this mechanism of jealousy.

Although the more dramatic and communicable problems of marriage have to do with "low" fidelity, a subtle form of imitation is high or exaggerated fidelity. In this there is a devotion and obeisance that can be oppressive, stifling and enraging. One mate may become a puppy dog to the other, following, imitating, obeying with such obsequiousness as to drive the other mad. A major part of the maddening process of this relationship is that it is very difficult to lodge a complaint. In this world of cruelty, alienation, and abandonment, how can one tell a judge that "my mate loves me too much"? Yet our poets and dramatists have told us the vagaries of loving unwisely. If, for some situations, love may not be enough, for others it can be too much. The observer soon sees that servile love is a sign of immaturity in the giver and an act of oppression to the object. It is a "killing with kindness" syndrome, really a grave insincerity which hides behind the euphemism of devotion.

This sort of "devotion" led one woman to seek psychiatric help. Her chief complaint was that her husband spent his time following her around the house. His overriding preference was to be with her every moment that he was home from work. Her company preempted all other social and recreational activities. His home was his castle; he seemed to have no other needs outside of it; he knew no one on the outside with whom he would rather be than the woman whom he had chosen and loved. At parties and social gatherings, her presence and conversation were always the most attractive and most stimulating. What friends they had were ones whom she had "found"; he was grateful that she assumed this social responsibility. Similarly, he relinquished his ties to his own parents and siblings, and seemed to prefer his in-laws.

The most oppressive aspect of his uxorious devotion was the imitative component. He liked to follow her in her interests and hobbies. When she signed up for a course in adult education, he immediately thought this would be a good idea for himself. When she undertook to play a musical instrument, he dusted off his adolescent violin. He similarly took his cues about political, religious and moral issues from her. She appeared to be, to say the least, like an overbearing wife and perhaps the promotion of this image was one of his underlying motives. She had never sought or demanded this sort of authority in the home. As a modern woman she cherished what she considered a reasonable degree of autonomy for herself but showed no particular lust to possess the will of her mate. This he seemed all too freely to relinquish; for her this was no valuable acquisition, but indeed a tiresome burden. He wished to effect a fusion with her in the hope of gaining needed support, but for her this was a severe threat to her own boundaries and integrity.

The observer could see his behavior as reminiscent of a boy tied to his mother's apron strings—a manifestation of extreme dependence on a woman, eclipsing needs to maintain the conventional image of the male as independent, strong, outgoing, and self-sufficient. Yet, in his own mind, he was nothing but loyal and loving. He was deeply hurt when she was annoyed with his behavior. Could he help it if he loved her so dearly? What he was unable to see was that in giving himself over to her, he was performing a religious act of adoration—one that should be reserved for one's Deity. He hoped thereby to obtain for himself the blessings that accrue to what might appear as unselfishness but which was really a lack of self.

Ironically, such total devotion may be a normal conventional expectation for a woman. Her emptying herself of all personal goals when she marries is looked upon as perfectly normal, and her docility is viewed as a prime virtue. When a male does it, it becomes a clinical case! Rarely, if ever, is there the complaint that a wife is too docile, too submissive, too much at home. She may without danger become her husband's devotee. We might conclude that "high" fidelity on the part of the male is considered highly "unnatural" for him and at best looked upon with a great deal of suspicion. Conversely, the usual expectation of fidelity on the part of the woman is part and parcel of her docility, submission, and consequent dependence on the authority of her husband. . . .

One generally hears of loyal servants or subjects, rarely of loyal masters or rulers. This can be applied to aspects of faithfulness in marriage where the rules of conduct as far as infidelity are concerned are much more stringent and condemnatory for the relatively powerless woman than for the man. . . . In the male-dominant society the infidelity of the male is generally excused whereas the woman's lapse has severe consequences. This well known double standard has been rationalized and vindicated in the fiction that the male of the species is basically polygamous, and therefore his transgressions are a part of his basic nature, whereas the woman's is a moral fault. This is another instance where power can write its own favorable rules supported by an ongoing mythology. We might have to agree with the cynic when he says that if one is powerful enough one does not have to be sexually faithful and yet at the same time can demand unswerving loyalty from another. The best safeguard for mutual fidelity may be a healthy balance of power. . . .

Fidelity, with its partner, trust, is a necessity for harmonious social relationships. Without it, no family, no community, no nation can long exist. Fidelity, although born in the family, permeates all subsequent relationships and understandings and must be prominent in the hierarchy of commitments—from marriage to business, to profession, to church, to country

Simone de Beauvoir (1964:57) has expressed with candor the question of fidelity as it arose between two "liberated" people. Although unmarried, she revealed the same problem of preserving basic faith, and at the same time the maintenance of autonomy of the individuals involved. Even with a great deal of abstract philosophy and highsounding intentions, she reveals plenty of banal hurt feelings, anxieties and suspicions when Sartre related his feelings for M. As an over-all philosophy for their relationship, she writes:

> Often preached, rarely practiced, complete fidelity is usually experienced by those who impose it on themselves as a mutilation; they console themselves for it by sublimations or by drink. Traditionally, marriage used to allow the man a few "adventures on the side" without reciprocity; nowadays, many women have become aware of their rights and of the conditions necessary for their happiness; if there is nothing in their own lives to compensate for masculine inconstancy, they will fall prey to jealousy and boredom.
>
> There are many couples who conclude more or less the same pact as that of Sartre and myself: to maintain throughout all deviations from the main path a "certain fidelity." "I have been faithful to thee, Cynara, in my fashion." Such an undertaking has its risks—it is always possible that one of the partners may prefer a new attachment to the old one, the other partner then considering himself or herself unjustly betrayed; in place of two free persons, a victim and a torturer confront each other.
>
> If the two allies allow themselves only passing sexual liaisons, then there is no difficulty, but it also means that the freedom they allow themselves is not worthy of the name. Sartre and I have been more ambitious; it has been our wish to experience "contingent loves"; but there is one question we have deliberately avoided. How would the third person feel about our arrangement? It often happened that the third person accommodated himself to it without difficulty; our union left plenty of room for loving friendships and fleeting affairs. But if the protagonist wanted more, then conflicts would break out.

Finally, something should be said about that word opportunity—so disdained in sophisticated psychological circles. It is easy to say that moral behavior is overwhelmingly determined by internal needs, defenses, prohibitions and values. We hear that the sound person will respond ethically to all and any temptations. Even if it is true that the morality or lack of it in any individual may be predictable, we can say so only with the qualification of "more or less." Only belief or illusion has absolute certainty. If it is so that we can say that a person will be "more or less" faithful, we must then take into account unpsychological factors such as proximity and opportunity. With lack of opportunity, the worst scoundrel would have to be a saint. Taking into account drives, ego needs and the vagaries of opportunity, one is justified in speaking of fidelity in human terms of more or less. The relationship without blemish is not to be condemned as rigid or compulsive. Nor is a lapse or two to be interpreted as a sign of deep and unalterable corruption of character. Inconstancy is not necessarily infidelity.

It was the genius of Freud that turned away from unalterable positions in favor of conceptualization in terms of fluidity—of progressions and regressions. Freud never did accept the vision of man's unswerving and unfaltering propulsion to heaven. One can be deemed faithful if he is more or less faithful in spirit and body.

The question of fidelity and jealousy that arises is inextricably tied to man's basic wish for the absolute, for the unalterable and infallible. Jealousy in a sense is the by-product of the breakdown of belief in another human being. His belief system has been shattered not only by actual infidelity but by the inherent incapacity of his fellow human beings to sustain and imitate the model of God.

Dr. Seidenberg's contribution reminds us that the experience and the interpretation of jealousy often hinge upon the *definition of fidelity* which is at work—in a person, within a couple, and in a whole society. If, for example, two partners in an intimate relationship do not operate from a common understanding of what constitutes faithful or unfaithful behavior, painful experiences of jealousy are made more likely. Definitions of fidelity are in part culturally derived, in part idiosyncratic. Most importantly, such definitions and the "ground rules" based upon them vary somewhat from person to person and from couple to couple. Thus the pain of jealousy can be minimized by means of candid and clear communication between the partners. For further discussion of this important issue, see the short article by Ben N. Ard, Jr. (Chapter 15).

Social psychology is the branch of psychology which concerns itself most self-consciously with the relationship of individual behaviors to the larger social context. Standing squarely in that tradition, the next article argues that an emotional experience has *two* indispensable components: (1) a mental set of socially-shaped *beliefs and feelings* by means of which to interpret (2) *physiological arousal*. That is, a true emotional experience involves the body *and* the mind.

Applying this paradigm, the next article argues that the emotion we call *jealousy* has two components: (1) a mental set of socially-shaped *beliefs and feelings* (about sex, love, marriage, the current state of the relationship, degree of dependency, present threat to the relationship, expectations of peer group, and dozens of other pertinent concerns) by means of which to interpret (2) *physiological arousal* (rapid heartbeat, accelerated breathing, and other impulsive body reactions). In other words: If you find yourself physiologically aroused in a circumstance in which you (and your friends) believe you *ought* to feel jealous, you are likely to label your feelings "jealousy" and begin to act out the various "jealousy scripts" stored in your head from past experience and learning.

8

The Social Psychology of Jealousy

Elaine Hatfield and G.William Walster

---

jealous/ 'jel-əs/*adj* (ME *jelous,* fr. OF, fr. (assumed) VL *zelosus,* fr. LL *zelus* zeal—more at ZEAL) 1 a: intolerant of rivalry or unfaithfulness b: disposed to suspect rivalry or unfaithfulness: apprehensive of the loss of another's exclusive devotion 2: hostile toward a rival or one believed to enjoy an advantage 3: vigilant in guarding a possession 4: distrustfully watchful: SUSPICIOUS *syn* see ENVIOUS—

Webster (1963)

We begin the section on "Sexual Jealousy" in our Human Sexuality classes with a simple question: What would you most like to know about jealousy? Students' answers are surprisingly redundant. They ask: "What

Elaine Hatfield, Ph.D., (1937-) is Professor of Sociology at the University of Wisconsin at Madison. Her article, "Adrenaline Makes the Heart Grow Fonder" (*Psychology Today,* June 1971), touched on jealousy and moved the editors of this volume to invite her (and co-author Ellen Berscheid) to contribute. G. William Walster, Ph. D., (1941 -) is also Professor of Sociology at the University of Wisconsin. The research reported in this paper was supported in part by the National Institute of Mental Health, Grant *1 RO1 MH26681-01.* This paper was written especially for this volume.

is jealousy?'' and—whatever it is—"How can you get rid of it?" A scattering of anthropologists, sociologists, and psychologists—as well as a tidal wave of novelists—*have* addressed these two questions. Unfortunately, their answers are unnervingly inconsistent.

> Jealousy is an enigma, the least known of all human emotions, the least spoken of human reactions.
>
> Sokoloff (1947:14)

WHAT IS THIS THING CALLED JEALOUSY?

Since Aristotle's time, theorists have been unable to agree as to what jealousy "really" is. They have insisted that jealousy should really be equated with "love/hate," "a perverse kind of pleasure," "shock," "uncertainty," "confusion," "suspicion," "fear of loss," "hurt pride," "rivalry," "sorrow," "shame," "humiliation," "anger," "despair," "depression." or "a desire for vengeance."

Probably most theorists can agree that jealousy possesses two basic components: (1) a feeling of bruised pride, and (2) a feeling that one's property rights have been violated.

> Il y a dans la jalousie plus d'amour-propre que d'amour. (There is more self-love than love in jealousy.)
>
> La Rochefoucauld (1665)

According to such analysts as Bohm (1967), Fenichel (1955), Freud (1922), Lagache (1947), Langfeldt (1961), Mairet (1908), or Mead (1960), jealousy is "really" little more than wounded pride. For example, Margaret Mead (this book:120) contends that the more shaky one's self-esteem, the more vulnerable one is to jealousy's pangs:

Jealousy is not a barometer by which the depth of love can be read. It merely records the degree of the lover's insecurity. . . . It is a negative miserable state of feeling having its origin in the sense of insecurity and inferiority.

> Jealousy is . . . a kind of fear related to a desire to preserve a possession.
>
> Descartes, quoted in Davis (1936)

According to such analysts as Davis (1936) and Gottschalk (1936), jealousy is "really" little more than one's fear that he may lose his property. For example, Davis (this book: 129) claims:

> . . . In every case it [jealousy] is apparently a fear . . . or rage reaction to a threatened appropriation of one's own, or what is desired as one's own, property."

At this point, however, theorists' descriptions of jealousy begin to diverge.

The man on the street shows similar confusion as to what jealousy "really" is. For example, Ankles (1939) asked university graduates:

> What are the emotions and feelings involved in jealous behavior? (Cross out those which do not apply)

(1) Anger	(8) Narcissism or self-love
(2) Fear	(9) Antagonism
(3) Ridicule	(10) Pleasure
(4) Joy	(11) Stupidity
(5) Cruelty	(12) Respect
(6) Hate	(13) Elation
(7) Self-feeling	(14) Shame

To Ankles' surprise, he found that at least a few of his respondents insisted that jealousy was associated with *all* of the preceding emotions. In a more recent study, Davitz (1969) interviewed 50 people and secured 50 different descriptions of jealousy.

CAN WE CONTROL JEALOUSY?

If we know what a social commentator thinks society should be like, we can pretty well predict whether s/he thinks jealousy is "bred in the bone" or can easily be stimulated—or extinguished.

JEALOUSY IS "BRED IN THE BONE"

Traditionalists insist that marriage should be both permanent and exclusive. Thus, *they* naturally prefer to believe that jealousy is a natural emotion.

> Even insects express anger, terror, jealousy, and love.
>
> Charles Darwin (1965)

Traditionalists generally begin their spirited defenses of jealousy by pointing out that even animals are jealous. They cite the "jealous" courtship battles of stags, antelopes, wild pigs, goats, seals, kangaroos, howler monkeys, and so on (See Bohm 1967). They go on to mention that even Kinsey and his associates (1948:411) believed that male jealousy had a mammalian basis:

> While cultural traditions may account for some of the human male's behavior, his jealousies so closely parallel those of the lower species that one is forced to conclude that his mammalian heritage may be partly responsible for his attitudes.

Generally they end their defense by reminding us that many societies simply take it for granted that jealousy is a basic emotion. (For example, in some societies, if a man catches his mate and his rival *in flagrante delicto,* he is allowed to kill them.)[2]

JEALOUSY SHOULD BE, AND CAN BE, EXTINGUISHED

Radical reformers such as Beecher and Beecher (1971) or O'Neill and O'Neill (1972) see things differently. They are convinced that people could evolve more loving personal lives, and more creative and productive professional lives, if they felt free to love all mankind—or at least a larger subset of it. Thus, *they* naturally prefer to believe that society has the power to arouse, or to temper, jealousy as it chooses.

Radical reformers generally begin their spirited attacks on jealousy by pointing out that not all men are jealous. They note that in most societies men are allowed to have more than one partner. Ford and Beach (1951) report that 84% of the 185 societies they studied allowed men to have more than one wife. Only 1% of the societies permitted women to have more than one husband. Most societies also look more tolerantly on "wife lending" or "mate swapping" and on extramarital sex than does our own. For example, Ford and Beach (1951) report that when Chukchee men (Siberia) travel to distant communities, they often engage in sexual liaisons

[1]East (1949) found that "jealousy" was the underlying motive in 23% of the 200 murders he investigated.

with their hosts' mates. They reciprocate in kind when their hosts visit their community.[2]

Radical reformers point out that, traditionally, our own society has strongly fostered marital permanence, exclusivity—and jealousy. Yet, in spite of the fact that our society tells men they *should* be jealous of their mates, many are not. For example, Kinsey and his associates (1953) found that if a husband learned about his wife's extramarital relations, his discovery caused "serious difficulty" only 42% of the time; 42% of the time it caused "no difficulty at all."

THE SOCIAL-PSYCHOLOGICAL PERSPECTIVE

What does social psychology have to say about these questions? Can we add to the existing confusion? Certainly.

Currently, Schachter's (1964) theory of emotion is probably the most popular social-psychological theory of human emotional response. Schachter argues that both one's mind and one's body must be engaged if s/he is to have a true emotional experience.

Mind: A person must feel that it is appropriate to interpret his/her feelings in emotional terms. A person learns—from society, parents, friends, and from his or her own experience—what emotions it is "appropriate" to feel in various settings. We know that we feel "joyous excitement" when a friend comes to visit, and "anxiety" when an enemy swaggers into town. The untutored may well experience the very same feeling on both occasions (a sort of anxious excitement). Schachter argues that a person will experience an emotion only if s/he interprets his or her "feelings" in emotional terms.

Body: A person must be physiologically aroused. Schachter argues that a person can experience an emotion only if s/he *has* some "feelings." Schachter argues that—*by themselves*—neither appropriate cognitions nor physiological arousal constitute a complete emotional experience.

Schacher tested his two-component theory in an ingenious series of experiments.

MANIPULATING PHYSIOLOGICAL AROUSAL

Schachter's first step was to manipulate the first component of emotion—physiological arousal. In one now classic experiment,

[2]See Bohm (1967), Forel (1931), Mead (1931), and Russell (1926) for other examples.

Schachter gave half of his participants (those in the *Unaroused* groups) a placebo. He gave the remaining participants (those in the *Aroused* groups) an arousing drug—epinephrine. Epinephrine is an ideal drug for producing a "high." Its effects mimic the discharge of the sympathetic nervous system. Shortly after a person receives an epinephrine injection, s/he experiences palpitations, tremor, flushes, and accelerated breathing. In short, s/he experiences the same physiological reactions which accompany a variety of natural emotional states.[3]

MANIPULATING "APPROPRIATE" COGNITIONS

Schachter's second step was to manipulate the second component of emotion—the participants' cognitions. In the Non-Emotional Attribution Groups, Schachter wished to lead volunteers to attribute their feelings to a non-emotional cause—the injection. In the Emotional Attribution Groups, Schachter tried to lead volunteers to attribute their tranquil (or stirred up) feelings to an emotional cause.

Non-Emotional Attribution Groups.   In these groups, Non-Aroused volunteers (who should have no reaction to the placebo shot) were given no information about how the shot would affect them. The Aroused volunteers were given a complete description of the shot's effects; they were warned that in a very few minutes they would experience palpitations, tremors, flushing, and accelerated breathing.

Emotional Attribution Groups.   In these groups, Schachter tried to lead volunteers to attribute their tranquil or aroused feelings to an emotional cause. For example, in some groups, Schachter arranged things so that, at the time the shot took effect, volunteers were caught up in a wild, abandoned, happy social interaction. In this setting, Schachter hoped that when the Aroused subjects felt the effects of the shot, and asked themselves, "What's happening to me?" they would answer, "I'm having fun—that's what."

[3] As Lazarus *et al.* (1970) observe, theorists fall into one of two camps: the Generalists and the Specificists. The theorists agree on the evidence, i.e., that emotions, if sufficiently intense, have both general and specific physiological components. [See Averill (1969), Ax (1953), Funkenstein *et al.* (1957), Lacey (1967), and Lindsley (1950)]. What they disagree about is whether it is emotional similarities or differences that are important. The Generalists—such as Cannon (1929), Duffy (1962) and Schachter (1964)—insist that emotions' physiological similarities are important. They attribute little theoretical significance to possible physiological differences.

Schachter is a Generalist. Thus, when Schachter says an emotional person must experience "physiological arousal," he means merely that one must experience *general* physiological arousal. One need not experience some unique complex of physiological patterning.

In other groups, Schachter arranged things so that, at the time the shot took effect, volunteers were involved in a tense, explosive, angry interaction. In this setting, Schachter hoped that when Aroused subject felt the effects of the shot, and asked themselves, "What happening to me?" they would answer, "I'm mad . . . mad as hell—that's what."

Schachter found support for his hypothesis. He found that *both* appropriate cognitions and physiological arousal *are* indispensable components of a complete emotional experience.[4] Additional support for the two-component theory of emotion comes from Schachter and Wheeler (1962) and Hohmann (1962).

This, then, in brief, is the Schachterian emotion paradigm. Can this social-psychological perspective give us some new insights into the complex and confusing nature of jealousy? Let us see how a Schachterian would answer the two questions with which we began.

WHAT IS JEALOUSY?

Interestingly enough, Schachter's "revolutionary" theory of emotion generates an equally revolutionary view as to the nature of jealousy.

From Aristotle to Schachter, almost all analysts simply assumed that emotions such as jealousy are somehow built into the organism.[5] They took it for granted that all persons, at all times, "really" experience the same thing. It was *their* job to ferret out the essential elements of those emotions. The fact that individuals' emotional descriptions were unnervingly inconsistent—the fact that some "jealous" persons insisted they felt "joyous anticipation of revenge" while others insisted they felt "depressed" and "lethargic" *or* the fact that some claimed they were suffering unbearably, while others stoutly insisted they felt perfectly

---

[4]It is interesting that Davis (1936:402), writing long before Schachter formulated his theory, conceived of a distinctly "Schachterian" definition of jealousy. Davis argued that (1) one's social experiences determine how he labels his feelings, and (2) jealousy is akin (physiologically) to a variety of emotions.

> . . . Doubtless the physiological mechanism is inherited. But the striking thing about this mechanism is that it is not specific for jealousy, but operates in precisely the same manner in fear and rage. The sympathetic nervous system plays, apparently, the usual role: increased adrenal activity speeding the heart, increasing the sugar content of the blood, toning up the striated and staying the smooth muscles.

> If we are to differentiate jealousy from the other strong emotions we must speak not in terms of inherited physiology but in terms of the type of situation which provokes it.

[5]For example, Plutchik (1970) echoed the prevailing sentiment when he argued that since subjective emotional reports are "unreliable" and "biased," scientists must define emotions "functionally" and "behaviorally."

content—was simply chalked up to the fact that human beings possess poor powers of observation and often deceive themselves.

The Schacterians would insist that a person's confidences should be treated with more respect. For the Schachterians, one's mind, as well as one's body, contributes to emotional experiences. One's beliefs about what a jealous person *should* be feeling, and what s/he *must* be feeling, should have a potent impact on what s/he *does* feel. If society's sub-groups have radically different ideas about the essential nature of jealousy—and they do—our labeling will necessarily reflect these differences. Thus Schachterians would argue that jealousy is "really" a vastly different experience for different people.[6]

CAN JEALOUSY BE CONTROLLED?

According to Schachter's two-component theory, society has the ability to shape *all* of our emotional experiences. If society wanted to do so, it could suppress jealousy in either of two ways: (1) Society could try to persuade people to *label* their feelings in a somewhat different way; or (2) society could try to arrange things so that the realization that we must share our "possessions" with others would arouse a far less intense physiological reaction.

Altering Labeling.   Societies vary from considering jealousy to be a natural human response to considering it to be an entirely illegitimate one. If our society wishes, it could change from one which encourages marital permanence and exclusivity—and jealousy—to one which insists that people should not, and must not, be jealous. Surely, the wily citizen would be clever enough to come up with a host of new, more acceptable, labels for his or her feelings. Social reformers would naturally hope that the once-jealous individual could be persuaded to re-label his or her feelings in positive, or at least neutral, terms (i.e., to label "jealous" feelings as "sexual curiosity," "pride that others value one's mate," etc.). Unfortunately for potential reformers, it is probably at least as likely that the persons would come up with alternative *negative* labels for their feelings (i.e., "chagrin at my mate's poor taste," "anger," or "depression at her neglect," etc.). From the reformer's point of view, such changes would really constitute no change at all.

According to the Schachterians, there is a second way society can eliminate jealousy: It can reduce the "jealous" person's physiological arousal—and this is a distinctly harder task.

[6]Interestingly enough, after a scholarly review of all that has been written on the emotions, Arnold (1960) comes to the same conclusion.

Reducing Physiological Arousal. If society works at it, it should be able to affect *some* reduction in the intensity of people's jealous feelings.

Currently, it is believed that one's value depends on the faithfulness of one's spouse, and on his/her possession of people and things, which accounts for some of jealousy's sting. Society *could* teach its citizens that self-worth depends on what one is and does—not on how many people one can control. If the association between "pride" and "a partner's exclusive possession" were reduced, jealous feelings should be less intense.

Unfortunately, society would have a harder time eradicating many of the links between "a mate's loss" and "physiological arousal." Currently the person who loses his or her mate is confronted with an enormity of practical problems. S/he loses the partner's love. S/he may have to endure the loss of friends—and worse yet, the loss of his or her children. One's daily life is disrupted in a thousand different ways. It is likely, then, that society might be able to make the jealous person's feelings somewhat less intense, but they are unlikely to be able to eliminate one's physiological arousal altogether.

"Jealousy"—by any other name, even at a reduced intensity—may still remain a painfully devastating experience.

Hatfield and Walster suggest that what we call the "basic emotion of jealousy" might be, in fact, a rather *neutral* impulse which is labeled and given direction by our feelings, beliefs, values, and expectations (which, in turn, are shaped by our associations with other people, with institutions, and with our culture). This interpretation would help account for the fact that circumstances which provoke jealousy in one person may not provoke it in another.

Of all those contextual factors which influence the processing of "jealous feelings," surely prevailing ideas about and attitudes toward *romantic love* must be counted among the most important. Romantic love has been with us for a long time, but it has not been around forever. Here is an excerpt from Morton Hunt's (1959:131) account of its advent and impact:

> Toward the end of the eleventh century A.D., a handful of poets and noblemen in southern France concocted a set of love sentiments most of which had no precedent in Western civilization, and out of them constructed a new and quite original relationship between man and woman known as. . . courtly love. . . [It] began as a game and a literary conceit, but unexpectedly grew into a social philosophy that shaped the manners and morals of the West. It started as a playful exercise in flattery, but became a spiritual force guiding the flatterers; it was first a private sport of the feudal aristocracy, but became finally the ideal of the middle classes; and with wonderfully consistent inconsistency, it exalted at one and the same time adultery and chastity, duplicity and faithfulness, self-indulgence and austerity, suffering and delight. Although satirists have slain and buried it in the tinsel costume of all its follies a thousand times over, it has not stayed interred for one night, and men and women throughout the Western world still live by and take for granted a number of its principal concepts.

The next selection explores the relationship between sexual jealousy and romantic love. Berscheid and Fei conclude that the prime candidates for the aversive experience of sexual jealousy are those unfortunate lovers who are very *dependent* on their partners *and* who are *insecure* in their relationships. Our society, they suggest, puts us in a double bind by placing high value on both independence and romantic love (which involves dependency).

9

Romantic Love and Sexual Jealousy

Ellen Berscheid and Jack Fei

It is amazing how little the empirical sciences have to offer on the subject of love. Particularly strange is the silence of psychologists, for one might think this to be their particular obligation. . . . Sometimes this is merely sad or irritating, as in the case of the textbooks of psychology and sociology, practically none of which treats the subject. . . . More often the situation becomes completely ludicrous. One might reasonably expect that writers of serious treatises on the family, on marriage, and on sex should consider the subject of love to be a proper, even basic, part of their self-imposed task. But I must report that no single one of the volumes on these subjects available in the library where I work has any serious mention of the subject (Maslow 1954:235).

It was over two decades ago that the distinguished psychologist and humanist, Abraham Maslow, admonished his colleagues for their neglect of love. But it is still amazing how little the empirical sciences have to offer on the subject, perhaps even more so now. Since Maslow wrote those words, scientists have not only flown us to the moon, they have also

Ellen Berscheid, Ph. D., (1936-) is Professor of Psychology at the University of Minnesota. She is a contributor to *Psychology Today* and author (with Elaine C. Walster) of *Interpersonal Attraction* (Reading, Mass.: Addison-Wesley, 1969). Jack C. Fei, B. A., (1949-) is a graduate student at the University of Minnesota and an instructor at the College of St. Catherine in St. Paul. Preparation of this paper was supported in part by National Science Foundation Grant #7205468 to the senior author. "Romantic Love and Sexual Jealousy" was written especially for this volume.

shattered the research taboos which kept our sexuality shrouded in mystery and myth. Nevertheless, romantic love, as well as its intimate associate, sexual jealousy, largely remain the empirical puzzles they were when Maslow came away from his library empty-handed.

Some progress has been made, of course. Researchers no longer jeopardize their scientific status by confessing a professional interest in the subject of love. For example, the social scientist who treads in the footsteps of the University of Minnesota psychology professor of the 1920s need not fear being dismissed, as he was, on grounds of moral turpitude. (Clear evidence of this researcher's depravity was provided by a questionnaire he had constructed which asked the Jazz Age flappers and their raccoon-coated companions such provocative questions as "Did you ever breathe into the ear of a person of the opposite sex in order to arouse their passion?")

The acceptance of romantic love as a legitimate topic of scientific inquiry is not, even now, endorsed by all segments of our society. For example, one U.S. Senator recently launched a highly publicized attack against the scientific study of love; he protested that the subject is properly the concern of poets and song-writers and ought to remain a mystery. Such political attacks, along with other difficulties researchers have experienced in attempting to give love the systematic effort and attention it demands, make it less surprising that empirical data on the topic is sparse, and that concrete information on the psychodynamics of sexual jealousy is virtually nonexistent.

While empirical data is lacking, fortunately there is no scarcity of theoretical ideas about the antecedents of romantic love.

THE SOIL OF ROMANTIC LOVE: UNFULFILLED NEEDS, DISSATISFACTION, DEFICIENCIES

Most theoretical treatises on romantic love are woven with the thread of "psychological dependency." A crucial relationship is believed to exist between our dependence upon another for our comfort, well-being, and happiness, and our love for him or her.

Maslow (1954) calls it "D-love." "Deficiency-love," he theorized, springs from our needs for love, for security, and for belongingness; when another gratifies our "deficiency" needs, we love him in return. According to Maslow, there is another kind of love—"B-love." But although all of us can aspire to love another simply for his "being" rather than for the satisfactions he provides, only very few exceptional "self-actualized" individuals may ever actually experience such love. The kind of love most of us experience in our lifetimes is, in Maslow's view, D-love.

Other theoreticians agree. Casler (1969), for example, speculates that love grows out of our needs for security, sexual satisfaction, and social conformity. Klein and Riviere (1953) concur; they too believe that love has its genesis in our dependency upon other people for the satisfaction of our needs. And Theodor Reik (1944), the dean of the romantic love theorists (who broke his relationship with Freud over a disagreement about the antecedents of heterosexual love), hypothesizes that a sense of our own deficit—a dissatisfaction with ourselves and our state in life—is our spur to love another.

Social-psychological theorists are more likely to discuss the antecedents of attraction in general rather than focusing specifically upon romantic love. The position most take, however, is not inconsistent with the view of those who have directed their theoretical attention specifically to romantic love. Most social-psychological theorists believe that attraction for another stems from the rewards we receive from, or associate with, that person (Blau 1967; Byrne 1969; French & Raven 1959; Homans 1961; Lott & Lott 1972; Thibaut & Kelly 1959).

There is little theoretical dissent, then, from the proposition that the desire to receive what another can give, to have what another has, is fertile ground for the growth of romantic love.

FALLING IN LOVE: THE GROWTH OF PSYCHOLOGICAL DEPENDENCY

It seems reasonable to suppose that, as another satisfies more and more of our desires and gratifies more and more of our needs, our positive feelings for him or her should grow in equal measure. Affection given to a person starved for it, like food given to a hungry man, should result in pleasure and happiness—and affection for the giver.

One might expect, then, that the growth of a relationship from the casual acquaintance of two separate and independent individuals into the increased pleasure-giving and mutual need-satisfaction associated with love should be an unalloyed delight. Any negative feelings we once might have had about the other ought to become fewer and fainter, pushed aside and overwhelmed by the growth of love.

Although it seems reasonable that falling in love should be a consistently pleasant experience, the reports of those who find themselves doing so tell us a different story. The novelist Lawrence Durrell, for example, writes, in *Justine* (1957:59) "But what made me afraid was that after quite a short time I found to my horror that I could not live without her. . . . I had fallen *in love*. The very thought filled me with an inexplicable despair and disgust."

Reik (1944:185), too, observes that very often "the person whom love approaches does not welcome it as a gift, but tries to chase it away as an intruder. Love appears first as an emotion which the person is afraid of, however desirable it may appear to the conscious mind. . . . It is as if the ego were afraid of a danger, of a threatening loss." Durrell describes the despair and disgust of which his character speaks as "inexplicable." Similarly, Reik characterizes the feeling of danger as "the mysterious fear."

The undercurrent of negative emotion—sometimes subtle, sometimes less so—which seems to accompany the growth of love is recognized by several other theorists. Blau (1967), for example, notes that a vacillation between positive and negative emotions even seems to be a defining characteristic of the "falling in love" process. He does not think it mysterious, however; he believes it to be a natural consequence of growing dependency upon another. Thibaut and Kelly (1959) also recognize that ambivalence and confusion between positive and negative emotions are frequent characteristics of developing heterosexual love relationships; they, too, theorize that these feelings are the result of growing dependency. Klein and Riviere (1953) agree. They hypothesize that the "anxiety of dependency" is an inevitable concomitant of love.

INSECURITY: AN INEVITABLE OUTGROWTH OF PSYCHOLOGICAL DEPENDENCY?

What is the "anxiety of dependency?" Where does the "mysterious fear" which accompanies love come from? How is it the "result" of growing dependence? One answer to these questions lies in the recognition that to grow dependent upon another person is to give a portion of ourselves away as hostage—and not simply to fortune in general, but to the other specifically.

As our dependency grows, we relinquish more and more control over our fate. The opposite side of the coin of dependence is independence. To be independent is to be self-sufficient and self-reliant. These qualities add up to freedom: freedom from another's influence, freedom from another's control. If the romantic love theorists are correct, love involves a loss of freedom and independence.

As we lose our independence, as our happiness becomes more and more vested in another, our awareness—and dread—of the conditions and circumstances which may take the loved person away from us, and threaten our happiness, may grow also. Casler (1969:20) puts it strongly: "Every increase in dependency increases the fear of losing the source of gratification."

We said that psychology does not lack hypotheses about love. But hypotheses are just hypotheses, and, as Maslow observed, psychology is an empirical science. One stumbling block to investigating such hypotheses as Casler's—that fear and insecurity increase with every increase in dependency, as well as the relationship between these two factors and romantic love—has been the task of measuring dependency and insecurity within a specific relationship.

DEPENDENCY, INSECURITY,
AND ROMANTIC LOVE

In order to begin at the beginning, we attempted to construct, in our laboratory, a scale which could assess a person's dependency upon another (see Fei & Berscheid, 1976). First, we asked young men and women to describe their relationship with the one member of the opposite sex they were currently "most involved with." We found that the major dimension underlying their responses to questions about their relationship was clearly their "dependency" upon the other. Their answers to such questions as "(X)'s presence makes any activity more enjoyable" and "I spend a great deal of time thinking about (X)" were especially representative of this "dependency" dimension.

There was a second dimension underlying the responses of these men and women. It was characterized by their answers to such questions about their relationship as "I often wonder how much (X) really cares for me" and "I worry about losing (X's) affection." This second dimension clearly seemed to represent the "insecurity" factor that so many theorists presume characterizes the growth of love.

We then examined the relationship between the degree to which the man (or woman) was dependent on the person he (or she) was most involved with and whether he reported that he was "in love," "not in love," or "didn't know" whether he was in love with the other. If the romantic love theorists are correct, the higher a man or woman scores on the scale which measures his dependence on the other, the more likely he or she should be to report that he is in love.

This was the case. Those persons who reported that they were definitely "in love" with the person they were most involved with were highly dependent on the other. Further, the men and women "in love" were significantly more dependent upon the other than were those who "didn't know" whether they were in love. In turn, those people who said they "didn't know" if their relationship was love scored significantly higher on the Dependency Scale than did those men and women who were confident that they were "not in love."

Previous theorists were clearly correct that high dependency on another does appear to be strongly associated with reports of love. (Supporting evidence also comes from Rubin 1970, who developed a scale to measure romantic love; he found that one dimension which appeared to be contained in his scale was an "affiliative and dependent need" factor.) But is it also true that those who are in love, and highly dependent, are experiencing insecurity, the "anxiety of dependency," "the mysterious fear" of which many theorists speak?

To find out, we compared the Insecurity Scale scores of the men and women who were sure they were "in love" with those who said they "didn't know" if they were in love, as well as with those who said they were sure they were "not in love" with the person they were most involved with. The results surprised us. The most insecure men and women were *not* those "in love" with their partner, but rather those men and women who "didn't know." In fact, the Insecurity scores of the people "in love" did not differ significantly from the scores of those who were sure they were "not in love."

This finding suggests that dependency is associated with insecurity only for those whose love is weak or growing; those who love is full blown appear to experience high dependency without necessarily suffering from high insecurity. To pursue this hypothesis further, we directly examined the correlation between a person's degree of dependency upon the other and the insecurity he or she felt in the relationship. We found that for those who are sure they are "not in love" with the other, there is a high and significant relationship between dependency and insecurity; the more the person is dependent on the other, the more insecure he or she is in the relationship ($r = .60$). For those who "don't know" if they are in love, there is also a positive relationship between dependency and insecurity; but it is significantly weaker than it is for those who are not in love ($r =$

.31). And for those "in love?" There is no relationship! (In fact, there is even a slight tendency for those who are highly dependent upon the other to be less insecure: $r = -.10$.) This means that some persons "in love" are highly insecure, but that some are not insecure at all—we cannot predict a person's degree of insecurity from his degree of dependency.

THE SOIL OF JEALOUSY: HIGH DEPENDENCY PLUS HIGH INSECURITY?

What does all this have to do with sexual jealousy? In theory, at least, a great deal. One of the dictionary definitions of jealousy is "vigilance in maintaining or guarding something." It follows that we are unlikely to be vigilant in maintaining something we do not value and do not need. But it does make sense that if we found a person who gives us great delight, who satisfies our needs, who makes up our deficit, who completes us, we should very much tend to be vigilant in maintaining our relationship with him or her. Dependency, then, would seem to be a necessary condition for sexual jealousy.

But dependency may not be the only condition for sexual jealousy. Even if we are highly dependent, we may have little reason to feel jealous. If we believe that the other considers us an important person in his or her life, and if we trust in the other's continuing affection for us, it may not be necessary to exercise vigilance in guarding our relationship. However, when we fear that we may lose the valued other—perhaps because of the intervention of a person, a hobby, or a career goal, for examples—and when the other's affection for us cannot be assumed, then we may feel compelled to be vigilant. Thus insecurity in a relationship, in addition to dependency, would also seem to be a necessary condition for sexual jealousy.

How is love related to sexual jealousy? Most of our "in love" persons were highly dependent on their partner. Dependency, we have reasoned, is virtually by definition a necessary condition for sexual jealousy. Thus romantic love and sexual jealousy would seem to be intimately related through their common link of dependency. It seems not unreasonable to hypothesize, then, that a jealous person may well be deeply "in love."

But is a person "in love" necessarily sexually jealous? Only some—not all—of our "in love" persons were highly insecure about their relationship. Since insecurity may also be a necessary condition for sexual jealousy, it follows that not everyone in love should experience sexual jealousy. We would guess that the prime candidates for the aversive experience of sexual jealousy are those unfortunate lovers who are highly dependent and also highly insecure about their relationship—and thus are highly sensitive to any threat another person or force may pose to it.

SEXUAL JEALOUSY: A SYMPTOM
OF PERSONAL INADEQUACY?

We feel compelled to end our discussion with a comment upon the pejorative light in which sexual jealousy is often viewed. Jealousy is frequently called "the green-eyed monster." Those who experience it are often considered to be "unreasonable" and "suspicious" individuals with "inadequate" personalities.

This condemnation of sexual jealousy is not surprising, for our society deals as harshly with dependency, which sets the stage for jealousy. Dependency upon another is frequently considered to be a sign of weakness and immaturity, particularly for men. We are socialized to suppress and to be ashamed of our need for others. Similarly, we are taught from an early age to cherish our independence and to cultivate the personal traits of self-sufficiency and self-reliance.

The lengths to which parents will go to foster the American ideal of independence in their children is described by former chief medical consultant to Project Head Start, Robert S. Mendelsohn (1975). The father of a three-year old boy told Mendelsohn that, because he had lost his job, his wife would be going to work at the same day-care center that his child was currently attending. Mendelsohn remarked that this would be a good arrangement, for it would be reassuring to the child to have his mother close by. Mendelsohn's response horrified the father. He and his wife did not want their boy to be *reassured*, he protested; they wanted him to be *independent*! In fact, to encourage their three-year old's self-reliance, they had already planned for the child and his mother to take separate buses to the day-care center.

It is ironic that our society, which makes such a severe moral judgment about dependency, also makes love a culturally prescribed requirement for marriage. For if the majority of romantic love theorists are correct—and the available evidence suggests they are—if it is true that heterosexual love grows out of our dependency upon another, then two of the most highly valued experiences in our society—romantic love and independence—are inimicable to one another.

Although we usually think of freedom from outside influence, and of maximum personal control over our lives, as unequivocally desirable, it is possible that men and women who believe (perhaps correctly) that they alone control their fates and fortunes may be depriving themselves of an opportunity for love. Dion & Dion (1973) found that such people were less likely to have ever experienced a romantic attachment than were those men and women who believe that forces beyond their control, including the actions of other people, are an important influence in their lives. This finding, coupled with the strong association between love and dependency, suggests that to be free and independent may mean to be alone—as Kris Kristofferson laments, "Freedom's just another word for nothing left to lose."

If the dependency view of romantic love is correct, we cannot have our cake and eat it too: To love is to need another and to take the continuing gamble that one's need will be answered—but not necessarily without ever experiencing "the mysterious fear."

Romantic love promises to re-create the all-encompassing one-to-one relationship that obtained between the infant and the mother. Once again the world is shut out; once again the demands of others can be ignored. Romantic love as described in song and story suggests that two lovers depend on one another to the exclusion of all others, that they fulfill one another totally, and that, if deprived of one another, they will die—or, at least, be very unhappy forever.

Romantic love legitimizes a "second childhood," a second period of self-centered dependency. If a constructive relationship with one's parents requires that the child transcend the narcissism and possessiveness whch are inevitable accompaniments of the natural dependency of infancy, so also, perhaps, a constructive relationship with a lover or a life partner requires that the adult transcend the narcissism and possessiveness which often accompany the socially-scripted dependency of romantic love.

Perhaps, as Sara Winter (1975:20) suggests, a certain amount of jealousy is inevitable for persons who seek to move away from the possessive romanticism with which we have been programmed. In order to explore this possibility, we need to look more closely at the ways in which jealousy is embedded in the social fabric, and, more specifically, at the understandings of jealousy characteristic of contemporary American society. The last three articles (Seidenberg, Walster & Walster, and Berscheid & Fei) anticipate the major concern of Part III: to discover the ways in which social and cultural patterns shape the experience, the expression, and the interpretation of jealousy.

III

Jealousy and Culture

One thing I can't stand in a guy is jealousy—it's not really love, it's a sickness. I broke up with two boyfriends over it. I could see it if they had a reason, but I've never cheated on anyone.

—Janet Lupo, Playmate of the Month
Playboy, November 1975

Most people tend to think of jealousy as a very private emotion, as an individual matter, as a psychological datum. The articles in Part III show us that jealousy also has powerful *social* implications: It is part of the cement that holds human groups together and, uncontrolled, it can be an explosive which blows them apart. Although the jealous *impulse* is natural and universal, the specific *patterns* through which that impulse is given expression vary considerably from one culture to another and among various subcultures within a given society.

Underlying this variety, however, is an apparently universal awareness of and concern about jealousy. Anthropologists have found no society in which jealousy is completely absent;[1] even in the societies with the least amount of jealousy, some individuals experience the emotion (Stephens, 1963). And where there is jealousy, there must be mechanisms for its control. As Yorburg (1973:191) has observed:

> No society has existed or can exist without norms regulating the continuous (nonseasonal) sex drive of human beings. Sexual conflict, rivalry, and jealousy must be at least minimally controlled in order to ensure the cooperation that becomes increasingly imperative in highly specialized and consequently increasingly interdependent technologically developed societies.

The articles in this section are the work of an anthropologist and four sociologists. Margaret Mead and Kingsley Davis consider jealousy in cross-cultural perspective; their articles can help us discover the constants and the variables in the jealousy equation. Robert Whitehurst focuses on the ways in which jealousy is fostered by the social structure and socialization practices of contemporary American society. Jessie Bernard and Brian Gilmartin suggest that recent and ongoing changes in our understanding and practice of marriage may even now be contributing to new conceptions of jealousy and to new understandings of its role in the formation and maintenance of viable intimate partnerships.

---

[1] Frazer (1910(1968)IV:88f.) notes that "the Eskimo of the Arctic regions and the Todas of Southern India, neither of whom are known to have ever engaged in war . . . appear to be almost free of sexual jealousy which has always been one of the most fruitful causes of dissension and quarrelling, of secret murder and open war among mankind."

We begin with an analysis of jealousy by anthropologist Margaret Mead. Anthropology has been defined—with humorous intent—as the social science which teaches us that anything we have done or imagined doing, no matter how at variance with the standards of our own society, is *normal somewhere*. This article shows that situations which provoke jealousy in one society may not in another—and that the modes of expressing and managing jealousy vary considerably from culture to culture. Here, as in so much of her work, Mead focuses on the malleability of human nature and on the wide range of institutions through which basic (universal) human needs can be met.

Mead, who was about 30 when she wrote this, did not give the article its title. In a brief preface to the original, she protested the title and challenged the assumption that there is such a thing as "civilized" jealousy.

10

Jealousy:
Primitive and Civilised

Margaret Mead

Some thinkers have included under the term jealousy all those defensive attitudes of fear, anger, and humiliation which center about the loss of some object, be that object lands or flocks, spouse or title, position or reputation. Some theorists, like Muller-Lyer, have, erroneously, I think, insisted that primitive man does not know sexual jealousy because he often submits with the best grace in the world to situations which would injure the ego of a present-day German citizen. Ernest Jones, claiming that the key to the meaning of sexual jealousy hangs side by side with all the other keys on the key ring of psychoanalysis, attributes sexual jealousy to a suppressed homosexuality which projects upon the suspected mate impulses of which the suspicious one is really guilty. The romantics have claimed that jealousy is the inevitable shadow cast by the perfect contours of real love. Here are contrasts enough: theories which would make jealousy any

Margaret Mead, Ph. D., (1901-78) is one of the most influential social scientists in the English-speaking world. She is Curator Emeritus of Ethnology of The American Museum of Natural History in New York City and the author of more than twenty books including *Male and Female* and *Sex and Temperament in Three Primitive Socities*. In her monthly column in *Redbook* magazine, Dr. Mead seeks to apply what she has learned in her studies of other societies to the problems of our own. "Jealousy: Primitive and Civilised" is reprinted from *Woman's Coming of Age*, edited by Samuel D. Schmalhausen and V. F. Calverton, with the permission of the publisher. Copyright 1931 by Horace Liveright, Inc. Copyright renewed 1958 by Liveright Publishing Corp.

reaction to threatened self-esteem, set it down as special pathology, or justify it and even endear it to the world by tacking it on like a tail to the kite of romantic love. In this paper I shall adhere to the more catholic and less special view foreshadowed by Shand:

"If it is difficult to define jealousy by its feeling, which sometimes inclines more to fear, sorrow and shame, at others to anger, suspicion and humiliation—we can still define it by its end or function. It is that egoistic side of the system of love which has as its special end the exclusive possession of the loved object, whether this object be a woman, or other person, or power, reputation, or property." I would only amend his definition to expunge the word "exclusive," for many people are jealous of a privilege which they share with others but which they maintain against outsiders.

Perhaps nothing illustrates more vividly the essentially egoistic and selfish nature of sexual jealousy than a comparison of the different cultural conditions under which one man may have first access to another man's wife. There is no evidence for claiming that an intensely proprietary attitude towards one's wife is characteristic of simpler or more complex cultures, for the most uncompromising exclusiveness has been found in all levels of society. Let us then investigate the contrasting attitudes of the French peasantry before the Revolution and the present-day Banaro of the Sepik River region in New Guinea. The French peasant resented fiercely the exercise of the *jus primae noctis* ["right of the first night"] by his seigneur [lord]. The proponent of jealousy as the inalienable ornament of the lover's spirit would say that it was outraged love which resented this intrusion of another male—that any man subjected to such a trial would be filled with the keenest and most righteous jealousy. But is it not equally plausible that it was outraged dignity which tortured the peasant? He was no party to the scheme; his set of ideas did not include any soothing philosophy that he thought his bride was dignified by the lord's embrace. The exercise of the noble's power simply underscored in the most vigorous way possible the peasant's social impotence.

Legal arrangements under which another man has first access to a man's bride do not necessarily give rise to feelings of jealousy. Where the custom is merely that the chief's daughter should be deflowered by another, the eloping young chief will not approach his bride during the elopement, but, if he intends to marry her, bring her still a virgin to his father's house, where he knows she will submit to the cruel public defloration ceremony. He is more concerned with his reputation for having married a virgin than for the intimate ordeal to which he is subjecting the girl.

Among the Banaro it is not only the defloration but a year's enjoyment of his bride, which the young bridegroom must yield to another man. Banaro society is divided into two exogamic moieties. Each of these moieties is subdivided into two divisions, making four divisions in all. In the other division of his own moiety, each man has a ceremonial friend, and it is the duty of this friend to initiate his friend's son's future wife into sex. This is done most formally in the "Goblin House" in front of the hidden sacred pipes upon which no woman may look, and the girl is then returned to her father-in-law's care. The ceremonial friend has access to her, always ritually, until a child is born, which is known as the "goblin child." Only then may the young man take his wife. Meanwhile he himself has been initiated by the wife of his father's ceremonial friend, whom he has been sent to seek out in the forest, carrying a charmed liana [plant] as invitation. Later on, on ceremonial occasions, the young bridegroom and *his* ceremonial friend of the other division will exchange wives, and their wives may even bear children to their husbands' friends, instead of to their husbands. So, in a lifetime, every individual has three goblin spouses in addition to a regular spouse.

This social situation is simply packed with occasions which among us would give rise to jealousy: an old man's jealousy because his wife takes a young lover, an older woman's jealousy of her husband's interest in a fresh young girl, a young man's thwarted desire for his young wife—for he has to accept the embraces of a woman of his mother's age while another enjoys his pledged bride's virginity. Yet we have peculiar testimony of the peaceful and satisfactory way in which this apparent set for jealousy really operates. All over New Guinea and the adjoining islands, wherever the white man has gone, recruiting offers an escape to those who are permanently or temporarily at odds with their society. Working for the white man provides a refuge, unknown in the old days, to the disinherited son, the betrayed husband, the discredited magician, the deposed leader. The eagerness with which men come forward to meet the recruiter's tempting offers is a measure of the peace and content within their respective cultures. And among the Banaro the recruiter has little luck; every one is too contentedly involved in the fantastic intricacies of Banaro social life.

Or let us consider another familiar situation which may give rise to the most intense jealousy or to which jealousy may be entirely irrelevant. If a guest seduces his host's wife among us, or indeed in any society where the crowd are ready to cry "cuckold," the husband betrays the most furious resentment and jealousy. But let us go instead to a society where wife lending is the rule, as among the Eskimo, a society which cries, not "cuckold" but "stingy," "inhospitable," "mean," to a husband who does not give his wife to his guest. Here the husband will upbraid the wife who is slow to respond to his guest, rather than resent the guest's demands. The most casual survey of primitive literature betrays the numerous ways in which exclusive sexual possession of the spouse is modified and contravened, and demonstrates how the self-interest of husband and wife is identified, not with the exclusive possession of each other, but with the appropriate carrying out, whether it be through wife lending, wife exchange, ceremonial license, or religious ceremony, of these very contraventions.

A conspicuous example of this is the attitude of women towards secondary wives in a culture where polygamy is the rule for the rich and influential. There is a case on record of a woman who actually haled her husband into court on the charge that she had been married to him three years and borne him two children, and he had not yet taken another wife. The native court allowed the husband six months in which to take unto himself without fail a second wife. Women urge their husbands to take other wives, which will add to their own prestige by conferring upon them the rank of first wife and also for the practical point of *providing labourers* and child bearers in the household. The self-esteem of the *chief wife* is enhanced by their entrance into the ménage and there is no occasion for jealousy—*unless* one of them tends to become the favorite and flexible custom permits usurpation of the first wife's dignities. In a society where there is emphasis upon virginity, a father will be jealous of his daughter's honour. In dissimiliar case is the Maori father who has offered his daughter to an honoured guest, only to have her churlishly refuse the guest her favours. The guest is then entitled by custom to fasten a log by a long vine, and naming the log after the ungracious girl, to drag it about his host's village, heaping the most definite and vigourous abuse upon this dummy. Such a father, although his daughter's virginity may be preserved, will bow his head in shame.

However varied the social setting, it will be seen to be the threatened self-esteem, the threatened ego which reacts jealously. Situations involving this self-esteem will, however, take widely different forms. One's reputation may be concerned with acquisition of wealth, display of wealth, distribution of wealth, or merely with having exchanged much wealth for value received. A man's personal reputation may be based upon the number of women he has purchased or the number of women he has captured, or, as among the Manus, upon the number of temptations which he has resisted—or again in certain parts of Micronesia, he may boast of the honourable scars which he has received from the shark tooth knives of belligerent and unwilling women. A woman's reputation may be tied up with absolute chastity, or with the type of pre-marital prodigality of favours which was so much admired among the ancient Natchez Indians that they pictured a spirit world entered by means of a bridge which was treacherously slippery beneath the feet of the over-virtuous maiden. There is hardly any limit of performance or apparent deprivation to which the individual may not be pushed by his society's standards. Whatever the social set, however, it will inspire him to zeal for his socially defined position. And if he feels his self-esteem is threatened, if his reputation as a gracious wife lender or as a successful ruler of a harem is in danger, jealousy will be the result.

The line between zeal and jealousy is a fine one; a line which the apologists for jealousy usually neglect to draw. An attentive interest in the attainment or the preservation of social or personal status is zeal, a positive attitude; a frightened, angry defense of such status, is jealousy, a negative attitude, always unpleasant in feeling tone. This can be seen clearly in a polygamous society. A zealous man anxious to enhance his own prestige will buy many wives. But the South African king, who, impotent himself, tries to draw a fast line of police about his two hundred wives, instead of winking at their amours as was the custom of over-married monarchs, is no longer merely zealous in carrying out the dictates of social usage, he is simply jealous.

The same distinction can be observed between the behavior of the zealous suitor and the jealous one. He who is zealous studies his mistress's face to learn her pleasure, seeks out special gifts to please her, tries to arouse her interest and fulfil her slightest wish; all of his behavior is positive, constructive, directed towards a goal. But the jealous suitor looks into her face only to read there his own dismissal or signs of his rival's triumph; he is far too busy worrying about his fate to be an acceptable tennis partner or dinner companion. Turned in upon himself, his whole duty is not to please the lady but to pity himself and to blame her or his rival for the humiliation which he is suffering. Although his goal is avowedly the same as his rival's, his whole behavior serves to prevent his attaining it.

Compare also the behavior of the woman, secure in herself, but anxious to please her lover, with the behavior of her who fears to lose husband or lover. Aldous Huxley has drawn a vivid picture of the tears and tantrums of poor Margery, every one of which served to precipitate her impatient lover into the arms of her rival. The jealous man or woman seldom comes bearing flowers, and if one does so, it is with such a look in the eye as warns the recipient that conquest of the rival and rehabilitation of the injured self-esteem was the prime motive when the bouquet was selected.

So often, conduct which is zeal in one age or in one society, because it is motivated by an eager and lively appreciation of the social pattern or the customary values in personal relationships, is motivated in another society by feelings of insecurity which lead to fear, doubt, and suspicion. The mediaeval crusader who cared so little for his chatelaine that he neglected to lock the metal girdle about her loins, would have been lacking in zea. and his wife might have felt just grounds for resentment, but the fifteenth century husband who kept up this practice would have been branded as a jealous monster.

The confusion between the two attitudes is increased by the inclusion in the romantic love pattern of certain conventional manifestations of jealousy. A failure to display a suitable amount of flattering anxiety, to greet a broken engagement with alarm, or a smile to another with glowering hostilities, if a man, with tearful pouts, if a woman, is written down as lack of zeal. But a closer scrutiny will always reveal the point at which the lover no longer acts to reassure his beloved but to reassure himself, from fear of loss or hurt to his self-esteem. Hence the ridiculous comment which is so often heard, "She likes him to be jealous of her." No one, not in some way pathological, likes to see another in an acute state of misery and humiliation. What such a commentator really means is: "She likes him to act in a way to, which others are only impelled by self-love because she knows he is moved to it by love of her." The husband who dances close attendance from jealousy, the wife who goes meticulously over the events of an absence, from jealousy, is not appreciated.

In similar confusion was a woman who remarked to me recently: "Most men expect you to be jealous, and if you're wise you will be." What she meant was simply that most men were flattered by an amount of flutter which simulated jealousy.

If, then, jealousy be not a matter of a normal man defending his natural rights, but of a frightened man defending himself against the infringement of rights not natural but merely guaranteed to him by his society, we can admit frankly that it is an unfortunate phenomenon with nothing to be said in its favour. Jealousy is not a barometer by which depth of love can be read, it merely records the degree of the lover's insecurity. And jealousy is notably an attitude which arouses no sympathy in others. If its display is really so strongly associated with true love, why should the world, having taken the lover to its bosom, evict the jealous lover? Is it not because jealousy, like all other forms of extreme egoism, is repellent, is necessarily of a sort with which others cannot identify themselves? Moreover jealousy defeats its own ends. It is a negative, miserable state of feeling, having its origin in a sense of insecurity and inferiority.

In turning to a consideration of the causes of jealousy, as an occasional or chronic state of mind of large numbers of the human race, it is necessary to consider two types of causation, one social, one personal. Any society which places groups of individuals at a disadvantage because of racial, religious, or class distinctions, will be laying the groundwork for many jealous citizens. Furthermore, any society which arranges social or family life so as to provide inevitable clashes of interest of the sort which cannot be avoided will be opening the way to jealousy. Examples of this type of clash are those which arise from primogeniture [the right of the eldest son to inherit the entire estate], emphasis on the blood kin at the expense of the marriage tie, or such social rules as that which decrees that the eldest daughter must marry first. In this sense jealousy is directly dependent upon social causes; and in proof of it, some primitive peoples are far more jealous that others. Although every homogeneous culture inures those born within its confining walls to an unquestioning acceptance of its most difficult dictates, still some cultures force situations which produce less pleasant emotions than others.

An example of a culture in which jealousy is a conspicuous characteristic of the normal individual, is the Dobuan culture of the D'Entrecastreaux Islands, east of New Guinea. Here the stage is set for jealousy and its expression in continual broils and dissension. The people are sorcery ridden and each maternal kin group of some half dozen families live to themselves in little villages where all others—even those married into the group—are regarded as strangers, and probably witches and sorcerers. There is complete pre-marital freedom, a freedom the exercise of which the old people insist upon by turning all the boys over twelve or thirteen out of the family huts at night. The boy is then forced to wander about among the various villages of his locality—for the girls of his own village are his "sisters"—until he finds some girl who will reply affirmatively to his plantive jews-harp which he sounds hopefully from house to house. Several years' amourous vagabondage assures a youth's having slept with practically every girl in the locality except those of his own village.

Into this habit of amourous and undiscriminating vagabondage, betrothal intrudes rudely, and not always by mutual consent. It is a fast rule that the boys must be up and away to their own villages by dawn. If a boy oversleeps and the mother of his partner of a night's intrigue, who sleeps in the same hut, considers him a suitable husband for her daughter, she can rise before him and sit in the house door. The villagers, early astir, knowing the significance of a woman's being so seated in her doorway, cluster about to gape rudely at the unfortunate youth who must finally emerge. He is now engaged. He and his fiancée must rigorously avoid each other during the day and meet only clandestinely, as before, at night. But meanwhile the engagement sets up a round of economic exchanges for which the boy and his relatives must work hard. He is away for days, fishing and hunting. And no longer may he even speak to the girls who last week were his carefree partners in love. The most strict fidelity is enjoined upon the engaged couple, as upon the married couple, in Dobu. And each partner is tortured by the suspicion that the other is returning to the so recently abandoned amorous adventures.

After marriage a new impetus is given to jealousy. In keeping with the general spirit of jealousy, the young couple are not permitted to settle down either in his village or in hers but are required by custom to live alternate seasons in each of the two villages. Here the one who does not belong to the village is treated as a stranger, must walk humbly, avoiding the names of all the "owners of the village." Meanwhile the vigilance of each spouse has been unflagging. A Dobuan husband follows his wife about everywhere, sits idly by while she does woman's work in the garden, counts her footsteps if she leaves the verandah for the bush. She is never allowed to go to another village alone. Such jealous surveillance, coupled with the strain of a marriage where one spouse is always resident among alien and suspicious kin, combined with the pre-marital habits of licence, all combine to produce rather than to prevent infidelity. And here, the man or woman, depending upon which one is resident in their own village, turns to village incest for intrigue—a type of intrigue not tasted before marriage. But where there is such close espionage, inter-village intrigues are hard to manage. Furthermore, a man who has been discovered as the seducer of another man's wife, is liable to have a spear thrust in his back. But against his wife's intrigue with one of her village "brothers" a man has no such redress. If he protests, his wife's relatives simply throw him out of the village. Should he slay a member of his wife's village, it would become a "place of blood" to him and he might never enter it again. In desperate case indeed is the man whose wife has betrayed him with a village "brother" and in such case also is the wife of the latter who also is only an in-law and a stranger in the village. In such cases the betrayed spouse has only one resource, a sort of pseudo-suicide in which fish poison, which may or may not be fatal, is taken. The kin of the unfaithful spouse, alarmed lest death will follow which will involve them in a blood feud, may then exercise pressure and reunite the pair. But marriages maintained by attempted suicides against odds such as these, do not make for security and happiness, but rather for suspicion and jealousy.

It is worth noting that this jealous attitude which the Dobuan displays, bred from intolerable social arrangements, also characterises his attitudes towards property and trade. He stays up half the night uttering incantations to protect his own yams and to seduce the yams of his neighbour's gardens into his own. If he attains a sudden supply of tobacco as a workboy returning from work for the white man, he will distribute it all, fearful of the jealousy and envy of others should he keep any for himself. He spends his life pitting his magic against the inimical magic of his neighbours, in a state of morbid anxiety and insecurity. Into this house divided against itself, the recruiter steps, perhaps acquiring in one trip a divorced husband who is leaving in furious chagrin and the brother of the former wife who wants to escape the extra work of helping with his divorced sister's garden.

Samoa is keyed to a very different note. Here instead of the tiny hostile kin groups of Dobu, are large villages the members of which are united in formal ceremonial and allegiance to a chief. Instead of the limited and unfruitful garden lands of Dobu, where no amount of spells and hard work will produce a really fine crop, there is fertile land, and enough for all. Although there is freedom before marriage, marriage itself is not viewed primarily as sexual, but as social contract between individuals who are old enough to turn their attention to more serious matters. Residence is within that household where the young couple fit most perfectly, in terms of temperament or carefully laid plans. Rank is so arranged that there are titles for all of those capable of holding them. And jealousy, as a widespread social phenomenon, is very rare in Samoa. Where it does occur it centres about those points in the system of rank which result in clashes of interest. So, occasionally, a Samoan wife is violently jealous of another woman who wishes to marry her husband, because as a divorced woman her rank is reduced and she has to sit among the young girls and the wives of untitled men. In Samoa divorce is far less frequent than in Dobu, where intolerable circumstances breed jealousy, which breeds infidelity and divorce.

When my husband was leaving the Dobuans, the attitude they displayed was characteristic. All other emotions on the part of the men who had been his sailing and living companions for months were obscured by their jealous rage that he should actually choose to leave them. Sullenness, wounded self-esteem, was written on every face. But in Manus, of the Admiralties, where we had both lived for months, the people gathered in the thatched pile house which we were deserting and stood there silent, nuddled together, possessing no customary phrase for so drastic a leave taking. As our canoe was poled, solemnly, by the elders of the village, outside the last row of houses, the people we had left behind beat out upon the great slit drum first the call which we had used to call our house boys and, second, the death beat. The dignified gesture was not marred by any injured self-esteem. And this perhaps is one of the chief reasons why sophisticated people should wish to ban jealousy from their lives, because it tends to blur the important issues, to obscure the fundamentals of personal relations, to muffle hurt in sullenness, and to deck separations in rags of bitterness and abuse.

Aside from the social causes of jealousy, the sets which decree that whole people, or a whole class will be ridden by a morbid doubt of keeping their winnings or winning their chosen prizes, there are the special reasons which predispose a given individual to react jealously to one situation after another. Some of these are purely culturally determined also. On the east coast of Africa, where marriageable girls are kept for months in the "Fatting House" and given a daily massage with butter to improve their physical attractiveness, the girl who refuses to put any weight upon her bones is at a social disadvantage which may well give her a haunting fear of failure and desertion. Among the Bush Negroes of Dutch Guiana the man who does not know how to carve, who has unfortunately no gift for handiwork will be scorned by the maidens who are in a position to scorn, and be accepted grudgingly by the others. Whatever the mode of beauty or bravery, there will be some individuals who deviate strongly from the desirable type. And these, with rare exceptions, jealousy has marked down for her own.

Consider the historic cases of jealous obsession, and one finds the two causes for insecurity, cultural discrimination against groups and narrow cultural standards of beauty and achievement, as the motivating elements. Othello is perhaps the best example in literature of insecurity born of belonging to a racial group judged inferior by the group from whom he won his wife. Keats is as outstanding an example of the other type of jealousy, as he remarks in the revealing phrase in a letter in which he discusses the local maidens: "But much they care for Mr. John Keats, five feet and a quarter." I do not claim that matter of race or social status on the one hand, of physique or natural aptitudes on the other, are the only causes of the insecurity which has its expression in morbid jealousy, but they are perhaps the strongest contributory causes to its chronic existence. It does not dignify Othello's jealous emotion to have to read it in terms of racial inferiority rather than the fair letters of true love, and the admirers of Keats could suffer more wholeheartedly with him under Fanny's cruelty were it not for the suspicion that he would have suffered with equal violence over others, because his jealousy was not relevant to Fanny but to himself and his self-doubts.

The only type of jealousy which can be regarded as strictly relevant to the personality of the lover and which cannot, in final analysis, be reduced to any sort of cultural causes, is the result of bad luck. The individual who has loved unhappily once, then twice, or perhaps oftener, develops a haunting fear of loss which is a comment neither upon an accident of birth nor upon his use of his own endowment, but rather upon forces which are completely out of human control. This same observation applies also to the artist, the scientist, or the business man, who, starting without any fundamental attitude of insecurity, is beaten into it by ill fortune. With pathetic violence, the unlucky cling to any good fortune which must of necessity appear to them as one lonely and unreliable spar salvaged from shipwreck. It is to be presumed that there will always be those who through a grain of unfortunate circumstances become chronically unsure and pitifully anxious to hold that which they have. In deprecating jealousy, one must include them, for jealousy adds to rather than mitigates their misery, but the revision of social or personal attitudes which give rise to jealousy can do nothing for these unfortunates for whose sake it is necessary to indict, not culture, but the nature of the universe.

It is also revealing to re-examine the terms upon which women have been indicted as "the jealous sex." Throughout history, with a few rare exceptions, women have been the *insecure* sex. Their status, their freedom of action, their very economic existence, their right over their own chldren, has been dependent upon their preservation of their personal relations with men. Into the field of personal relations have been thrust all these other considerations not germaine to it. The wife threatened with the loss of her husband's affection, fidelity, interest, or loyalty, whichever point her society has defined as the pivot of wifely tenure, sees the very roots of her social existence being cut from beneath her. She has been in the position in which a man would be if he had to read in his wife's averted shoulder the depreciation of all his stocks, a loss of his business reputation, eviction from whatever position he holds, both social and political, as well as the loss of his home and possibly of all control over his children. If women's superior morbid anxiety concerning their relations with the all-necessary male purveyors of economic and social goods be read in these terms, it becomes a truism that women probably always have been "the jealous sex." It is also possible that the inescapable fact that women age earlier than men, and are more handicapped by child bearing and child care, will always render them relatively more insecure than men, and therefore relatively more anxious to keep their lovers and husbands. But the disassociation of social, economic, and legal security from the field of personal relations should go a long way towards giving women a security which is as great as that which their culture permits to the men born within it. . . .

Margaret Mead and other anthropologists show us that jealousy is different in different societies. A situation that provokes strong jealousy in one society may not provoke jealousy in another. Variations in jealousy reflect variations in marriage rules, the adultery taboo, and norms regarding the protection of relationships that are threatened.

Cross-cultural research also reveals something that Mead overlooks: the universality of the institution of marriage and the adultery taboo. In every society, a distinction is made between those who are married and those who are not. In every society, a distinction is made between children born to married women and those born to unmarried women. In every society, sex is permitted within marriage and prohibited, for married people, outside of marriage. Even societies that are very permissive regarding premarital sex are much more restrictive regarding extramarital sex.

Despite variations in some particulars, all societies prohibit (but do not eradicate) adultery. Despite the prevalence of a double-standard that punishes women's infidelities more harshly than men's, all societies prohibit (but do not eradicate) adultery for men as well as women. Although some societies permit polygamy or concubinage and some are more tolerant of affairs than others, every society seeks to minimize sex outside of marriage.

Jealousy is universal because the institution of marriage and the threat of adultery are universal. Jealousy protects marriage (and other valued relationships) from adultery (and other threats). Jealousy cannot disappear from human society unless humans stop forming marriages (and other valued relationships) or stop caring about sexual and emotional exclusivity in marriages (and other valued relationships). Even swingers and practitioners of open marriage seek to preserve their primary relationships against emotional betrayal with other sexual partners (see Gilmartin, Chapter 14). Jealousy would be useless only for the small minority who are sexually very permissive and unable or unwilling to form a primary relationship.

Margaret Mead overlooked the universality of marriage and the adultery taboo, thereby overlooking the social usefulness of jealousy. In several confusing paragraphs that the editors have deleted from this edition, Mead denounces jealousy as "undesirable, a festering spot in every personality so afflicted, an ineffective negativistic attitude which is more likely to lose than to gain any goal." She would like to eliminate it. She suggests that we could exclude jealousy from our lives if we would be more like the Samoans, "eliminating strong emotion, high stakes, emphasis on personality, interest in competition" — but she concludes that this would be too high a price to pay for serenity. Then, confusing jealousy and envy, she suggests that perhaps the experiments then (1931) under way in the Soviet Union will reduce "jealousy" or that living in a cosmopolitan city like Paris or New York might reduce "jealousy." While continuing to use the term "jealousy," Mead has shifted the discussion to envy. Such confusion is typical of those who overlook the social usefulness of jealousy and thus view it only in negative terms.

Margaret Mead's article displays the wide spectrum of ways in which jealousy is expressed and managed in other cultures. The next selection invites us to look more carefully at the ways in which jealousy actually *works* in human societies. Here again the perspective is cross-cultural, not parochial. Kingsley Davis's account of the social structuring of jealousy is pertinent to many different kinds of societies. As we follow his general analysis, we may begin to "fill in" particulars from our own experience.

Davis argues that jealousy has a function not only with reference to the individual's emotional balance but also with reference to social organization. The ways in which jealousy is experienced and expressed reflect the norms and institutional structure of the larger society *and* the statuses and roles of the individuals involved. Jealousy, then, is not *only* a personal matter; it is also *inter*personal and *social*. In order to understand jealousy, we must understand the social structure within which it is experienced and expressed.

11

Jealousy and Sexual Property

Kingsley Davis

Descartes defined jealousy as "a kind of fear related to a desire to preserve a possession." If he had in mind what is customarily called jealous behavior, he was eminently correct. In every case it is apparently a fear or rage reaction to a threatened appropriation of one's own or what is desired as one's own property. Sexual property differs from economic property in many respects but nevertheless bears some resemblance to it. Among other things, sexual property is institutionally defined and regulated. Let us begin, then, by viewing jealousy in relation to sexual property.

Conflicts over property involve four elements: Owner, Object, Public, and Rival or Trespasser. A popular fallacy has been to conceive the jealousy situation as a "triangle." Actually it is a quadrangle because the public, or community, is always an interested element in the situation. The

Kingsley Davis, Ph.D., (1908-97) is Ford Professor of Sociology and Comparative Studies and Chairman of International Population and Urban Research at the University of California, Berkeley. "Jealousy and Sexual Property" was first published in 1936 in the journal *Social Forces*, 14:395-405. A revision of the article was included in Davis's influential introductory textbook *Human Society* in order to demonstrate the utility of the sociological perspective for the understanding of seemingly private matters. Abridged by the editors, this selection is reprinted with permission of the author and Macmillan Publishing Co., Inc. from *Human Society* by Kingsley Davis. Copyright 1948 by Macmillan Publishing Co., Inc., renewed 1976 by Kingsley Davis.

failure to include the public or community element has led to a failure to grasp the social character of jealousy. The relationships between the four elements are culturally regulated. They are current in the given society and constitute the fixed traditional constellation of rights, obligations, and neutralities that may be called sexual property. They are sustained and expressed by the reciprocal attitudes of the interacting parties. . . .

RIVALRY, TRESPASS, AND SOCIAL CLASS

While the love-property situation contains a relationship of intimacy, it also contains a diametrically opposite kind of relation—namely, that of power. The power relationship which obtains between the lover and his rival or trespasser is not a value in itself but a means to an ulterior end; and it connotes an absolute opposition of purpose in the sense that if one succeeds the other fails. The rival or trespasser may be a stranger or a close friend; in either event, so far as the common object is concerned he is an enemy.

Here as elsewhere in the discussion it makes a difference whether the enemy is a trespasser or a rival. Rivalry is most acute in the early stages of acquisition, and jealousy is at this point a fear of not winning the desired object. Toward one's rival one is supposed to show good sport and courtesy, which is to say that society requires the suppression in this context of jealous animosity. Regulated competition constitutes the *sine qua non* of property distribution and hence of stable social organization. But as one person gets ahead and demonstrates a superior claim, his rivals, hiding their feelings of jealous disappointment, must drop away. If any rival persists after the victor has fortified his claim with the proper institutional ritual, he is no longer a rival but a trespasser.

Jealousy toward the trespasser is encouraged rather than suppressed, for it tends to preserve the fundamental institutions of property. Uncles in our society are never jealous of the affection of nephews for their father. But uncles in matrilineal societies frequently are, because there a close tie is socially prescribed between uncle and nephew. The nephew's respect is the property of the uncle; if it is given to the father (as sometimes happens because of the close association between father and son) the uncle is jealous (Malinowski 1932:100-111). Our malignant emotions, fear, anger, hate, and jealousy, greet any illicit attempt to gain property that we hold. We do not manifest them when a legitimate attempt is made, partly because we do not then have the subjective feeling of "being wronged" and partly because their expression would receive the disapproval of the community. The social function of jealousy against a trespasser is there-fore the removal of any obstacle to the smooth running of the institutional machinery.

Discussions of jealousy usually overlook the difference between rivalry and trespass. Rivalry implies a certain degree of equality at the start. Each society designates which of its members are eligible to compete for certain properties. While there are some properties for which members of different classes may compete, there are others for which they may not compete. In such cases the thought of competition is inconceivable, the emotions reserved for a rival fail to appear, and the act is regarded not as rivalry but as a detestable thrust at the class structure. Thus, at one time, it was inconceivable that a Negro could be the rival of a Southern white man for the hand of a white girl. The white man would have him lynched. Southern society did not permit Negroes as a class to compete for the affection of white girls.

But jealousy against a trespasser is another matter. Since a trespasser by definition is a breaker of customary rules, the more he breaks, including the rules of class structure, the more of a trespasser he is. A violator of property rights may for this reason occupy any position on the social scale.

The fact that men of native races sometimes prostitute their wives to civilized men without any feeling of jealousy while they are extremely jealous of men of their own race (Malinowski 1929:271), is sometimes pointed out as showing that men are jealous only of their equals. This is true only in so far as jealousy of rivals is meant. The civilized man is not conceived by the natives as a rival, nor as a trespasser. He *may* be con-ceived as a trespasser—if, for example, he attempts to retain the wife with-out paying anything. In the case mentioned he is not a trespasser but merely one who has legitimately paid for the temporary use of property. His very payment recognizes the property rights of the husband.

One may argue that the nearer two people are in every plane, the more intense will be the *jealousy of rivalry*; while the further apart they are, the greater the *jealousy of trespass*. . . .

THE SOCIAL FUNCTION OF JEALOUSY

Into every affair of love and into every battle for power steps society. The community has an inherent interest in love not only because future generations depend upon it but also because social cohesion rests upon the peaceful distribution of major values. Doubtless the physiological mechanism operating in the jealously aroused person is inherited. But the striking thing about this mechanism is that it is not specific for jealousy, but appears to be exactly the same in other violent emotions such as fear and rage. The sympathetic nervous system seemingly plays the usual role: increased adrenal activity speeding the heart, increasing the sugar content of the blood, toning up the striated muscles and inactivating the smooth muscles.

If we are to differentiate jealousy from the other strong emotions we must speak not in terms of inherited physiology but in terms of the type of situation which provokes it. The conflict situation always contains a particular content, which varies from one culture to the next. The usual mistake in conceiving jealousy is to erect a concrete situation found elsewhere (often in the culture of the author) into the universal and inherent stimulus to that emotion. This ignores the fact that each culture distributes the sexual property of the society and defines the conflict situations in its own way, and that therefore the concrete content cannot be regarded as an inherited stimulus to an inherited response.

This mistake is made, I think, by those theorists who seek to explain certain human institutions on the basis of instinctive emotions. In the field of sexual institutions Westermarck is the outstanding theorist who has relied upon this type of explanation. He disproves the hypothesis of primeval promiscuity and proves the primacy of pair marriage largely on the basis of allegedly innate jealousy (1922,I:Chap. 9). He assumes, indeed, that all types of sexual relationship other than monogamy (as he knows it in his own culture) are native stimuli to instinctive jealous retaliation.

As soon, however, as we admit that other forms of sexual property exist and that they do not arouse but instead are protected by jealousy, the explanation of monogamy breaks down. Whether as the obverse side of the desire to obtain sexual property by legitimate competition or as the anger at having rightful property trespassed upon, jealousy would seem to bolster the institutions where it is found. If these institutions are of an opposite character to monogamy, it bolsters them nonetheless. Whereas Westermarck would say that adultery arouses jealousy and that therefore jealousy causes monogamy, one could maintain that our institution of monogamy causes adultery to be resented and therefore creates jealousy.

Had he confined himself to disproving promiscuity instead of going on to prove monogamy, Westermarck would have remained on surer ground. Promiscuity implies the absence of any sexual property-pattern. Yet sexual affection is, unlike divine grace, a distributive value. To let it go undistributed would introduce anarchy into the group and destroy the social system. Promiscuity can take place only in so far as society has broken down and reached a state of anomie.

The stimulus to jealousy, moreover, is not so much a physical situation as a meaningful one. The same physical act will in one place denote ownership, in another place robbery. Westermarck appears to believe that it is the physical act of sexual intercourse between another man and one's wife that instinctively arouses jealousy. But there are cultures where such intercourse merely emphasizes the husband's status as owner, just as lending an automobile presumes and emphasizes one's ownership of it.

We may cite, for example, the whole range of institutions whereby in some manner the wife is given over to a man other than her husband. These run from those highly ritualized single acts in which a priest or relative deflowers the wife (the so-called *jus prima noctis*) to the repeated and more promiscuous acts of sexual hospitality and the more permanent and thoroughgoing agreements of wife-exchange; not to mention the fixed division of sexual function represented by polyandric marriage. In societies where any institution in this range prevails, the behavior implied does not arouse the feeling of jealousy that similar behavior would arouse in our culture. Jealousy does not respond inherently to any particular physical situation; it responds to all those situations, no matter how diverse, which signify a violation of accustomed sexual rights. . . .

CONCLUSION

It should now be clear that a genuine understanding of jealousy requires that it be studied and analyzed from a comparative sociological point of view. A theory of jealousy which derives its empirical facts solely from the manifestations of jealousy in our own culture can hardly be a satisfactory theory, no matter how plausible it may seem to people who live in our culture. When a comparative point of view is adopted it is seen that the situations calling forth a jealous response vary tremendously from one culture to another. Jealousy is an emotion which has a function as a part of an institutional structure. Not only is it normatively controlled but it gives strength to the social norms as well. To understand the *social function of jealousy*, to see the significance of its variable but inevitable appearance in different societies, one must have some conception of the cultural definition of social situations in terms of the statuses and roles of the participants; some notion of means, ends, and conditions; and some idea of processes of interaction such as rivalry, competition, and trespass. It is not contended here that the sociological approach to jealousy is the only one that is needed. Jealousy must also be studied from the point of view of the personality as a unit. But it is contended that for a full understanding of jealousy the sociological approach is indispensable because it addresses itself to a real and important aspect of jealous behavior—the social aspect.

Kingsley Davis suggests that the individual's experience of jealousy depends upon the nature of the institution of marriage, which in turn depends upon the social and economic needs of a given society. We are warned not to assume that our understanding of marriage and our experiences of jealousy are universal. As Lévi-Strauss (1969:37) has written:

Social and biological observation combine to suggest that, in man, these [polygamous] tendencies are natural and universal, and that only limitations born of the environment and culture are responsible for their suppression. Consequently, ... monogamy is not a positive institution, but merely incorporates the limit of polygamy in societies where, for highly varied reasons, economic and sexual competition reaches an acute form.

The analyses of jealousy offered by Mead and Davis lead us to ask: What conditions in society contribute to the rise and development of jealous feelings and behaviors? Like Davis, Albert Ellis concludes that one important condition is the idea of possessiveness, or property rights: "Wherever women are conceived as property, and where men have the patriarchal right to command their sexual favors, jealousy tends to exist." In his influential book, *The American Sexual Tragedy* (1954; second edition, 1962), Ellis argues that sexual jealousy is implicit in the romantic monogamic ideology by which most people in our society try to live.

After surveying the anthropological literature, the content of the popular media in the 1950s and the 1960s, and the self-revelations of his psychotherapy clients, Ellis (1962:152) concluded:

> Sexual jealousy is not a completely innate emotion, since it varies among different peoples of the earth, and is far less prevalent in some cultures than in others. It is largely rooted in human cravings for socio-economic and sexual monopoly and possessiveness, and in the insecurities, anxieties, and feelings of inadequacy that are engendered when the fulfillment of these cravings is threatened. But desires for sexual monopoly, even though they may possibly have an innate or unlearned element, are closely related to attitudes developed through social learning. Such attitudes appear to be particularly pronounced in cultures which favor romantic and monogamic philosophies of sex, love, and marriage, and to be less pronounced in cultures which favor less romantic and less monogamic philosophies.
>
> In the last analysis, then, although monogamy and romanticism may not justifiably be said to create sexual jealousy out of whole cloth, they do appear to inflame and intensify it.

In the selection that follows, Robert N. Whitehurst explores the ways in which North American social structure and sex-role socialization foster jealousy. This article, written more than 20 years after the first edition of Ellis's *American Sexual Tragedy*, supports and extends some of Ellis's conclusions and also treats some of the implications of the "sexual revolution," the women's liberation movement, and other developments of the intervening years.

12

Jealousy and American Values

Robert N. Whitehurst

Jealousy is often considered to be a natural accompaniment of loving another person. It is usually seen as inborn and common to all people, or as so deeply entrenched in human affairs that there is nothing anyone can do about it. Recently, however, writers in the area of alternative life-styles have raised some questions about jealousy that cast doubt on its inevitability.

Although many writers have argued that jealousy is largely a function of feelings of personal inadequacy, I see jealousy as largely a function of social structure and sex-role socialization. In the discussion that follows, I will show that cultural and normative considerations can help us understand how jealousy is fostered in North American society.

SEX, LOVE AND MARRIAGE

Let us look first at those values and norms which are directly pertinent to our understanding of sex, love, and marriage. The ways in which we are

Robert N. Whitehurst, Ph. D., (1923-   ) is Professor of Sociology at the University of Windsor in Canada and co-editor (with Roger W. Libby) of *Marriage and Alternatives*. He is currently (1976-77) on leave in Denmark, where he is studying the effects of sex roles and changing sexuality on separation and divorce. "Jealousy and American Values" was written especially for this volume.

prepared for adult life make it virtually inevitable that we will become dependent upon each other in adulthood. Socialization of males encourages them to lean heavily on a woman's supportive services. Men are raised to be relatively helpless in taking care of themselves, their clothes, their household, and their dietary needs. In a myriad of other ways, they are taught to call upon women for help. Women, on the other hand, learn that it is not good to compete with men in the marketplace of jobs, and that one cannot be a complete woman without a man. They learn to support his ego, cater to his needs, and defer to his judgment in important decisions.

This "division of labor" fosters, in both men and women, a basic sense of inadequacy, a fear of facing the world alone. Few men are jealous of the position of their wives, even though on occasion they may voice envy at the easy life women presumably have at home. In a number of ways, however, wives reflect the uneasiness of their positions vis-à-vis husbands. This uneasiness often surfaces in the form of jealousy. Only true sex-role equality and education for a higher degree of independence can in the long run eradicate many of the marital problems which nurture jealousy.

The importance of comprehending American society as a *paired* (and family oriented) society cannot be overestimated. The single person is a "deviant" and therefore suspect. Strong pairing norms make for a heightened sense of ownership (*my* wife, etc.) and exclusivity. They encourage vigilance and overprotectiveness. As those around us divorce and remarry, we fear that we, too, may be deserted. All this adds much to our potential for experiencing jealousy.

The relative *isolation* of people in marriages may tend to create a shortage of affect and a feeling that others may have something they feel is missing in their lives. This sense of having to meet many of one's most serious problems alone and unsupported, of being out of touch with others, may lend itself to feelings of neglect and alienation that can easily be relabeled and redirected against one's spouse.

In our culture, jealousy is seen as a measure of love. If one does not become jealous, at least on occasion, the quality of one's love becomes suspect. "If you loved me, you'd be jealous. You must not care what I do." Our understanding of "true love" demands expressions of jealousy, expressions which, paradoxically, far from enhancing relationships, sometimes help them disintegrate.

Traditionally, extramarital involvements have been viewed as more legitimate for men than for women. This is but one reflection of the greater freedom of self-expression which men have enjoyed. This *double standard* creates latent jealousies in wives and deepens the inevitable trivial jealousies which arise in any relationship. Until recently, few wives challenged this imbalance. Even today, many women tacitly grant their husbands prerogatives they deny themselves and thus unwittingly intensify their own experiences of jealousy.

OWNERSHIP, COMPETITION, AND PERFECTION

Many of the general, taken-for-granted values and norms of American society affect individual interpretations of sex, love, and the family, and so are pertinent to an understanding of jealousy. Our concepts of *ownership and private property* tend to make us very protective of people as well as things. The spouse may come to be seen as a possession. This norm may lead to feelings of insecurity since, obviously, control of a person has to be more tenuous than control of other possessions. A sense of paranoia is rarely manifested in an extreme form, but mild feelings of jealousy are obviously rooted in this aspect of American culture.

Related to the property concept is the emphasis on *novelty* and the search for "kicks." The pressures conveyed through the popular media to have, do, experience, and buy "the latest" affect our interpersonal lives as well as our economic pursuits. Needs for the new and the familiar, adventure and stability, are at odds with each other. In achieving a workable balance in a relationship, there is much potential for jealousy.

The American way is essentially characterized by *competition*. We compete for scarce jobs, for money, for prestige, *and* for the affection and the support of people. The norm of individualistic competition tends to support a narrow and uncertain style of monogamous relating in which it is often difficult to maintain a sense of easy assurance with one's partners. Our relationships often depend upon implied competition with an unknown number of others "out there" who may be able to replace us as better lovers, breadwinners, or spouses. Competition as an ethic in this society does not lend itself to the acceptance of people for what they intrinsically *are*. It is rather what they can *produce* in the way of goods and services that may be in demand. Thus, jealousy and competition tend to reinforce and support each other.

Our strong needs for acceptance and the desire to have a *perfect* relationship with someone tend to make us susceptible to jealousy. This may grow out of inordinate fears of rejection: No one wants to have an "average" relationship. Americans have a passion for passion. The fact is that this is either not readily attainable in the average relationship, or it occurs so infrequently that it does not fulfill our appetites. No relationship can realistically remain at the high peaks we would seem to demand, but we still cherish the expectation. This expectation makes relationships always a bit edgy and uncertain. This instability may easily result in jealous feelings in the event of failure to meet this heavy expectation.

All of these aspects of contemporary American social existence tend to aggravate the feeling and expression of jealousy. Furthermore, a highly mobile and affluent society provides many opportunities for meeting others and for developing significant relationships outside of marriage. Working with and liking others enhances the probability of other sorts of involvements with them. As more and more women enter the work force, more and more affectional and sexual possibilities are built into the work situation.

Meanwhile, traditional forms of social control are becoming weaker. Church and community no longer define acceptable standards of behavior with the force of moral authority they once enjoyed. We are freed from many of the traditional restraints on our behavior and relationships. With this freedom comes a sense of uncertainty and a greater burden of personal choice and responsibility. There is much more to comprehend on one's own and much less that is patterned, institutionalized, and predictable.

The societal values and norms discussed in this article work against our integrating the feelings of jealousy which are likely to arise. This, in turn, leads to the existence of a "secret society" of subterranean sexuality, not quite acceptable but so common and statistically normal as to be visible in many quarters of "respectable" society. This secrecy further undermines trust and exacerbates jealousy.

Through this analysis of norms, values, and social context I have sought to show that jealousy is a *social* phenomenon and not merely a private one. Attempts to reduce the incidence of jealousy and to minimize its painful consequences must take account of these cultural considerations. If jealousy is so deeply rooted in our social existence, we should not be surprised if it proves difficult to eradicate.

For a useful general discussion of the relationship between sex-related values and social structure see Philip E. Slater, "Sexual Adequacy in America," in Kenneth C. W. Kammeyer, ed., *Confronting the Issues: Sex Roles, Marriage, and the Family*. See also Slater's *The Pursuit of Lo 'iness*, Chapters 3 and 4.

If one assumes that jealousy is "natural," one might argue that monogamous marriage was invented to control it. But Kingsley Davis reversed this argument and suggested instead that marriage, as we know it, causes adultery to be resented and so *creates* jealousy—and uses it as a support for the institution of marriage. Whether one accepts Davis's inversion or not will depend largely upon the layperson's own prejudices on the matter and upon the scholar's prior choice of a discipline or methodological perspective—the two being functional equivalents. But at the very least, Davis's argument invites us to consider in more detail—and with contemporary data—the very complex dialectical relationship between our conception of marriage *and* our experience and understanding of jealousy. Although we cannot measure their mutual effects with hydraulic precision, it seems safe to conclude that *the way we view marriage and the way we feel jealousy*—both social constructions rather than "natural" phenomena—*affect one another*. Changes in one produce changes in the other. *And* each is capable of influencing the other; neither is inert or constant.

The principle of such a two-way relationship between views of marriage and understandings of jealousy is further elaborated in the next selection. Jessie Bernard suggests that because of recent and ongoing changes in the patterning of marriage in the United States, the incidence of marital jealousy is declining.

13

Jealousy and Marriage

Jessie Bernard

The present volume offers the first serious systematic scrutiny of jealousy as related to marriage since Kingsley Davis's classic statement forty years ago (this book, Chapter 11). One searches in vain through both the systematic and research literature on marriage since that time for serious discussion of the subject. For one reason or another, students of the subject of marriage seem not to be concerned with it. Nor does jealousy as a serious theme seem to interest novelists or dramatists today. Equally interesting is a related change in terminology: The non-pejorative term "extramarital relations" has pre-empted use of the term "adultery." Marriage has apparently changed so markedly with respect to sexual exclusivity that jealousy is no longer viewed as a necessary prop to enforce it, and hence it becomes of relatively little interest. Community support for the norm of sexual exclusivity which jealousy formerly buttressed has itself suffered serious attrition.

Jessie Bernard, Ph. D., (1903-96) Research Scholar Honoris Causa, Department of Sociology, Pennsylvania State University. She is the author of *The Future of Marriage, The Future of Motherhood*, and several other books on sex roles, marriage, and the family. She currently resides in Washington, D.C. This article was written especially for this volume.

TWO PARADIGMS

Two paradigms—one basically psychological, the other sociological—have been offered to explain the relationship between jealousy and marriage. One begins with an instinctive emotion, jealousy, which makes marriage, especially although not exclusively monogamy, inevitable; the other begins with marriage or the institutionalized right to sexual exclusivity and sees jealousy as the result of a violation of that right. The two models are not actually as different as they seem. Both view jealousy as performing the basic function of protecting marriage. But their implications differ. If one accepts the instinctive view, then the limits within which change in marriage can take place are seriously circumscribed; if one accepts the derivative view, marriage has a longer tether.

THE INSTINCTIVE PARADIGM

Charles Darwin, on the basis of what he saw about him in Victorian England, believed that male jealousy was the basis of marriage: ". . . looking far enough back in the stream of time, and *judging from the social habits of man as he now exists*, the most probable view is that he originally lived in small communities, each with a single wife, or, if powerful, with several, whom he jealously guarded against all other men" (1888,II:394, emphasis added). Edward Westermarck concurred. He also believed that jealousy prevented promiscuity and thus buttressed and supported marriage (1922,I:334). William Stekel held that the inability to share, which characterized jealousy, was a "tragic characteristic of all people" (1938:328). He agreed with Freud that those who deny they are jealous are only afraid to admit it. Kinsey and his associates also subscribed to an instinctive theory of jealousy: "While cultural traditions may account for some of the human male's behavior, his jealousies so closely parallel those of the lower species that one is forced to conclude that his mammalian heritage may be partly responsible for his attitudes" (1953:411).

Westermarck was at great pains to survey the research on preliterate societies of his day to show the universal existence of jealousy. He had to find it everywhere in order to validate his thesis, which denied primitive promiscuity. He managed to explain away whatever cases he found where it was reported as absent. Even where jealousy was said to be illegal and punishable by death, Westermarck quoted his source as being positive that most of the quarrels he observed resulted from jealousy (1922,III:304). The Iroquois might boast that they had no jealousy, "but those who are most acquainted with them, affirm that they are jealous to excess" (306). If one observer reported that Canadian Indians were "cold and incapable of jealousy," Westermarck was sure that "this hardly agrees with his statement that the married women 'had as good be dead as be guilty of adultery' " (306). He admitted that jealousy might be feebler among Eskimos than elsewhere, "but it is not absent" (307). And so on. He felt he had to have jealousy in order to explain the universality of matrimonial institutions.

If one accepts the view that institutions are the expression of "human nature," this view makes sense—and any hope to change marriage runs against the stone wall of human jealousy. This was, in fact, Stekel's position. Although he himself saw a decline in normal jealousy, he still held that "every attempt to renew the forms of marriage and to pour new wines into the old bottles will come up against an unconquerable resistance on the part of the jealous" (1938:33).

One may hold to the belief that jealousy is instinctive rather than an institutional product, or at least that it has an instinctive component, yet polygamous societies do manage to control it, as do many of the persons in our own society who experiment with postmonogamous life-styles (Smith and Smith 1974:81, 95, 207). Bertrand Russell believed jealousy to be instinctive, yet he noted that it "can be controlled if it is recognized as bad and not supposed to be the expression of a just moral indignation" (1929: 143). That is precisely the point. It can only be recognized as bad when it is no longer performing an important function—as, apparently, it is not today.

THE DERIVATIVE PARADIGM

If one holds to the view that "human nature" reflects institutions or culture, then an interpretation precisely the opposite to the instinctive can be made. Contrary to Westermarck's thesis that matrimonial institutions rested on the bedrock of male jealousy, Kingsley Davis has suggested that actually the reverse is true: Jealousy is derivative, the product of monogamy, not its cause. Jealousy is generated by monogamy, not monogamy by jealousy. He argues that if human beings are reared in a monogamous society, they are socialized to expect to have the exclusive right to the attention and sexual favors of their spouses. If a partner or a trespasser deprives them of this privilege by engaging in adultery, they feel they have been wronged and that they are justified in their jealousy. "Our institution of monogamy causes adultery to be resented and therefore creates jealousy" (1949:189). If monogamy had not conferred the exclusive right to the sexual favors of the spouse, there would be no occasion for jealousy.

Briffault emphasizes the importance of community support. The claim to the exclusive attention of a spouse depends "upon the established usages of the social environment; a man claims as a right what the law, current custom, and opinion entitle him to claim" (1927,II:121). Like Davis and Briffault, Borel also sees jealousy as a social creation, as "an impression of age-old, primitive, collective, social mores and beliefs" (1952:29).

The human species has had its present biological equipment for at least several millennia and conceivably longer, but during that period of time it has had a strikingly variegated institutional history. Human beings now have, as they have always had, the biological equipment for experiencing a wide variety of emotions—love, hate, anger, grief, joy, and jealousy, among others. Yet some of these emotions have been more prevalent at one time and place, others at different times and places. Although emotional experience *seems* to be independent of the surrounding society and *feels* peculiarly private, subjective, intimate, and personal, nevertheless, the channeling and differential emphasis on emotions by the surrounding culture specifies when and how they should be experienced. This gives them an objective reality. It is, for example, a cliché that cultures prescribe when to laugh and when to cry. Some call for tears at a funeral, some for dance. Joy and gaiety are discouraged in some times and places; in others, they are encouraged. The orchestration of the emotions of a people can ordinarily be seen as part of a total institutional system. For example, the blue-nose solemnity usually attributed to New England puritanism is sometimes tied up with the Protestant Ethic, an ethic that created the thrifty population needed to accumulate capital for industrialization. Emotions become, in effect, institutionalized. We *learn* when to express them and when not to—and also how to do so.

In literature, for example, the classic style prescribed that emotions be relatively superficial: wit and artifice were valued; rules were important. In the Romantic Age which followed, passion and emotion were exalted; the individual became more important than the rules. The more vehement the emotion the better. The emotions taken for granted in moving pictures of the past are different from those taken for granted in the 1970s. In brief, *emotions are themselves cultural phenomena with histories of their own.*

The biological basis for the experience of jealousy is, then, very old. But its history is quite checkered. Jealousy has been insisted upon in some times and places, and accepted but not required in other times and places. It seems now to be in a process of attrition.

We do not have to make a choice between the two paradigms—jealousy as the cause of monogamy versus monogamy as a cause of jealousy—to recognize that there has been a close relationship between them. Whatever form marriage takes in any society—whether monogamous or polygamous—all the other institutions of that society will operate to create a "human nature" that responds to its requirements. The surprising lack of interest in the subject of jealousy in recent years may presage a form of marriage partially, if not completely, emancipated from jealousy.

JEALOUSY AS DETERRENT

In both the instinctive and the derivative paradigms, jealousy serves not only to punish violation of a right after it has occurred but also—and preferably—to deter it. Punishment after the fact cannot undo the damage—the humiliation, the suspect paternity—but it may make deterrence more credible. If men are forgiven even for killing to defend their honor, as, for example, in Sicily, this can serve as a powerful deterrent to jealousy-provoking behavior. Westermarck rested his case to a large extent on both the punitive and the deterring function performed by jealousy.

This inhibitory influence can succeed only if jealousy is accepted by the community as a legitimate response. If or when the community accepts extramarital relations, thus denying the husband's right to exclusivity, then the husband has no "right" to be jealous. The community, far from supporting him, may criticize him for making a nuisance of himself. The jealous husband can appeal to the community for support only when it accepts his right and validates his claim that he has been injured.

Jealousy as a deterrent to extramarital relations implies more than merely subjective experience. As the Constantines have concluded from their research, jealousy is not "an emotion but rather . . . behavior, an expression of a great variety of intrapsychic experiences" (in Smith and Smith 1974:281). If the response to a violated right—anger, grief, resentment, rage, withdrawal, what-have-you—has no interactional outcome, if one is not permitted to *express* it, it performs no deterrent function. Although it may be of psychiatric or psychological concern, it can scarcely have sociological implications.

If jealous behavior is anticipated, the tempted wife will restrain her impulses; the seducing male will inhibit his advances to the attractive wife. To the extent that jealous behavior is anticipated, it deters violation of the husband's right and thus supports exclusivity in marriage. It performs a policing function; it enforces community norms.

The increase in extramarital relations today seems to document the fact that in our day and age, anticipated jealous behavior retains little deterrent effect. As our society moves away from the old monogamous pattern, the nature and incidence of jealousy itself have changed and may be expected to continue to change. Today, we seem to be in about the same position attitudinally with respect to *extra*marital relationships as we were 50 years ago with respect to *pre*marital relationships.

FEMALE JEALOUSY

Most of the literature on the subject of jealousy and all of the discussion here so far have dealt with male jealousy. Westermarck did make a bow in the direction of female jealousy in connection with polygyny [the marriage of one male with more than one female]. But overall he spent thirty-seven pages on male jealousy and only seven on female jealousy. He believed that male jealousy prevented promiscuity but he did not explain why female jealousy was not able to prevent polygyny.

Since the right to expect sexual exclusivity was not, apparently, a right conferred on women, there was no functional need for female jealousy to enforce it. There were fewer rationalizations for demanding that men restrict their sexual relations to one partner. There might even be justification for demanding just the opposite. The custom of plural wives increased the baby supply of the community as well as the labor supply of the individual household. Polygyny made provision for the protection of surplus women when there were any, and of widows—as in the case of the levirate. Whatever the reason, female jealousy has been a quite different phenomenon from male jealousy.

There is no reason to believe that women cannot experience the same emotions as those men experience when they have to share the attentions of their spouses. Although among preliterate peoples women might welcome the entrance of new wives into the household to share the work and increase its wealth, there is evidence that even when polygyny is highly institutionalized and prescribes that there be no favoritism among the wives, there may still be jealousy among them. Schapera (1939:279) tells us that among some African tribes the term "jealousy" *means* polygamy.

In our society, where women have been so dependent on husbands for economic security, the stimulus for jealousy is probably less likely to be sexual deprivation than fear and anxiety. One study of swinging found that husbands reported jealous concern about their wives' popularity but that "when wives reported jealousy it was more likely related to fear of losing their mate" (Denfeld in Smith and Smith 1974:264). Like the man, the woman may be subject to humiliation, but she is also subjected to the threat of loss of the husband's support if the other woman wins him away from her. Equality and independence on the part of women will go a long way toward removing this aspect of female jealousy.

There are other than sexual forms of jealousy that may be equally devastating to women. The work and careers of men, for example, have been serious competitors for the time and attention of men. The time a man spends on his career may deprive a wife of as much time as if it were spent with another woman—and his attention may be even more difficult to win back. As one wife put it, "If he were seeing another woman I'd have a better chance. But what chance do I have against his work?" Freud reminded us some time back that women paid for civilization. The time men spent on their trips to the moon, on their new electronic marvels, and on all their other technological toys was time that could have been spent with women.

Of course, it is not only women who suffer these nonsexual kinds of jealousy. A husband may feel jealous of the time a new baby demands of the mother, time of which he is deprived. He may be jealous of his wife's ties with her mother. Today some husbands show jealousy of the time and attention career wives devote to their work. Men have felt that they had not only a right to exclusive access to the sexual favors of their wives but also a right to their total time and attention.

We have already begun to challenge the life-style that demands so much of most men, and to question the almost obsessive achievement drive to which many are subject. And, conversely, we are more and more accepting the idea that women may invest time and attention in their own careers. We are already poking malicious fun at the man who will permit his wife to take a job provided she promises to have dinner on the table when he comes home. Even these kinds of jealousy seem to be on the way out.

JEALOUSY IN THE LIFE CYCLE

Age as well as gender makes a difference in attitudes toward exclusivity. There is some evidence that tolerance for extramarital relations grows with age. Three scraps of evidence seem to warrant this conclusion. One comes from the Kinsey data: "In time," Kinsey and his associates noted, love, jealousy, and morality "seemed less important, and the middle-aged and older females had become more inclined to accept extramarital coitus and at least some of the husbands no longer objected if their wives engaged in such activities" (1953:417). In some cases spouses actually came to welcome extramarital relations. A second clue comes from the clinical practice of a psychiatrist, Milton R. Sapirstein. Among his older patients, extramarital relations on the part of a spouse were often accepted as the lesser of two evils (1948:174). Tolerance of such relations was preferable to the trauma of divorce. Such acceptance of extramarital relations may be the only alternative for women socialized to complete dependence, left wholly unprepared for an autonomous life. The most recent and in many ways most persuasive bit of evidence for changes over the individual life cycle is the work of the Constantines on multilateral relations: "Jealousy was . . . a function of age: all respondents under age thirty-one listed jealousy as a problem, but only nine of fifteen over thirty-one years old did. This was highly significant . . . and suggested that in this context non-jealousy and maturity may be related, a suggestion later supported by interviews and prolonged interaction with groups" (in Smith and Smith 1974:281). It is interesting to note that although there is some evidence that the incidence of extramarital relations among younger couples is increasing (Bernard 1970:16-17), there seems to be no noticeable increase in jealousy.

THE FUTURE OF JEALOUSY:
A VANISHING RIGHT?

Almost forty years ago, William Stekel concluded that "normal jealousy is on the decline" (1938:127). I am inclined to accept this opinion, although there are no direct and conclusive data to support it. There are no studies dealing directly with the subject, no measures available, and no base-line against which to compare trends. All the supports for this point of view are, of necessity, therefore, inferential. The evidence that seems most persuasive to me lies in the changing attitudes toward sexual exclusivity now becoming prevalent. If the belief in exclusivity is declining, jealousy has less justification. Grief, pain, and humiliation may be experienced at the loss of exclusive love and favors; but if the community does not sanction one's feelings, they can hardly express themselves as jealousy.

The legal right to sexual exclusivity is conferred by the community through marriage. If, as the Davis paradigm specifies, jealousy is the result of a frustrated expectation of exclusivity, then it is legitimate only if one had the community-conferred right in the first place. When or if such a right can no longer be taken for granted, if it is not supported by the community, then jealousy itself is no longer viewed as legitimate. At the present time there seems to be a trend in the direction of denying the right to sexual exclusivity in marriage. Jealousy resulting from a violation of that right seems to have lost much community support.

We know that adultery is less and less frequently used as a ground for divorce, despite the fact that we know from the Kinsey data that adultery occurs in about half of all marriages. As counterpoint to this reluctance to use adultery as a ground for divorce, there is also, perhaps, a reluctance to claim that adultery is so devastating to the "innocent" party. The attitude toward adultery characteristic of many contemporary marriages is increasingly permissive.

The change in terminology referred to above—"extramarital relations instead of "adultery"—is part of the desacralization process. The very fact that a researcher undertakes to study the problem scientifically undercuts the power of the taboo. The researcher proclaims his objective, non-moralistic stance by calling the object of his study "extramarital relations" rather than use the pejorative legal term, "adultery." The end result tends toward an implicit defense of extramarital relations.

Elsewhere (1969) I summarized several other "straws in the wind" that seem to indicate changing attitudes, values, and behavior with respect to sexual exclusivity in marriage. One is the greater tolerance of extramarital relations shown by some theologians and ethicists. Another index of changing attitudes is to be found in recent divorce legislation: The whole concept of "fault" has been dropped in several states. Thus, adultery is no longer considered a ground for divorce. Another clue is the increasing emphasis on the positive aspects of extramarital relationships. Kinsey and his associates (1953:432-435) were among the first to mention these; contemporary advocates of sexual alternatives in marriage make many of the same points (see Smith and Smith, 1974, passim).

Jealousy seems helpless to guarantee exclusivity in marriage as, according to the Westermarck and Davis paradigms, it should. Since its usefulness and efficacy rested on its institutionalized nature, it has, with changing community attitudes, lost its functionality. The sexual rights which marriage once conferred on spouses—the violation of which justified jealousy—no longer have sacred sanction or total community support. Sexual exclusivity no longer looms as large as it once did.

Whereas the attrition of normal jealousy with changing attitudes toward extramarital relations seems likely, the same cannot be said for pathological jealousy. Pathological jealousy has little relationship to consensual reality and can scarcely be said to perform *any* social function. It might, indeed, serve in dysfunctional ways, as when a person sees a threat to or violation of his right to sexual exclusivity in any gesture or smile from another. In short, jealousy may decline as a sociological concern, but it is likely to remain as a psychiatric concern.

This article invites us to consider the possibility that the amount of jealousy which is functional for a marriage may decrease over time—as the relationship grows stronger and deeper. One writer (Secades 1957) has suggested that jealousy is "delightful during courtship, practically essential to the first year of marriage, but after that, Chinese torture." Be that as it may, the assumption that a decrease in jealousy means the erosion of love—rather than the growth of trust—might often serve to manufacture insecurity and intensify jealous feelings, to the detriment of all concerned.

Jessie Bernard suggests that we are in a transitional period during which attitudes toward extramarital sex are being liberalized, with a resulting decline in the importance of jealousy. Clearly, such liberalization is not the case for all or even most married persons. There is, however, a growing literature that describes married persons who do not demand sexual exclusivity of their mates, persons who engage in extramarital sex with the knowledge and consent of their spouses. Careful study of such marriages might reveal the conditions under which sexual jealousy is eliminated or, at least, rendered nonproblematic. Such study might also detect the persistence of subtle forms of jealousy even among those who have sought to eradicate it from their relationship.

Of persons engaged in various forms of consensual adultery, those most accessible for research purposes are the "swingers"— married persons who, with the knowledge and often in the presence of the spouse, engage in extramarital sex for recreational purposes. Most regular swingers claim to have jealousy under control—at least as long as both partners stick to the "ground rules" the couple has (explicitly or implicitly) adopted. A rather common ground rule prohibits emotional involvement with an extramarital partner.

But swinging, no matter how well managed, does require that participants confront rather directly the extramarital sexual activities of the mate, a confrontation which for most married persons would produce some sort of jealous response. Swingers, then, are of interest in the study of jealousy *both* because they have a lot of experiences most other people would find jealousy-provoking *and* because they claim to be relatively successful in managing destructive jealousy.

14

Jealousy Among The Swingers

Brian G. Gilmartin

To most Americans it is inconceivable that a person could allow his/her partner to engage in casual sexual intercourse in their own home with a stranger or acquaintance. To swingers—husbands and wives who together engage in sexual mate exchange—this is considered an acceptable form of social recreation. Why do some people experience strong feelings of jealousy over extramarital sex, while other people seldom if ever experience such feelings? From 1969 to 1972 I conducted a study of 100 suburban California couples who practice swinging. This study included a group of 100 "control" couples who were of the same age and socioeconomic status as the swingers and lived in the same neighborhoods.

THE MEANINGS OF ADULTERY

From studying these couples it would appear that one's *belief structure*—the internalized system of norms and ideas which create

Brian G. Gilmartin, Ph. D., (1940-   ) is Visiting Assistant Professor of Family Development at Virginia Polytechnic Institute and State University, Blacksburg, Virginia. His research on swingers has appeared in *Psychology Today* (February 1975) and in *Beyond Monogamy*, edited by James R. Smith and Lynn G. Smith. He is currently working on a monograph on comarital sexual behavior and conducting research on shy heterosexual males who do not date at all. "Jealousy Among the Swingers" was written especially for this volume.

meaning for an individual—plays a large role in one's susceptibility to feelings of jealousy. An overwhelming majority of the swingers agreed that it was possible to engage in a great deal of extramarital sexual intercourse without being at all unfaithful or untrue to their marriage partner. Very few of the nonswingers believed this was possible.

Three times as many nonswingers agreed that when adultery occurs it is usually symptomatic of the fact that the marriage is not going well. With this association in their minds, with this interpretation of the *meaning* of adultery, it is not surprising that most middle-class suburbanites view the mere thought of their spouse engaging in any kind of adultery with a strong sense of threat to their ego, security, masculinity or femininity, and self-esteem.

Suppose, I asked my respondents, your spouse admitted to occasionally experiencing sexual intercourse "on the side," and indicated to you that it was purely by reason of a need for sexual variety, that s/he loved you no less than before, and that s/he definitely planned to continue occasionally enjoying such extramarital sex. Assume that the marriage had been happy and satisfying to you up to this point. (A) Would you consider a divorce? (B) Would you consider a separation? The swingers were far less likely than the nonswingers to feel that such adultery would be sufficient to prompt them into considering a divorce or a separation.

Swingers seem to have what in American society is an unusual ability to dissociate both intellectually and emotionally the concept of *person-centered sex* from the concept of *body-centered sex*. To most swingers, body-centered sex is defined and viewed as a form of social recreation and convivial play. They dissociate the idea of sex from the idea of romantic/conjugal love. And they come to regard both of these forms as constituting valuable and highly rewarding human experiences. Sexual intercourse for the swinger in the context of the party situation is viewed as being purely body-centered, and hence, as not posing a threat to the integrity and security of the marital relationship.

To the swinger, sexual play at mate-sharing gatherings is very much the same in its overall significance as a game of bridge might be for a non-swinging couple. At bridge parties it is quite common for the participants to select someone else's spouse as a partner; this state of affairs is seldom perceived as threatening by those involved. For mate-sharing swingers, taking someone else's spouse as a sexual partner has much the same lack of emotional significance.

Swingers attempt to avoid jealousy feelings by structuring the *context* of extramarital sex to minimize the threat to their primary relationship. They pursue sex as a shared leisure activity with others. They express concern that the couples they "swing" with have a reasonably happy marriage which they want to maintain. Most swinging groups will not permit single men to participate, nor do they allow married men to attend parties without their wives. (Yet, strangely enough, many swinging groups welcome single women. This is a common inconsistency.)

Almost all swinging groups have strong norms prohibiting their members from falling in love with one another. Some groups permit the expression of tender feelings, but normally expressions such as "I love you" are strongly disapproved and feared (within the context of swinging festivities). The idea, of course, is to protect and defend the marital unions of everyone involved, yet still enable everyone to enjoy playful, recreational sex.

To be sure, most swingers value the emotion of friendship with the couples with whom they share their recreational pursuit. The expression of warm friendship and sincere human concern within the context of sexual mate exchange is not ruled out. But there is a very marked difference between the warmth of friendship and the emotional desire for sexual and social exclusivity that comes with the initial stages of the romantic falling-in-love experience.

Some swinging groups also make a conceptual distinction between "committed love" and "noncommitted love." Such groups tend to be comprised primarily of the younger, better educated, more iconoclastic couples. These people do not see deep, long-lasting friendships with their swinging partners as competitive with the *committed* type of love characteristic of a sound marriage. Friends who see each other very often are regarded by such people as "loving" one another, but in a noncommitted way. They do not live together, pay each other's expenses, or have children by each other. The psychological exclusivity that comes with committed love is still reserved for the spouse. Many such younger spouse-sharing cliques have been heavily influenced by the ideas of Robert H. Rimmer, author of *The Harrad Experiment, Proposition 31,* and *Adventures in Loving.*

INTERNALIZING SWINGER NORMS

Adopting new beliefs about the meaning of adultery is, however, only the first step in the process of reducing jealous feelings so as to allow multiple extramarital relations. These new beliefs must be internalized on an emotional level. Normally it requires much longer for a set of nonconformist norms to become internalized on this deeper emotional level than for them to become internalized on an intellectual level. When strong feelings of jealousy *do* emerge among swingers, it is not, typically, because the norms against falling in love were violated. Most often, the problem is this: One or more of the participants had accepted the swinging norms on an imperfect, intellectual level and not on a deep, emotional level.

Not everyone at a swinging gathering is likely to be a long-time swinger. Sometimes upon hearing about sexual mate-exchange a man will become extremely excited and will enthusiastically bring the matter to the attention of his wife. Such a man will quite often perceive himself as being very much in need of sexual variety, and he will fantasize about all of the real or imagined rewards he might derive from becoming a swinger. The problem of course, is that such a man will very often direct so much of his psychological energy toward reforming his wife that he completely forgets about himself and the real implications of what he thinks he wants to do. He does not confront the fact that he is going to see his wife undressed and engaging in sexual activity with other men. If, as often happens, she enjoys the experience, his expectations are upended and he loses his balance. Jealousy attacks him in his guts with the force of a strong blow.

Experienced swingers also report occasional feelings of jealousy. These feelings are usually milder than those of the novices—and less likely to issue in rage. The veteran swingers usually keep their feelings to themselves until they get home. There, very often, the expression of jealousy becomes a sexual "turn-on"—even though they are physically tired after having spent several hours in an orgiastic social setting.

Seeing or visualizing the mate with another person often serves to activate a swinger's sexual interest in his/her own mate. Indeed, this pattern occurs so regularly among swinging couples that it may be viewed as an integral part of the swinging ideology which becomes actualized in behavior. When so many of their swinging friends talk enthusiastically about how they arrive home from a party even more erotically charged toward their spouse than when they left, the expectation of similar feelings in themselves arises even in those who are relatively new to swinging. Sociologists have long argued that even very intimate feelings tend in large measure to be a predictable by-product of the normative ideology of the most meaningful reference groups of which a person is a member.

SEXUAL AND MARITAL HAPPINESS

Swinging couples do indeed tend to engage in more sexual intercourse *with their own spouses* than nonswingers of roughly the same age. I asked each of my 400 respondents to provide me with an estimate of the number of times they are likely to copulate *with their own spouse* in the course of a typical week. (Husbands and wives were asked this question separately and the discrepancies were very small.) Of the swingers, 23 percent were found to average six or more copulations per week with their own spouse, compared to only 2 percent of the nonswingers. Similarly, 32 percent of the swingers compared to only 14 percent of the control group averaged four or five copulations in the course of a typical week. At the other extreme, only 11 percent of the swinging couples reported only one (or less than one) copulation weekly, compared to 48 percent (almost half) of the control couples.

If the emotion of jealousy—and the related feeling of having one's primary relationship placed in jeopardy—constituted a frequent problem among the swingers, we would expect to find that swingers would rate the overall happiness of their marriages as low by comparison with ratings of couples who do not practice any form of adultery. This did not turn out to be the case.

Among the nonswinging, suburban couples studied, in 34 percent of the cases one or the other partner had at one time been involved in conventional, deceptive adultery. (In 5 percent of these marraiges *both* the husband and the wife had had some previous experience with adulterous sexual intercourse.) Those who had not, those who had remained "sexually faithful," were far more likely than those who *had* experienced adultery to view their marriages as happy and satisfying. Curiously, the swinging couples, who had engaged in far *more* extramarital sex, were even *more* likely to perceive their marriages as being "very happy" than the nonadulterous control couples. The adulterous controls showed the *lowest* ratings for marital happiness. It would thus seem that if any strong jealousy feelings did result from the swingers' sexual behavior, such feelings did not afflict their marriages with any overpowering problems.

It has already been shown that swingers copulate with their lawful spouses far more ofteñ than do nonswingers of the same age and socioeconomic status. But how about just plain old spontaneous displays of love and affection? Once again the swingers turned out to be more satisfied with the amount of affection the spouse spontaneously displays around the house. They also were slightly more satisfied with the amount of time they spent with the spouse and the amount of interest which was shown in them by the spouse. The swinging couples also gave significantly larger estimates of the amount of time they spend together engaged in informal conversation.

Hence, it would appear that the swinging couples whom I studied were in most cases deriving the warmth and emotional nurture they needed out of their conjugal, husband-wife relationship. Jealousy feelings are likely to emerge only when a spouse's exclusive franchise upon the "person-centered" *emotional* sex-love relationship is perceived as being threatened. In short, a copious quantity of "body-centered" sex with other people does not appear to be sufficient in and of itself to arouse jealousy feelings.

The happily married couple is viewed as the safest practitioner of sexual mate exchange. Such a couple is the least likely to want (consciously or unconsciously) to violate major norms such as "falling in love" with someone else's spouse. The happily married person's only desire in the context of sexual mate exchange is to experience for himself and to share with his or her spouse the rich and wide range of erotic feelings. Such a person values rich sexual variety as a good and valuable thing in its own right.

IMPLICATIONS FOR NONSWINGERS

Swingers are quite conventional in some ways. Their ideology exalts "togetherness," the sharing of activities between husband and wife— *including* the sharing of extramarital sex. The swingers accept love, romance, the family, marriage, residential and psychological monogamy (as opposed to strict *sexual* monogamy). But intellectually and emotionally they separate romantic sex from recreational sex. Jealousy, they believe, is relevant only to romantic sex. Recreational sex is viewed as nonthreatening. The one is seen as having nothing to do with the other except as a possible means of increasing erotic competence and of heightening sexual interest. Swingers believe that jealousy is largely a *learned* emotion and they have set out to *un*learn it. What are the implications of their efforts for persons *not* interested in swinging?

The study of swingers shows us the importance of re-examining and redefining the *meaning* we assign to extramarital relations. Extramarital sex does not necessarily mean that "something is wrong at home." If we continue to assume that it does, we are more likely to feel threatened and jealous.

This study also shows that even when we have suspended or changed our beliefs, we may still find ourselves reacting with gut-level jealousy. It takes time and experience to learn, and to integrate on an emotional level, the fact that the sky will *not* necessarily fall on our heads if we (or our partner) have sex with another, that our relationship will *not* be ripped asunder, and that we will continue to love each other no less than before.

The experiences of the swingers demonstrate the importance of a secure relationship with one's primary partner if outside relationships are to be explored with a minimum of jealousy. Emotional (as well as sexual) involvements with others may or may not need to be ruled out, depending on one's value system and the strength and commitment of one's primary relationship. Ground rules which serve to limit the threat of multiple relations may take many forms.

This research also shows the importance of social support and the power of social disapproval. As long as jealousy is justified by our cultural norms, as long as the "wronged party" is seen as a "cuckold," as long as individuals are excused for "crimes of passion," we may expect jealousy to pervade our interpersonal relations.

Even among swingers, jealousy still occurs, although it is usually kept to manageable proportions. If we hope to completely eliminate it from our lives, we are probably being unrealistic. If we hope to reduce its power and minimize the role it plays in our social relations, the swingers show us that this is, in fact, possible.

IV

Managing Jealousy

Jealousy is a sign that something is wrong, not necessarily rotten, in the organism of love.

—Theodor Reik
Psychology of Sex Relations, p. 173

Having explored the psychology and sociology of jealousy, we are now prepared to directly address the question: What can be *done* about jealousy? The very notion of *doing something* about jealousy—rather than simply letting it have its way with us—is a new idea. It is part of what we earlier called the *active orientation* toward our most important relationships, an attitude grounded in the belief that we can *understand* those relationships and consciously change them for the better.

Because we have only just *begun* to approach jealousy in this way, our formulations of ways of working with the emotion will necessarily be tentative, incomplete, and perhaps even flawed. The contributors to Part IV are among the pioneers in the understanding and management of jealousy, and yet neither they nor the editors of this book are prepared to offer any surefire plan. The reader seeking "the conquest of jealousy in five easy steps" will be disappointed. If this material is to be useful to you, you must sift through it carefully, seeking those insights and techniques most pertinent to your situation. *You* must weave them together into a way of working with jealousy that fits your needs, your values, your expectations. No one else can do this for you. It requires work and it requires *risk*.

Jealous feelings become a problem when they interfere with successful functioning in a chosen life-style or relationship (Constantine, this book, p. 191). When this happens, you have several options (adapted from Winter 1975:22):

1. You can get out of the relationship.
2. You can ignore and/or tolerate the behaviors which are making you jealous, perhaps hoping to maintain a measure of control through complaints, sarcasm, and/or veiled threats.
3. You can try to get your partner to stop (or otherwise modify) the behaviors which make you jealous.
4. You can work on your own jealousy.

Obviously, the last three strategies can be employed in combination. The decision to focus on your own jealousy often comes when strategies 2 and 3 have been tried without success.

Many people decide to work on their jealousy when they realize two things: (1) They *will*, in fact, continue to feel jealous from time to time (regardless of the nature of the particular partnership, no matter how considerate the partners); (2) conventional strategies for dealing with jealousy are very unattractive and inadequate. Consider the *normal* reactions to jealousy, the behaviors which are statistically commonplace and socially tolerated: repression (which is self-deception), denial (which is lying), fright, flight, fight, retaliation, manipulation, rationalization, and paranoia, from mild to rather wild.

Generally speaking, you ought not attempt to work on your jealousy unless the following conditions (Winter 1975:22) are met:

1. The relationship touched by jealousy is good for you in many ways; it is *worth* some effort.
2. You are not simultaneously trying to handle other major life crises.
3. You can count on support and nurture from your partner.
4. You can count on getting some help from other people besides your partner (friends, a therapist, etc.).

You must begin your endeavor with realistic expectations. Otherwise, whatever growth you experience will disappoint you. You must realize from the beginning that jealousy probably cannot be completely eliminated. You may well *minimize* the pain and disruption of jealousy. You may discover constructive and creative ways to redirect the jealous impulse. But you almost certainly will not eradicate it totally.

For some utopians, the repression and denial of jealousy are the chief means for its management. At Twin Oaks in Virginia, sexual freedom is the Community's norm and jealousy is a common problem. Kat Kinkade (1972:168), one of the founders, describes jealousy management at Twin Oaks:

> The biggest bulwark against jealousy is our heavy communal disapproval of it. . . . Nobody gets group reinforcement for feeling or expressing jealousy. A surprising amount of it is wiped out by that fact alone. . . . [M]ost of us here do not approve of our bad feelings when we have them. Just as a person with a puritan conscience can often control his erotic impulses by reference to what he believes, so a person with a communitarian conscience can control his possessive impulses by reminding himself of what his principles are.

Similarly, Bruno Bettelheim (1969:245) reports that children in the Israeli kibbutzim are expected to repress their jealousy of other children for the sake of the group goal. In the process, he suggests, positive feelings are also repressed.

Although we acknowledge the value of using group pressure to discourage or redirect certain undesirable jealous *behaviors*, we are not prepared to concede that jealous *feelings* are "wiped out" by communal disapproval. There is value in giving thought to the design of institutions, communities, and whole societies in which the hurt of jealousy is minimized, but we ought not put all our emotional eggs in one Skinnerian basket. The experience, expression, and interpretation of jealousy is an enormously complex dialectical process. This suggests that it might afford us a number of points for intervention. The repression and/or denial of jealousy might be functional (at least in the short run) for the solidarity of the *group* (a commune, a kibbutz, a swingers group, a couple) while at the same time making it *less* likely that the *individual* will confront and work with very real feelings of jealousy. Managing your jealousy begins with the acknowledgement that you are jealous. Repression or denial may only make things worse (Sokoloff 1947:252).

When a person declares that he has never been jealous, he is probably telling us less about his feelings and more about his participation in the cultural pattern which dictates that he not admit jealousy. Women sometimes deny jealous feelings, but this appears to be a special problem for men. Recent explorations into the nature of male role socialization have made many more conscious of the "strengths" a man is expected to display. These include stoic toughness, invulnerability, and self-control (see Farrell 1974).

The management of jealousy involves two major elements: Learning to deal constructively with *one's own* jealousy *and* learning to behave so as to *provoke* as little jealousy as possible in others. Jealousy cannot be treated in isolation. *Your* jealousy is not *your* problem alone. It is also a problem for your partner and for the person whose interest in your partner sparks your jealousy. Similarly, when your partner feels jealous, you ought not to dismiss the matter by pointing a finger and saying, "That's *your* problem." Typically, three or more persons are involved in the production of jealous feelings and behaviors. Ideally, all three should take on part of the responsibility for minimizing its negative consequences.

The modification of jealous feelings and behavior involves work at three levels: the *personal*, the *relational*, and the *situational*. Although all three persons in a jealousy-charged system may work at any or all levels, each of the principals has a *primary* responsibility for one of these.

The person who feels jealous has primary responsibility for work at the *personal* level. You may get help from your partner, from a psychotherapist, from a friend, or, in rare cases, from the third party. *But*, in the last analysis, *you* are responsible for your own perceptions, interpretations, and feelings. You must explore the roots of your jealousy and assay the legitimacy of your jealous response. You must discover the ways in which your self-esteem (or absence thereof) and your feelings about your relationship affect your jealousy. *And* you must ascertain whether or not some modifications in your own outlook might help reduce your jealous feelings. The article by Albert Ellis suggests some techniques for the kind of personal exploration and reassessment which is necessary for the understanding and modification of your own jealous response.

The *partner* of the person who feels jealous has primary responsibility at the *relational* level: This involves reassuring the jealous one that the relationship between the two of them is secure, that the bond connecting them is not threatened by the interest of/in the third party. Such reassurance must not merely be verbal. It must involve lots of shared time and activities—including some of the activities (such as gift-giving, eating out, going to new places, etc.) which often characterize a new relationship. Reminiscences of important moments in the history of the relationship may also be useful.

Because jealousy often reflects a somewhat irrational absence of self-esteem and of faith in the relationship, the jealous person will typically require much *more* reassurance than seems "reasonable" to the partner. And, for this same reason, if the reassurances are not sincerely *felt* by the partner, they will almost certainly fail to help the jealous person move past the jealous feelings. Needless to say, the failure of the jealous person to transcend the jealousy immediately constitutes no proof that the partner is insincere. These matters require considerable patience on the part of both partners.

Several of the articles in this section touch on the relational dimension of jealousy. The contributions of Ben Ard and Ron Mazur are especially useful in this connection.

One convincing evidence of the partner's ongoing commitment to the jealous person is a willingness to modify his or her behavior in the relationship with the third party. The partner and the third party together share responsibility at this, the *situational* level. Ideally, they will realize that the jealousy being expressed does not come *only* from within the jealous person: It is somehow *triggered* by the situation *they* have helped to create. From this recognition it follows that jealousy might be minimized if they were to modify their behavior, or, at least, their *public* behavior. A willingness to do this, at least until the jealousy is brought under control, simultaneously reduces the actual provocation of jealousy and *symbolizes* the partner's willingness to give the primary relationship the benefit of the doubt. Unless the third party is intent upon breaking up the primary relationship—or takes malicious delight in the suffering of the jealous person—he or she will almost certainly be willing to consider some modification of behavior for the purpose of minimizing the jealous reaction of another. After all, unless they are willing to resort to concealment and deception, the partner of the jealous person and the third party are most apt to have an enjoyable relationship if the jealousy is minimized. If you want to feel less jealousy, *provoke* less jealousy. The articles by Larry Constantine and by Bob and Margaret Blood are useful resources for an understanding of this situational dimension.

As we have seen, the experience and understanding of jealousy varies from culture to culture, and from time to time. It also varies from couple to couple within a given society—especially in a rapidly changing, pluralistic society such as the United States today. A situation which generates jealous anguish in one marriage may cause no trouble at all in another. There is, in other words, no single external standard by which all couples can measure the jealousy potential of certain situations and behaviors, no single set of criteria by which most jealous responses can be judged OK or not OK. This means that each couple must establish their own definition of appropriate behavior, their own sense of the legitimacy of a jealous response in a given situation. To do this requires candid and explicit communication of needs and expectations.

The next selection offers some guidance for the kind of communication that will help minimize jealousy in all sorts of intimate partnerships. Ben Ard suggests that *what* a couple decides is less important than. *how* they decide it. The partners should spell out for each other in some detail just what their assumptions are about the limits of acceptable behavior with the opposite sex. It is suggested that many difficulties that center around jealous reactions could be reduced if couples were more explicit about their needs and expectations.

15

Avoiding Destructive Jealousy

Ben N. Ard, Jr.

Jealousy has troubled relations between men and women for as long as recorded history. What causes jealousy? What can be done about it?

What one does about jealousy—and even one's feelings—depends to a great extent on one's assumptions. If an individual assumes that jealousy is a natural, normal, justified response to a given situation, that will lead to certain actions and consequences. If, however, jealousy is seen as not always justified or normal, then different reactions can be expected.

As an illustration of how one's *assumptions* influence behavior, consider the man or woman who assumes that unless their partner shows some jealousy now and then, it follows (in *their* mind) that the partner does not love them. They assume that jealousy must always accompany love.

Obviously this kind of assumption is incorrect. One man known to me in my practice as a marriage counselor was always very proud of his beautiful wife. When he was out of town (which was a lot since he was a railroad engineer), he never objected when his wife went out to dinner with

Ben N. Ard, Jr., Ph. D., (1922-   ) is a psychologist in private practice in San Francisco and Professor of Counseling at San Francisco State University. He is editor of *Counseling and Psychotherapy* (Palo Alto: Science and Behavior, Second Edition, 1975) and past President of the California Association of Marriage and Family Counselors. This article is reprinted from *Sexology* (December 1967) with permission of the author and the publisher.

men friends of theirs. He always said that he trusted his wife completely. Did this mean (since he wasn't jealous) that he did not love her? Not at all. He just defined acceptable behavior on the part of his wife in broader ways, perhaps, than other men might.

Other clients of mine have said, "I don't mind my spouse dancing, kissing, necking or petting with others, as long as he (or she) comes home to me at night. I want to be the one he (or she) sleeps with." Each person would probably draw the line of acceptable behavior for their partners at a different place.

There are no absolutes here, in the sense of limits that are universally agreed upon everywhere and at all times. The Eskimo practice of lending one's wife to the visiting guest should be sufficient to remind us of this.

What is important for each couple (if they are to avoid unpleasant jealous reactions) is that they spell out for each other in explicit detail just what their assumptions are about the limits of acceptable behavior on the part of their partner and themselves with the other sex.

This should be done early in the game rather than late. Too often a person merely assumes that his partner agrees with him without ever checking it out. Then when behavior seems to violate the underlying (but unspoken) assumptions, all kinds of tragedies may result. People have been beaten up, shot and killed because of just these unspoken assumptions and the resultant jealous reactions.

When a person is dating casually, he or she may not like it if the date pays too much attention to others while they are out together, but usually does not feel entirely justified in making too much of an issue about it since obligations are fairly limited here.

As one progresses from steady dating into engagement and marriage, however, the limits of acceptable behavior narrow down considerably. Many difficulties that center around jealous reactions possibly could be reduced if couples were more explicit about their expectations as they move through various stages of commitment. What was acceptable during casual dating may not be equally acceptable during engagement or marriage.

Certainly by the time a marriage is contemplated, a certain basic trust would seem to be required. If marriage partners cannot trust one another, there is little hope for the future of the marriage. And partners who are really committed to one another should not have to (or feel the need to) continually check up on one another.

It might not be a bad idea to discuss hypothetical situations ahead of time, just to check out each other's expectations. For example, what would you do if you walked into your home unexpectedly and saw your spouse kissing a stranger? Would you hit first and ask questions later? Go get a gun? Or would the thought occur to you that it just might be a long-lost kissing cousin returned from the foreign legion or the Far East?

Checking out the assumptions one has regarding acceptable behavior on the part of a partner probably is one of the best ways to avoid any unfortunate jealous reactions later on which one might regret. Easy ways to discuss such possible situations, for example, are after seeing movies, reading novels, or even observing other people's behavior at cocktail parties (where, perhaps, some hanky-panky is observed).

Talk it over first while it is other people's behavior that is involved, since it is usually easier to remain fairly calm and detached about their behavior than about one's own or one's partner's behavior.

Another example of how someone's assumptions can lead to trouble as far as jealous reactions are concerned is one that is very common: what happens when a husband looks with approval at some woman other than his wife and his wife "catches him at it."

Often the wife assumes that her husband would like to have sexual relations with the other woman (she might be right here); she then assumes that he must not love her any more (not necessarily true since he probably did not go blind when he got married); she may assume that "all men are polygamous by nature" (she might be right here); and that therefore no man can be trusted (a mistaken assumption that can lead to real trouble in a marriage).

It is a commonly held belief in our culture that it is just as sinful to lust after another man's wife (even if you don't do anything about it) as it is to actually commit adultery with another man's wife. And this very assumption often leads to jealousy and recriminations and even self-blame, none of which helps a couple to maintain good relations in their marriage.

The crux of the matter depends, as far as jealousy is concerned, on what actually is seen to be a threat to the relationship. All sorts of behavior may take place which one set of partners would not consider a threat at all, while another set of partners would break up their relationship immediately at the first occurrence of even one item of such behavior.

Where you would draw the line is not as important to the stability of the relationship as is the *explicit communication of expectations* to the partner. That is, clearly bringing to the surface and spelling out in detail the *underlying assumptions and expectations* about the roles each expects the other to play.

Merely "being in love" is *not* enough. Explicit communication of one's basic values, assumptions, and expectations is required. And it is so much easier to do this *before* situations have arisen in which one's jealous emotions are aroused.

Of course, no scheme can completely eliminate the possibility of self-deception and the deception and manipulation of the other in discussion of such a highly charged matter as jealousy. Indeed, many couples may find themselves incapable of constructive interaction around this issue. But many others will find that jealousy and jealousy-provoking behavior *can* be discussed and that the pain of jealousy can be reduced. Couples who have no history of candid discussion of important issues may find help in the book *The Intimate Enemy: How to Fight Fair in Love and Marriage* by George R. Bach and Peter Wyden (New York: Avon, 1968).

Learning to talk about jealousy with your partner is an important first step, but it does not guarantee that jealousy will be brought under control. Indeed, such explorations sometimes serve to make one more conscious of one's pain and dissatisfaction. The next selection presents techniques for the analysis of your own jealousy and offers some suggestions for working with it. Albert Ellis believes that jealousy (like most other forms of emotional upset) is rooted in irrational beliefs which cause us to misinterpret—to our own detriment—what goes on around us. His method emphasizes the *disputing* of those irrational beliefs and their replacement by reality-based (rational) beliefs.

Ellis is a maverick in the psychotherapy profession, opinionated and controversial. He is one of the few therapists who has written a step-by-step guide for working with one's own jealous feelings.

16

Rational and Irrational Jealousy

Albert Ellis

In the late 1930s I was living with a girl to whom I was quite devoted. I was exceptionally busy and had practically no time for adventures outside our relationship. Not so my inamorata. She was unemployed, knew a good many attractive males who had lots of time off during the day, and had sexual problems of her own which made it highly desirable that she acquire additional experience outside our double bed. So, being at least theoretically "free" in this regard, I consented to her doing whatever she felt like doing with other males.

At first, I had something of a rough time. I wrongly concluded—as practically everyone tends to do in this connection—that if my beloved couldn't find me one hundred percent satisfactory sexually, there must be something wrong with me, and that that was pretty awful! Fortunately, I was already (at the age of twenty-five) somewhat into using rational methods of psychotherapy on myself. I was not a therapist, nor even

Albert Ellis, Ph. D., (1913-   ) is the Executive Director of the Institute for Advanced Study in Rational Psychotherapy in New York City. He is the author of over 400 articles and 37 books and monographs, including *The American Sexual Tragedy* and *Humanistic Psychotherapy: the Rational-Emotive Approach.* This selection is abridged from *The Civilized Couple's Guide to Extramarital Adventure*, published by Peter H. Wyden, a division of David McKay Co., Inc. Copyright © 1972 by Albert Ellis. Reprinted with the permission of the publishers.

intending to be one; but I had had a considerable background in philosophy, and had particularly given thought to the philosophy of human happiness.

So I figured out—with the help of Epictetus, Marcus Aurelius, Spinoza, Bertrand Russell, and several other sensible philosophers—that there was no need to upset oneself seriously about anything, and that although it was highly dislikeable to have my sex-love partner off with some other male, it was hardly catastrophic. It didn't really mean anything about *me* as a person, but mainly meant something about *her* and *her* tastes and preferences. Besides, as I also figured out after she had tried it a few times, and had come home at two or three in the morning straight from somebody else's bed, her absence did have some advantages for me. I could work more steadily on the book I was then doing. I could (if I wished) try to make it with other girls and thereby enhance my own experiences. I could work to change my self-deprecating, nonsensical ideas, and thereby help myself considerably. And I could see whether sexual freedom, which I theoretically espoused, actually worked in (grim!) practice.

Well, I won that battle with myself, and in fairly short order. The first night my partner stayed out until early morning, I gave myself a pretty hard time, and kept myself awake until she finally returned. "Poor me!" I thought to myself. "Here, I act so nicely to her and then she not only seeks other sexual outlets, but makes little effort to work concertedly on bettering our own sex life! If only she did that, then her adding other lovers wouldn't be so bad. But imagine—copping out on *us*, first, and *then* spending time with others! What nerve! How could she do a thing like that?"

For a couple of hours, I really worked myself up into quite a self-pitying state. But then, philosopher that I was even in those days, I realized that that's the way she was, and that there was no reason why, with her nuttiness, she *had* to be any different. Besides, I figured out, she was so avoidant and anxious, sexually, that other experiences could probably only do her, and our relationship, good rather than harm. It was too bad that she didn't work things out between us, as I was sure she could if she persisted. But she wasn't persisting at that; so outside affairs might actually do us some good.

By the time she returned, I had calmed myself down, and done myself a lot of good. This, as I have noted, was in my pre-rational therapy days, and I was several years away from even thinking about becoming a therapist. But it was one of those occasions when I worked on myself so well that later on, when I began to do therapy, I could much better help others with similar problems. As a result of my sensible thinking, I was able to greet my paramour quite agreeably when she finally returned, be genuinely interested in her outside adventure (which she told me about in detail and which enabled me to understand her, sexually and otherwise, somewhat better), and have more enjoyable sex with her that very night than we normally had.

With about two more repetitions of the same kind of thing, I truly was in control of my sexual jealousy. I figured out, correctly, that her varietism had very little to do with me; it was mainly a reflection of her own tastes and problems, and didn't interfere seriously with my own life. And for the next six months that we lived together I was able to take it with equanimity. When we finally parted (for nonsexual reasons, since we had by then worked out most of our sex problems with each other, and she actually had benefited considerably from her outside affairs), I can't say that I had become totally unjealous; but I had certainly reached the stage of discriminating clearly between rational and irrational jealousy. And I had conclusively proved to myself that civilized adultery, even when one-sided, is definitely feasible for people who make this kind of differentiation.

What we call jealousy or sex-love fearfulness almost always has, to begin with, a distinctly sane or rational component. If you, for example, love your mate and enjoy having sex relations with him or her, you are rarely going to be completely overjoyed when you know that he or she is keenly interested in (or actually having an affair with) someone else. The reasons for this are pretty obvious. If you care for someone, you will not want your relationship to be seriously jeopardized. And if this individual is thoroughly enjoying sex, love, companionable, professional, or other intense participations with one or more members of your own sex, why should you be deliriously happy about the relatively high probability of (1) your being alone when your partner is preoccupied with someone else; (2) his or her interest in you being considerably diluted; (3) your being at times sexually deprived when you are in a let's-hop-into-bed mood; (4) your having less of a living-together, sharing partnership than you previously had; and (5) your losing this partner entirely, in case he or she finds another consort more enjoyable or agreeable than you and decides to make him or her the main mate?

Rationally and empirically, then, when you know that your mate has intense sex-love feelings for another, you are likely to be jealous in the sense of concluding; "I don't like this situation very much. I wish he (or she) were devoted only to me. What a pain in the ass this is, at least in some respects! Let me see how I can cement our relationship and make pretty sure that we become more exclusively devoted to each other or at least see that our relationship is minimally jeopardized by any outside affairs.''

This kind of jealousy is rational because it is usually based on logico-empirical observations. It is more or less depriving or frustrating to have your beloved less intensely devoted to you. It probably *would be* more satisfying if he or she were one hundred percent interested in your own one-to-one relationship. And you well *may* lose him or her completely if one or more of the simultaneously ongoing affairs turns out to be unusually satisfying as compared to your own partnership.

You would be pretty irrational and ostrich-like, therefore, if you ignored these realities and were not in any manner, shape, or form jealous of (or irritated by) your mate's other relationships. In fact, if you were *completely* unjealous, we would suspect that you really didn't care very much for this partner, you were quite absorbed in extramarital adventures yourself and therefore not *that* interested in your original relationship, or you were exceptionally busy with nonsexual pursuits (such as business or art) and consequently rather happy about having to devote less time and energy to your mate.

Rational jealousy, consequently, is reality-based, and it is unlikely that it will be reduced to near-zero when two individuals truly care for and eagerly look forward to steady contact with one another. Irrational jealousy, on the other hand, is quite different. When you are intensely or insanely jealous of your consort's extramarital affairs, you are almost always believing something like this: "Isn't it *awful* that he or she is interested in someone else! I *can't stand* it! What an incompetent and what a slob I am for allowing him or her to get so absorbed elsewhere! And how can that ungrateful louse do a thing like that to me!''

Irrational jealousy, in other words, is one of the common forms of emotional disturbance. And, in accordance with the theory and practice of rational-emotive psychology, it follows the regular A-B-C scheme of practically all emotional upsets. At point A there is an Activating event: your beloved shows real interest in or attention to another individual. At point C you feel an emotional Consequence, which we usually call intense jealousy, hurt, or rage. Quite commonly, you falsely attribute C to A—that is, you erroneously contend that "*Because* my mate is carrying on a hot affair with So-and-so, *that* makes me jealous and hurt.''

Bullshit!

There is no magic by which any outside event, such as your spouse's being intensely involved with another person, can wriggle its way deep into your gut and hurt or upset you. There is no doubt that he or she can, by various kinds of actions, frustrate, thwart, or deprive you: since you frequently want xyz satisfactions from him or her and you are actually given xyz minus, say ten or minus one hundred. So what you want you are not getting; and, in a sense, he or she is arranging matters so that you are deprived or balked. Therefore you can justifiably conclude: "His or her actions are thwarting my desires; therefore, I am being frustrated."

Intense jealousy, hurt, and emotional upset, however, are *not* deprivation and frustration. They are your idiosyncratic *reactions* to someone's blocking you. And since you have a distinct *choice* of reactions, and since ninety-nine other people who are deprived in exactly the same manner as you are also have this choice and frequently react quite differently to frustration, we cannot legitimately conclude that it is the balking *in itself* that hurts or enrages you. Much more accurately stated: you choose to hurt or enrage yourself *about* the circumvention of your desires that someone else (such as your mate) is arranging. He or she, of course, also chooses to thwart you or not; but once this thwarting occurs, you have a wide range of possible reactions, and you have considerable choice in taking rational or irrational pathways.

Your choice is at point B—your Belief system. The rational or sensible set of Beliefs that you could have chosen is the same as I listed a few paragraphs back, namely: "I don't like this situation very much. I wish he (or she) were devoted only to me. What a pain in the ass this is, at least in some respects!" Had you chosen to believe this, and *nothing but* this, you would have had a fairly intense feeling or emotional Consequence, at point C; but it would *not* have been insane jealousy, hurt, or rage. It would have been keen disappointment, sorrow, regret, annoyance, or irritation. And although such feelings can be very powerful at times, they are not by any means similar to feelings of hurt or rage. Indeed, they are significantly different.

What, then, caused your hurt and rage, if they could not have stemmed from your rational Beliefs? The answer is: your irrational Beliefs. And they were? Most probably, what I also noted a few paragraphs back: "Isn't it *awful* that he or she is interested in someone else! I *can't stand* it! What an incompetent and a slob I am for allowing him or her to get so absorbed elsewhere! And how can that ungrateful louse do a thing like that to me!" Once you believe *this* kind of nonsense, I will practically guarantee that you will feel insanely jealous, hurt, and angry.

Why are these Beliefs arrant nonsense? Because they not only have no empirical referent and not only are illogically derived from your rational observations and Beliefs; they are set up in such a magical, tautological fashion that there seems to be no possibility of their *ever* being included in a logico-empirical universe of discourse. They are dogmatic, absolutistic, faith-unfounded-on-fact statements, exactly like those in which orthodox religionists devoutly believe, and they are probably totally unverified and unverifiable.

To show how unrealistic and idiotic these irrational Beliefs are, you need only go on to the D of rational-emotive psychology, which logically follows its A-B-C. D consists of Disputing your irrational Beliefs—or questioning and challenging them, and asking *where is the evidence* for them and what is their scientific validity. Thus, if you go on to D, or Disputing, you would question your magical Beliefs or assumptions as follows:

1. "Why is it *awful* that my mate is interested in someone else?" Answer: "It clearly isn't! For *awful* means, first, that something is painful, unpleasant, or inconvenient, which my beloved's getting very interested in someone else may very well be. But it means, second, that this thing is *more than* one hundred percent painful, unpleasant, or inconvenient; which *nothing* possibly could be. *Awful* also means (if I'm honest about it) that *because* my mate's having an affair with someone else is distinctly painful, unpleasant, or inconvenient, this pain absolutely *should* not, *must* not exist; and it is *awful* that she is doing to me what she *should* not, *ought* not do. But, obviously there *are* (as far as I can scientifically ascertain) no absolute *shoulds, oughts,* or *musts* in the universe; and it is a complete non sequitur for me to claim that because I don't like something, it must not exist! *Awfulness,* consequently, is a pure devil, a demoniacal fiction, that I foolishly invent in my head. And *by* inventing it, I will almost inevitably make myself *feel* 'awful.' So I'd better stop this asinine kind of fictionalizing and inventing!"

2. "Why can't I *stand* my spouse's keenly wanting or actually having an extramarital affair?" Answer: "I damned well can stand it! I may never *like* it, of course; but I certainly can *lump* it! When I claim that 'I can't stand it!' I am really contending that I'll fall apart at the seams, die of it. Well, *will* I? Or am I insisting that because I may be *less* happy, with her having this affair, than I am with her refraining from it, I can't be happy *at all* if she has it? Well, why *can't* I? Because, childishly, I *think* I can't. I am insisting, demanding that I get total, one hundred percent happiness— *everything* that I want. And I am *determined* to feel utterly miserable if I get 99 percent, 70 percent, or 30 percent of my desires fulfilled. Well, that is my *choice*: to be happy as I possibly can be, considering the real frustrations involved with my mate's having an outside affair, or to be as utterly miserable as I can pigheadedly make myself. Shall I stupidly insist on taking this second choice? Hell, no!"

3. "Where is the evidence that I am an incompetent and a slob for allowing my mate to get so absorbed elsewhere?" Answer: "There can't be such evidence. It is quite possible—even probable—that my *behavior* is rather incompetent or slobbish and that consequently my beloved is choosing to have this affair. But it is also likely that my behavior has little to do with his or her choice, and that this choice is motivated by a desire for variety, novelty, or adventure that has virtually nothing to do with me. I could be King Solomon or the Queen of Sheba, and my mate might *still* not feel like being completely dedicated to me. How does his or her pluralism prove my ineptitude or inadequacy? It clearly doesn't!

Even suppose that I am deficient in some significant respects and that *therefore* my mate wants another lover, too. Does this prove that *I am* an incompetent or a slob? Of course not! It merely proves, at most, that some of my *acts* are incompetent or slobbish. And, being a fallible human, it would be incredible if I did no such acts. *An* incompetent or *a* slob is a concept that is invariably a magical overgeneralization. For if I were *a* slob or a *nogoodnik* it would mean that (a) I were *totally* incompetent; (b) I would *always* have to behave in this manner; and (c) I should rightfully be damned, denigrated as a human, and consigned to some kind of hell for *being* that way. None of these propositions, especially the second and the third, are really provable. And even if it were possible to prove the first two—namely, that I was incompetent in *every* way and would have to continue to be so *forever*—I would hardly be condemnable or damnable. I would merely be an exceptionally handicapped human who would get very little out of life, and that would be highly deplorable. But I hardly, except by any arbitrary theological definition, would therefore be a totally rotten, condemnable *person*; I would merely be a person *who unfortunately consistently acts badly*."

4. "In what way is my sex-love partner an ungrateful louse for doing a thing to me like having an extramarital affair?" Answer: "In no way, whatever. First of all, I can't even prove that his or her infidelity is poor, unethical, or lousy behavior. I can prove that *I* think it is; but that hardly necessarily makes it so. She or he really can't, as a human being, absolutely *promise* to care for me and only me till death do us part; so why is it a rotten act if my mate decides to care for someone else, too?

"Even if I could prove undesirable actions—if, for example, he or she kept lying to me about this outside affair, and thereby took away some of my freedom of action in responding to it—that would only indicate that his or her *deeds,* but not *person,* are unethical or reprehensible. So I can never legitimately refer to personal lousehood, but merely to lousy *behavior*. While behavior can be assessed or measured, he or she, as a total human, really can't be. And when I condemn a *person* for this person's *acts* I am foolishly and unfairly overgeneralizing—just as I am doing when I condemn *me* for my *acts*. I'd better stop that nutty overgeneralizing and stick to merely measuring a partner's *performances* and how much I dislike *them*. Then I can rationally decide whether it is worth my remaining intimately involved. Even if I decide that it isn't worth it, that hardly makes my mate a lousy individual, nor one with whom I could not have reasonably friendly relations in the future." . . .

Many people may consider it utterly impractical for spouses who love each other to achieve a state where they are essentially unjealous (or at least not insanely jealous) of one another; and rational-emotive psychology, which says that such a state is possible, may be viewed as an idealistic or utopian philosophy. A similar view has been independently expressed, however, by various Eastern sages, such as Krishnamurti, who never heard of RET. One of Krishnamurti's questioners asks: "Is it possible for a man and woman to live together, to have sex and children, without all the turmoil, bitterness, and conflict inherent in such a relationship? Is it possible for there to be freedom on both sides? I don't mean by freedom that the husband or wife should constantly be having affairs with someone else. People usually come together and get married because they fall in love, and in that there is desire, choice, pleasure, possessiveness, and tremendous drive. The very nature of this in-loveness is from the start fillec with the seeds of conflict."

Krishnamurti replies: "Is it? Need it be? I very much question that. Can't you fall in love and not have a possessive relationship? I love someone and she loves me and we get married—that is all perfectly straightforward and simple, in that there is no conflict at all. (When I say we get married I might just as well say we decide to live together—don't let's get caught up in the words.) Can't one have that without the other, without the tail, as it were, necessarily following? Can't two people be in love and both be so intelligent and so sensitive that there is freedom and absence of a center that makes for conflict? Conflict is not in the feeling of being in love. The feeling of being in love is utterly without conflict. There is no loss of energy in being in love. The loss of energy is in the tail, in everything that follows—jealousy, possessiveness, suspicion, doubt, the fear of losing that love, the constant demand for reassurance and security. Surely it must be possible to function in a sexual relationship with someone you love without the nightmare which usually follows. Of course it is."

Krishnamurti, in answer to another question from one of his followers, also points out that loneliness, bleakness, and wretchedness that you supposedly feel as a result of being in love actually existed before you fell in love. "Your problem is not this relationship but rather it is the problem of your own emptiness . . . Whatever is happening inside you—anger, depression, jealousy or any other conflict at all, drop it instantly. Stop it."

Krishnamurti seems to be saying that insensate jealousy, under any condition, is your *own* problem and does not stem from the circumstances of your loving, being in love, or having other deep feelings for your spouse, your extramarital partner, or anyone else. It stems from *your* thoughts and feelings, over which *you* really have control. Consequently, as we would say in rational-emotive psychology, *you* can change or eliminate it.

At first it may seem incongruous that Ellis—whose approach to psychotherapy is rational and conscious in the extreme—should find an ally in the Eastern sage, Krishnamurti. And yet, the stoic attitude counseled by Ellis (with its roots in Epictetus and Marcus Aurelius) has some affinity with the Eastern philosophy which one westerner has summarized thus: Don't just do something; *stand there*. In this tradition the solution to the problem of jealousy is to be found not in *action* but in letting go, that is, in freeing oneself from the dependency which gives jealousy the power to wound. Consider this advice from a Buddhist meditation *On Love* (Adapted from Orage, n.d.:17-19):

Take hold tightly; let go lightly. This is one of the great secrets of [happiness] in love. One may be afraid to "let go" for many reasons: because this relationship appears to be the last hope, or because too much time has already been spent on it, or because it has been the best relationship to date, or because his "ideal," created by education, demands eternal fidelity even when it is not possible (because it is not desired by both); or because the flesh being willing the spirit is weak; or because circumstances are unfavorable (as when the parties must continue to see each other at work or in the neighborhood); or because of imagination (as when one or the other pictures the happiness of the partner without him or her). There are a thousand explanations, and every one of them, while sufficient as a cause, is quite inadequate as a reason, because when one of the partners desires to separate, the other's love-duty is to "let go." Great love can both let go and take hold.

Jealousy is the dragon in paradise; the hell of heaven; and the most bitter of the emotions because associated with the sweetest. There is a specific remedy for jealousy, namely, conscious love;[1] But this remedy is harder to find than the disease is to endure. But there are palliatives: the first is the recognition of the disease and the second is the wish to cure oneself. In these circumstances let the sufferer deliberately experiment. Much may be forgiven him or her during this process. He may, for instance, try to forward the new plans of his former beloved—but this is difficult without obvious hypocrisy. Or he may plunge into new social activities. Or he may engage himself in a new work that demands all his energy. Or, in his imagination, he may regard his former beloved as dead; or as having become his sister; or as having gone away on a long journey; or as having become enchanted. It is best, however, if he "let go" completely with no lingering hope of ever meeting her again.

Be comforted. Our life is but one day of our Life. If not today, tomorrow! Let go!

---

[1]By *conscious love* the writer means a strong, wise, mature kind of love that is rarely achieved—and then only as a result of much self-discipline. It sounds rather like Maslow's Being-love (see this book, p. 9f.), the love characteristic of "self-actualizing" persons. This sage knows, too, about what Maslow calls Deficiency-love. He writes: "Conscious love. . .is rare among humans. . . because. . . the vast majority are children who look to be loved but not to love" (Orage n.d.:9).

We commonly use the single word *jealousy* to name several different kinds of feelings, reactions, and conditions. The distinctions among these are often subtle, and for most purposes the general label *jealousy* is adequate. But, for the kind of deeper understanding that is prerequisite to the management of one's own jealous feelings, more precise language may be required. Up to a point, the more *words* we know about something, the more we know about it—and the more we know about it, the more we can do with it.

The next selection identifies several varieties of jealousy. Each type is seen as the polar opposite of a positive value, the cultivation of which helps minimize that form of jealousy. The typology presented here is not the only one that could be formulated. Other typologies (explicit and implicit) appear elsewhere in this volume. More important than the choice of one taxonomy as the "truest" or "best" is the *process* through which we come to appreciate the components and intricacies of something previously viewed as an undifferentiated, incomprehensible blob. Each typology, then, is suggestive rather than definitive. Taken together, they can inform the reader's *own* framework for understanding the experience of jealousy and for minimizing destructive jealousy in relationships.

17

Beyond Jealousy
and Possessiveness

Ronald Mazur

. . . For those who are strongly motivated to outgrow jealousy, three questions are critical: what is the nature of jealousy; can jealousy be totally and permanently eradicated from a person; and how do persons go about understanding and deconditioning jealous feeling and behavior patterns?

Before answering such questions, it is helpful to assume a casual and positive attitude toward jealousy in persons: it's there; it's something to deal with; somebody is experiencing deep feelings, and the task is to understand them in the context of what that person is trying to learn or communicate. Joan Constantine and Larry Constantine,[1] in their research and work with multilateral or group marriages make observations about jealousy applicable to other lifestyles.

Ronald Mazur, S.T.B., (1934-   ) is a Unitarian clergyman and health educator. He is Director of the Peer Sex Education Program, University Health Services, and Lecturer, School of Health Sciences, at the University of Massachusetts. He is also the author of *Commonsense Sex* (Boston: Beacon Press, 1968). "Beyond Jealousy and Possessiveness" is abridged by the editors from Ronald Mazur, *The New Intimacy: Open-Ended Marriage and Alternative Lifestyles,* Chapter 7. Copyright © 1973 by Ronald M. Mazur. Reprinted by permission of Beacon Press.

Editors' Note: See Chapter 18 in this volume.

"If all jealousy is simply rejected as undesirable or immature, the affect goes underground and interferes with group functioning and the exchange of other feelings. If jealousy is lauded or facilely accepted, growth in important dimensions can be hindered. Thus it is necessary for participants in group marriages to differentiate among various forms of jealousy. Jealousy, if approached properly, becomes an opportunity to discover new information about individuals and their relationships" (1971).

Jealousy must be recognized, admitted, and worked with if it is to lead to personal growth and relational enrichment.

What, then, is the meaning of jealousy and how can it be recognized? While nineteenth-century American dictionaries clearly indicated both negative and positive meanings of the word, the 1970 paperback edition of *The American Heritage Dictionary of the English Language* gives predominantly *negative* denotations of "jealous." To be jealous is to be "1. Fearful of loss of position or affection. 2. Resentful in rivalry; envious. 3. Possessively watchful; vigilant." What seems clear is that the word itself has borne the burden of too many meanings; there is a great deal of legitimate difference and semantic confusion surrounding its historical usage. The trend also seems to be to use it only in a negative way.

Regardless of how contemporary lexicographers define it, jealousy is more than a word; it is usually a gut-feeling experience filled with anxiety, resentment, threat, fear, and other hurtful emotions. It comes like a flash flood, undoubtedly causing various physiological manifestations, Jealousy is a complex emotion, and perhaps the only way to understand it and to control it—not eliminate it—is to analyze its various forms. Perhaps, if we analyze its various forms, we will find that jealousy can be defused of its demonic potential.

The following is a typology of jealousy intended for use by all those who are disturbed by unwanted feelings of jealousy—who want to work toward eliminating it in relationships. . . . The task is to recognize, understand, and deal openly and creatively with whatever kind of jealousy is experienced. It must also be emphasized that the forms of jealousy are interrelated with some common causes and consequences. . . .

POSSESSIVE-JEALOUSY VERSUS AUTONOMY

Emotional space for each partner to be autonomous is a necessary condition for any type of creative marriage or intimate relationship. For the recognition and growth of our own self—our integrity or wholeness—we need emotional space. Poet Kahlil Gibran advises lovers: "Love one another, but make not a bond of love. Rather let it be a moving sea between the shores of your souls," and he speaks of "spaces in togetherness." This is startling for young lovers to hear, for they think of their love as an eternal bond. But Gibran jars the thoughtful into serious consideration of unspoken realities. . . .

Possessiveness is culturally sanctioned but is nevertheless a dehumanizing process. The possessive person does not know the inherent value or even the identity of the person possessed. The possessor is also possessed by private versions of reality—a reality requiring order, reassurance, and respect from without, and a sense of power and control. This allows for predictability, homage, and manipulation, but negates the qualities of spontaneity, authentic self-esteem, and mutuality of relationship. By perceiving the other merely as an extension of one's own life—even when romantically intended—that other person is deprived of dignity, individuality, and freedom to be and become with integrity. Possessiveness can, of course, be symbiotic in the sense that both spouses build their lives around it and feed off each other. This is so much the case that possessive marriage has superseded religion as the "opiate of the masses"; it is a stupefied security without joy, enthusiasm, or adventure.

The double-standard reinforces the sanctions for possessiveness in accordance with the best interests of males. When the male is possessive-jealous, the female is supposed to feel proud and grateful. When the female is possessive-jealous the male flaunts it as a sign of his desirability and attractiveness as long as the female doesn't push too hard. But when the female becomes too demanding she is demeaned as being nothing but a castrating bitch.

Possessive-jealousy is perhaps the most raging and wrathful form of jealousy, leading to acts of cruel vengeance and even murder. "You belong to me and if you cross me I'll get even with you. If I can't have you nobody is going to have you." That sentiment sounds as if it comes from one of those unbelievably trite movies. Yet, the sentiments of possessive people *are* unfortunately trite, and potentially destructive.

Is it possible to be monogamously committed to someone without possessiveness? We pose the question because many couples seem to confuse commitment with belonging to. Possessiveness is commitment without trust. Conversely, commitment with trust celebrates the autonomy of the other; rejoices in the uniqueness of the other; is aware of the privacy needs of the other. There need be no contradiction between mutual commitment and the mutual allowance for emotional space.

EXCLUSION-JEALOUSY VERSUS SHARING

The most painful type of jealousy is exclusion-jealousy: being left out of a lovely or critical experience of a loved one. . . . It's easy to feel jealous when you are excluded. It's not a matter of wanting to deny one's partner a new or enjoyable experience with someone else. Rather one wants to be included in the experience. It is also not a matter of possessiveness as such. For one can be genuinely nonpossessive and yet be overcome by exclusion-jealousy. It can happen for two reasons: being shut out of a good time and/or not having similar pleasure with another while the spouse is involved elsewhere. It sometimes comes down to a matter of, "Damn it, how come you have all the opportunities while I seem to be stuck in a rut?" Or it could be something like, "Why did you go there with your friend when you never like to go there with me?" Exclusion-jealousy is especially intense when a partner feels—or is—neglected in comparison to the time, finances, interest, and enthusiasm the spouse is lavishing upon someone else. Then there are those inevitable disappointing conflicts in plans when one partner says, "Oh, by the way, I'll be out with so-and-so on next Thursday evening" and the other replies, "Hell, I was hoping we could do something special together that evening." That "something special" is usually quite specific and it means changing plans with the friend or disappointing the spouse. With a little practice, however, couples can avoid such conflicts.

Different couples will handle the problems of exclusion-jealousy in different ways. Some couples, for example, feel strongly that they can always include the spouse, even when the spouse is not present, by sharing their experiences verbally and by having their friends always meet the spouse. This inclusive approach might possibly work for couples with similar needs who are able to verbalize experiences and always enjoy meeting each other's friends. Other couples, however, will not find this a satisfying solution—their needs for privacy and emotional space may be strong, they may find verbal analysis of their experiences superficial. Such couples would rather confront the fact of exclusion directly. They are willing to say, "Yes, it's true we have experiences with others from which our spouse is excluded. We don't experience all of each other's intimate friendships, but we rejoice in the persons we are and in the richness of our relationships. We simply have to learn to live with the freedom to have partially separate lives—and we really wouldn't want it any other way."

COMPETITION-JEALOUSY VERSUS SPECIALNESS

Marriage partners who are self-actualizing may at times be jealous of each other's achievements and will compete for recognition and success. At its best, this can be creative tension; at its worst, undercutting oneupmanship.

The arena of competition, however, is not restricted to status and success. This is not to say that this contest is unimportant or trivial. On the contrary, it's imperative for women to refuse being consigned to suportive roles, to unleash their full creative potential for the benefit of themselves and for all people. If this kind of competition makes men uncomfortable, that's *their* problem. Women for too long have apologized for bruising frail male egos, and such men are just going to have to grow up and stop expecting their wives to be their mothers.

Negative forms of competition stem from a lack of self-confidence or self-esteem leading to jealousy of the partner's achievements, attractiveness, friends, or sexual performance. Behind competition-jealousy is the attitude: "You think I'm not good enough for you, but I'll show you!" This projection of inadequacy demands constant reassurance from the partner, but the reassurance is always suspected of being mere condescension. What is needed to overcome this form of jealousy is the development of self-esteem in combination with the sense of being essentially *special* to one's partner. This sense of specialness rests on the attitude: "Sure, I'm aware you know some fantastic people who also think you're great, but that makes me happy for you because I also know I'm uniquely special to you, that the quality of our relationship is one of the highest shared values in our lives." To be glad for the other without feeling like a second-rate person does indeed require a high degree of self-esteem. And, ironically, that self-esteem is easier to develop when two people lovingly help each other to be special through mutual respect, sensual pleasuring, admiration, approval, support, and sometime forgiveness.

EGOTISM-JEALOUSY VERSUS ROLE FREEDOM

Role flexibility or interchangeability is a new personal freedom and a new feature of contemporary interpersonal relationships. The rigid stereotypes of masculinity and femininity have already been shattered, opening new avenues for self-realization and interpersonal openness. There are, to be sure, casualties of this shattering of sex stereotypes, and there are those who defensively hide from its impact. A time of transition is confusing and difficult for many. Nevertheless, the change is relentless and there is no turning back to the comforting absurdities of conformist man-woman, woman-woman, or man-man relationships. There is a new role freedom for all persons who will no longer allow themselves and their potentialities to be defined by cultural conformity or the insensitive expectations of others. This freedom also allows problems to surface: men who become enraged or embarrassed because their wives challenge them in public; women who become enraged or embarrassed because their husbands seem openly affectionate to other males. Examples of anger or embarrassment over a conflict in role expectations are endless.

Egotism-jealousy is a denial of role freedom. It is, in a sense, wanting a girl/boy just like the girl/boy that married dear old dad/mom. Rather than see the crisis of role interchangeability as an opportunity for growth, some people are ashamed of their "unfeminine" wives or "unmasculine" (note that the word is usually "effeminate") husbands and are jealous of other people who have "ideal" husbands/wives.

Egotism-jealousy can also be turned against the spouse with the ability for role flexibility who exposes the rigidity of the less flexible partner.

Egotism-jealousy is related to one's ability or inability to expand one's ego awareness and role flexibility. When both men and women can be persons in whatever ways that make them happiest, regardless of what and how tradition defines them sexually, they will invest less of their egos in social roles and status.

FEAR-JEALOUSY VERSUS SECURITY

Jealousy can be just plain fear: fear of losing someone special; fear of being lonely, of being rejected. To the extent that one's own value depends upon a partner's devotion, one will be vulnerable to the fear of desertion. If there is a classic form of jealousy, this probably is it, although an equally strong case can be made for possessive-jealousy. Fear-jealousy doubts the commitment of the other; it breeds on insecurity. It torments with anxiety and anguish. "What if my lover finds someone else better than me? What will happen to me?" Underlying such fearful feelings is the assumption that one is satisfying to the lover only as a desirable product—when something "better" comes along one will be abandoned. It's a hell of a way to live, but fear-jealousy is one foundation on which many marriages precariously endure.

The only security in a healthy relationship is to be a person, not a product. None of us is desirable or enjoyable in every way on every day, and if our relationships depend on the fear of having our lovers discover the attractiveness of others, then we do indeed shape dull and emotionally crippled lovers. Let your lover look at you with all of your blemishes and shortcomings and let your relationship be a dynamic exploration in living and becoming rather than a wedding exchange of personality packages. The strongest and most joyful relationships are those in which partners are not afraid to let each other go; attempting to control the duration of a relationship because of insecurity sacrifices the magnificence of every *now*. Bless and celebrate each moment of joy and loving with thankfulness, and let the future take care of itself.

Jealous behavior continues to be socially sanctioned in "appropriate" forms, but there are reasons to believe it will diminish as it ceases to serve a useful function in interpersonal relationships. Jessie Bernard (1971:209)[2] believes: "If it is true that marriage is indeed moving away from the old monogamic format in the direction of some as yet unclarified form, jealousy in the classic form would no longer be required to support it and we could expect its gradual diminution. But until we know with more certainty the nature of the model—or models—of marriage we are moving toward, jealousy in some form or other may continue to crop up in the clinician's office." It is probable, also, that even as models of marriage are clarified and become culturally accepted, forms of jealousy will be experienced by most people to some degree some of the time.

Whether one believes that jealousy is inevitable or eradicable, normal or neurotic, is ultimately not the most important issue. What is important is to ask the most helpful question: "What *kind* of jealousy affects my relationships?" It is of no practical use to try to decide once and for all whether or not one is a jealous person. But if one understands the various types of jealousy something *can* be done to control and minimize it—to disarm it if not dissolve it. So much more of the expectations and satisfactions of a relationship could be understood, communicated, and creatively acted upon, if couples could understand the specifics of jealousy. What is it that you *really* resent? Are you afraid? Envious? Excluded? Competitive? Possessive? Does your ego hurt? What do you *really* want to communicate to each other? It doesn't help merely to say "I'm jealous." Jealous how? Can we *do* something about it? Should we renegotiate our expectations of each other? How can we grow from here? . . .

[2]*Editors' Note:* See Chapter 13 in this volume.

Like Ron Mazur, several of the professionals who lead jealousy workshops utilize typologies to help their clients focus their attention on the particular *kind* of jealousy which is a problem for them. In the "open relationships" workshops at Sandstone Center (Paige 1975) near Los Angeles, participants are told that jealousy is learned behavior, a reaction to a loss or threat of loss (real or imaginary) which comes in a variety of forms. These are:

a. *Time jealousy:* The feeling that one does not have enough time with the partner.
b. *Person jealousy:* One partner may be threatened (or irritated) by the specific person the mate has chosen to relate to but not be threatened by others.
c. *Opportunity/situation jealousy:* One person may have unique opportunities/experiences which exclude the partner, who then feels cheated, *or* one person may be invited to participate in experiences with people at times or in places which exclude the partner.

Such a typology may help a person isolate and work with his/her *specific* problem. Without such a focus, time, energy, and good intentions are often wasted—and disappointment results.

Jealousy workshops are a new phenomenon. Their emergence reflects a growing concern to understand jealousy and to *control it* rather than to be controlled by it. Those who participate in jealousy workshops are not only trying to change themselves rather fundamentally but, more than that: *They are trying to take conscious control of what many have long assumed to be a "natural" function.* They are seeking to *relearn* that which had been viewed as virtually *instinctive.*

Biofeedback research has shown that we can exercise at least ɔome measure of conscious control over pulse rate, body temperature, brain wave patterning, and other body functions which were, until recently, believed to be automatic or involuntary (See e.g., Brown 1974; Kamiya 1971). By monitoring jealousy workshops we may learn something about our ability to assert at least some measure of conscious control over jealous feelings and sentiments—and, by extension, over other potentially destructive emotions.

If pioneer experiments with jealousy workshops are successful, we may expect that psychologists, marriage counselors, and growth centers will offer therapeutic small group experiences focused on the management of jealousy. Different people would bring different needs to such workshops. Some would wish to deliver quite conventional and otherwise happy marriages from the disruptions caused by jealousy over rather innocent flirtations. Others may want to open their marriages so as to permit each partner to develop meaningful platonic friendships with members of the opposite sex. Some may also wish to find the resources to liberalize their shared ground rules so as to allow extramarital sexual intimacy. A few may already be in the depths of unreasoning, pathological jealousy; these persons will, of necessity, be referred for more intensive work with a competent and sympathetic therapist or marriage counselor. Groups would probably be most effective if composed of couples whose experiences and goals were somewhat similar—although diversity of experience may also be valuable to the group process if creatively managed.

Larry Constantine's jealousy workshops have been attended by more than 160 people at Cornell University, Iowa State University, and elsewhere. In the workshop context, jealousy is not labeled "good" or "bad." Rather, "the object is to remove the pejorative connotation from jealousy and view it as a *behavioral cue* signaling an opportunity for exploration into the nature of the relationship." Participants are advised *not* to repress or deny their jealousies. The reduction of jealousy, according to Constantine, requires a clear sense of its causes and effects in specific contexts, and such awareness is not served by denial of feelings.

18

Jealousy: Techniques for Intervention

Larry L. Constantine

Jealousy is a defensive response to a particular kind of situation, a structural context which is perceived as threatening to a valued relationship: one person is threatened by the loss of something in a relationship with another person through the agency of a third party. The process called jealousy begins with perceptions, leading to interpretations, which generate feelings that may or may not be expressed behaviorally. The effect of jealous behavior on the structural context is to defend the boundary of the pair system. Through research on group marriages (Constantine & Constantine 1973), therapy with couples, and numerous workshops on jealousy, the sequential transformation of context into behavior has been elaborated by Joan Constantine and the author into a complete model or theory of jealousy.[1]

Larry L. Constantine (1943-   ) is a family therapist in private practice in Acton, Massachusetts. As an Instructor in Psychiatry at Tufts University School of Medicine he helps train new family therapists. He is co-author, with his wife Joan M. Constantine, of the book *Group Marriage* (New York: Macmillan, 1973). His recent publications include *Treasures of the Island: Children in Alternative Families* (Sage Monograph, 1976) and *Drugs and Therapy: The Psychotherapist's Handbook of Psychotropics* (Boston: Little, Brown, 1976). This article was originally published in D. H. Olson, ed., *Treating Relationships* (Lake Mills, Iowa: Graphic Publishers, 1976) and is reprinted in abridged form by permission of the author, the editor, and the publisher.

[1]This model is presented in detail in Larry L. Constantine, "Jealousy: From Theory to Intervention," in D.H. Olson, ed., *Treating Relationships.*

This model is in marked contrast to prevailing views which generally consider jealousy from a strong value stance. On the one hand are theories which regard jealousy as natural, necessary, and a sign of healthy monogamous commitment. On the other hand are those which treat it as a manifestation of possessiveness, objectification, and neuroticism. We feel that our theory clarifies the issues in a value-free manner. Jealousy and jealous behavior are neither intrinsically healthy and good nor unhealthy and bad. Jealousy becomes a problem when it interferes with successful functioning in a chosen life style or relationship. Insofar as it consumes emotional resources excessively, or antagonizes, alienates, and obfuscates, jealousy will tend to work to the disadvantage of all. Extreme jealousy may be dysfunctional, as may jealousy in response to imagined threats. But where the danger is real, jealousy may indeed be a functional response.

Jealousy can be a highly useful interpersonal process. It can serve to limit the complexity of interpersonal situations to a level which the principal players can tolerate. Jealousy may be an *early warning signal* that some aspects of a relationship need to be clarified and worked out more thoroughly. Jealousy may serve to draw attention to differences in assumptions and expectations by the partners, to changing assumptions, or to the need to change the couple's implicit contract.

Often the usefulness of jealousy will be a function of what the people involved do with it. If they can use conflict to build their relationship, to clarify personal differences, and to increase respect for what each finds important, then even extreme and highly stressful jealousy can be growthful. We have found that those people who have the most successful open relationships are not necessarily less jealous, but they use jealousy as an opportunity to learn more about themselves and their relationships.

TYPES OF JEALOUS BEHAVIOR

Jealous behavior may be classified according to its target (one's partner or the third party) and its effect on the relationship between the primary partners. One would predict that jealous behavior directed toward the third party would be most likely where s/he is accessible and where one cannot effectively regulate one's partner's behavior. Whether directed toward the partner or the third party, jealous behavior almost always takes the form of negative sanctioning, although positive sanctions might sometimes be equally or more effective in boundary maintenance.

An essential question concerning the effect of jealous behavior on the primary relationship is whether the mode of expressing jealousy maintains contact between the primary partners. By remaining in contact, there is at least hope of reaching an effective resolution and the reintegration which is essential for continued health of the pair system.

Whitehurst (1971) has proposed a typology of jealous behavior which includes isolation, antagonism, redefinition, and resolution. Our clinical and workshop studies verify the heuristic value of this typology.

Isolational behavior includes separation, withdrawal, withholding, silence, and refusal to fight or negotiate. *Antagonistic* behavior includes fighting, quarreling, violence, and attempts to take revenge. Oftentimes antagonistic jealousy will be more functional than isolational behavior because it maintains the couple in contact and facilitates problem solving unless the antagonism is so severe as to disrupt the pair system. Isolation often preserves peace at the expense of potential resolution and may create even greater mutual withdrawal.

Redefinition externalizes the problem through intellectualizing and rationalizing away the significance of the jealousy situation and the accompanying emotions. By redefining the problem as "infidelity" or "seductive men" or "the breakdown of the American family" the pair unites against a common enemy. The pair-boundary may be temporarily maintained, although again potentially at the expense of real resolution.

Resolutional behavior involves joint problem solving, direct attempts to explore the feelings, issues, and causes of the jealousy, realistic negotiation, and identification of personal stakes. Areas of mutual as well as conflicting interest leading toward "no-lose" resolution of the problematic situation also need to be discussed. Although this mode of jealous behavior may be uncommon and difficult to learn, it is clearly likely to be the most functional for all parties. Understanding the function and structure of jealousy also permits the dysfunctional aspects of isolation, antagonism, and redefinition to be minimized.

TECHNIQUES FOR INTERVENTION

There are various points of entry for intervention in a system where jealousy is a problem. Clarifying the contextual structure of jealousy can help one's partner to "decode" jealous behavior. This may also counter the effect of an excessive delay that allows resentments to reach unmanageable proportions before they are expressed.

Typical interventions involve an explanation of the contextual structure of jealousy, and inquiries about the details of specific past experience with jealousy: Who was doing what with whom? Exactly what immediately preceded the jealous behavior? We find it useful to have clients act out without words the ways they behave when jealous. This abstracts and accentuates the behavior and frequently makes it easier for each to get in touch with the feelings they associate with the behavior and the context in which these occur.

The structure of jealousy also reveals that the relationship between the jealous person and the third party can be a key factor in determining the degree of threat. In general, we find it productive to promote this relationship. Real human beings, known for all their uniqueness and vulnerabilities, are considerably less threatening than fantasied creatures. Furthermore, by bringing these two persons together, the person in the middle of the triangle is prevented from playing one off against the other. Getting husband and lover together, for example, may reveal and end a game being played by the woman to avoid dealing with things in *both* her relationships. Bringing all three parties into a therapy session may be initially opposed, especially by the partner in the middle, but it is almost always freeing. The insights so gained can substantially increase the options of all concerned.

Clarification of individual boundaries and those of the couple system as perceived by each partner has proven highly useful. The negotiation of any rules or limits on outside activities and relationships should be deferred until these boundaries are well understood by both parties. Most people are not consciously aware of their own and partner's boundaries or their strategies for maintaining them. Without this awareness, rules and agreements are not likely to work or to benefit the partners. A boundary sculpture (Duhl, Kantor, and Duhl 1974) is one of the most efficient ways to elicit information about these boundaries.[2]

It is also important to help the partners sort out their priorities in terms of the various dimensions in which their boundaries are maintained. An individual may experience an encroachment or invasion in one dimension of his/her life as much more threatening than in other areas. One husband, for example, had no jealous reactions about his wife's involvement with another man until, as a consequence, she was late for a dinner he had especially prepared for her. When his reactions were explored in therapy, it emerged that, to him, time was an especially important dimension of relatedness. Carrying over from his family of origin, he felt it especially important for everyone to begin dinner at the same time because dinner was to be an uninterrupted "family" time. When the husband felt that this

---

[2]*Editor's Note:* For a description of this technique see the next selection, page 201.

point of sensitivity was understood and respected, other annoyances about that relationship diminished in importance to him.

It is useful for the therapist to recognize that *anything* one values in the relationship with his/her primary partner may be the entity which one perceives as being lost. Careful and precise clarification of the context triggering one's jealous behavior may reveal a surprising or minor relationship element at stake. Key questions to ask are, "What are you afraid of? What unpleasant outcomes might you fantasize as the result of your partner's other relationship?" Or, "What is your stake in this other relationship? How does it affect you?" Some things which one does not want to lose may in fact be unhealthy to retain, such as dominance over one's partner.

Listed below are some elements of relationship we have found to be involved in jealousy situations.

1. Loss of face, status, or ego-enhancement.
2. Loss of need gratification, including sexual, intellectual, emotional, and other needs.
3. Loss of control over one's partner, of control of one's own life, of power in relation to one's partner.
4. Loss of predictability, the dependability of one's partner's behavior.
5. Loss of privacy, territory, or exclusive access.
6. Loss of actual time with one's partner, or reduced contact.

We do not find the security domain to be an efficient point of clinical intervention. Individual security, essentially one's sense of completeness and self-worth, is not likely to be affected except through long-term therapy. Focusing on the successful history and assets in the primary relationship could conceivably *raise* the threshold of insecurity in relation to the couple system. For some couples just learning that jealousy becomes less of a problem as they and their relationship mature reduces non-specific anxiety, which itself might have been making jealousy more likely.

Even in the most mature individuals and relationships jealousy does not disappear altogether. Jealousy is still apt to be expressed over basic functional issues, such as need gratification, privacy, or time together, that is, over things which are functionally necessary for personal integrity and the maintenance of a healthy couple system. In contrast, things which are more important for their symbolic content than their real effect on a person—status, sexual fidelity, and the like—tend to become less salient as triggers for jealousy as maturity develops.

It has been our experience that symbolic meanings do not change rapidly and are not normally accessible to purposive change, either by one-self or by an outside facilitator. This, it appears, may account for some of the inability of couples to reduce jealousy through the adoption of an ideology or intellectual set which maintains that jealousy is destructive, connotes possessiveness, or implies objectification of people. Deeply ingrained meanings change very slowly, if at all, despite surface intellec-tual changes. Clarification of differences in symbolic meanings may, however, be very useful as this will help the partners to understand the cir-cumstances under which jealousy is likely. Open-ended questions with a written response may be helpful. For example, "What does sexual intercourse with someone *mean* to you?"

Exercises to facilitate "synergic perception" are also extremely useful in working with jealousy. Synergic perception refers to the perception of opposites as being integral and inseparable rather than antithetical, a way of looking at things which diminishes problems with jealousy. These exer-cises are designed to show the ways in which *each* partner may experience positive gains from the outside relationship.

> *Bringing in Positive Energy.* The partners are seated facing each other so that they can maintain body contact. The partner who is to be the "giver" selects a gift for the partner. This should be something from the "outside" relationship, a specific event or a general aspect which s/he believes the partner will like or appreciate.
> *Examples:* "Paul and I talked about your paintings tonight. He agrees with me that you have real talent with water colors." Or "I've discovered with Jean an intellectual side to myself that I had neglected. As a result I can enjoy talking philosophy with you more than in the past."
> The "receiver" then "values" the gift, talking about what he likes about it and the feelings it evokes. The therapist should be alert to possible sabotaging of the exercise by the giver, who may send disguised "zingers," or by the re-ceiver who does not accept the gift. The partners' stake in sabotaging the exer-cise needs to be explored.
> *What's in it for Me.* In this exercise, partners take turns talking about the other's outside relationship. One partner describes specifically and in detail a way in which s/he benefits from the other's outside relationship.
> *Examples:* "What I like about your relationship with Don is that I've found a new golf partner." Or, "I really appreciate the fact that after you have been with Ann you seem more accepting of me and the children."

A person who perceives reality in a highly synergic manner is more likely to see his own interests as interdependent, rather than in conflict with the in-terests and wishes of a partner.

The most effective intervention at the final transformational step concerns training in effective resolutional behaviors. Effective problem-solving requires that each be able to identify and "own" their feelings, to communicate these in personal rather than projective statements, to articulate the structure of their relationship, and to identify and negotiate issues and elements at stake.[3] An example of a constructive dialog may aid in understanding this process of problem solving.[4]

Beth was an anxious wife who coped with uncertainty by taking control. She would talk incessantly and attempt to maneuver situations into predictable outcomes, whether pleasant or not, rather than face uncertainty. Soon after she became involved with Alan, Alan's wife, Andrea, began to develop a relationship with Beth's husband, Bryan. Though Alan and Beth had started the cross-marital relationships and were the early enthusiasts of a group marriage, their relationship was soon eclipsed by the one between Bryan and Andrea. The four of them and their three children had moved in together in an old farmhouse, but more and more, Andrea would persuade Bryan to go with her along on various junkets. She had never before had a deep sexual relationship except with Alan and after eleven years of marriage was totally absorbed by the novelty of her relationship with Bryan.

When Bryan and Andrea walked in after spending a weekend camping together, they found their spouses waiting. Alan seemed on the verge of exploding as he paced in tight ovals in front of the fireplace; Beth sat on the arm of an overstuffed chair, smoking nervously.

"You look like a caged tiger," Bryan said, addressing Alan. "What's up?"

"Nothing's up, that's just it. You guys were supposed to be back from your cavort with Mother Nature an hour and a half ago so we could all take the kids into town," Alan answered angrily, but he was interrupted by Beth.

"Listen, what about me? Nobody seems to be interested in what *I* feel, you just walk past me and start up with Alan. Look, I think we all ought to sit down and have a big talk. There are a lot of things that people aren't talking about." ("Like what?" Andrea asked as Beth went on oblivious-

---

[3]For more on such problem-solving techniques see Constantine & Constantine 1973; Thomas Gordon, *Parent Effectiveness Training,* an excellent guide to no-lose relationships of many kinds; and George Bach and Peter Wyden, *The Intimate Enemy.*

[4]The following illustration is reprinted with the permission of Macmillan Publishing Company, Inc. from *Group Marriage* by Larry L. and Joan M. Constantine. Copyright © 1973 by Larry L. Constantine and Joan M. Constantine.

ly.) "Andrea, why don't you put on some coffee while the boys move the chairs out to the porch. I want you all to start facing the issue. I think. . . ."

"Wait!" Alan interrupted, "Just what *is* the issue? No, wait, don't answer. Something strikes me funny, Beth. What are you doing?"

"Putting out my cigarette."

"No, before that, I mean. Weren't you doing just what you did when the neighbors dropped in last Thursday, talking like an express train and choreographing everyone and everything?" Alan paused and glanced at Bryan. "She does that when she's nervous, doesn't she?"

"Look, ask her. She's right here."

Andrea intervened and addressed Beth. "You look pretty nervous and uptight, Beth."

"Yeh, well I guess I am. Wouldn't you be? I mean, after all, I tell Bryan to get home by six and I depend on him to do things and he doesn't seem to care about what *I* want and. . . ."

"You're acting pretty jealous if you ask me," Bryan put in as he lit his pipe.

"Cool and collected as usual, ready with the labels," Beth sneered.

Andrea raised both hands above her head in a gesture of attention. "Hey, you guys!" she exclaimed. "Look, Beth, both you and Alan are acting pretty jealous. That ought to be a clue for us. Something *is* going on. What is it? What are you feeling? Like Alan said, you're behaving the same way you did with the snoopy neighbors. What do you feel?"

Beth smiled. "Give me a chance and maybe I can tell you." She paused and put a hand on Andrea's arm, making it clear she was not mad. "I feel—well, I feel like nothing's happening the way I plan it. Everything is getting away from me. I'm angry at Bryan. And I'm angry at you because Bryan wasn't supposed to respond to you this way. You two are running amuck and I don't know where it's going to lead."

"Maybe you're afraid you might lose Bryan," Alan put in.

Bryan walked over to Beth. "Is that it? Do you think I'll leave you for Andrea?" She didn't answer but frowned slightly. He went on, "You keep talking about not being able to depend on me, about me not doing what you want, stuff like that. What's that sound like to you?"

"Control stuff. Sounds like I'm losing control over you. Or afraid I will. But," the calm certainty in her voice changed again to nervous tension, "what about Alan? He's not losing control over Andrea. What's his issue?"

Alan snorted. "Never had control." He sat down, looked puzzled for half a minute and then began hesitantly, "I can't quite put my finger on it.

I get this uncomfortable, angry knot in my stomach at some times but not others.''

"Do you remember other times when you felt jealous about someone Andrea was into?'' Beth prompted.

"Well, not some*one,* some*thing.* Remember,'' he asked Andrea, "when you first got into yoga? It was yoga this, yoga that. Exercises for an hour and a half before bed, yoga classes three times a week, all day Saturday reading a book on yoga. I hardly even saw you. It's the same now.''

"You mean, honey, you're not seeing enough of me?''

"Right, I just don't have any time with you. It was okay as long as the four of us would spend time together and I would at least sleep with you every few nights, but now you two are always off by yourselves. I don't care so much what you and Bryan do together, but I want some of you, too. Funny, that goes for you, too, Bryan. We haven't talked or worked on the boat in two weeks. . . .''

This group is well on its way to improving their situation for all concerned. They will be working on the control issue for a long time and they will again find themselves with problems in distributing time, but they are well past the level of labeling behavior and the alienation which that brings about.

Though what we have presented is somewhat compressed, the interaction among Bryan, Andrea, Beth and Alan is representative of what we have seen emerging from the more highly functional multilateral marriages. We see no reason why this technique cannot be applied in conventional dyadic relationships. The object is to remove the pejorative connotation from jealousy and view it as a *behavioral cue* signaling an opportunity for exploration into the nature of a relationship. Undertaken repetitively, the effect is not only to illuminate the fears and insecurities over immediate threats, whether objectively real or merely perceived, but to build security and confidence in the ability of the relationship to cope with threat.

Bob and Margaret Blood have been offering jealousy workshops since 1974. Like Larry Constantine, they do not label jealous feelings "good" or "bad." They seek to meet workshop participants where they are and to help them achieve goals they have set for themselves. The Bloods' clients are a bit more diversified in age than Constantine's—and somewhat more conventional in their values and needs.

19

Jealousy Workshops

Robert and Margaret Blood

For several years we have used this flyer to recruit participants for experiential weekend workshops on jealousy:

> With the increasing openness of on-going partnerships to outside friendships, more of us more often have occasion to feel jealous about our partner's relationships with others. We feel hurt, threatened and inadequate within ourselves, angry and judgmental toward our "unfaithful" partner and toward the "other wo/man," and perhaps guilty for feeling so jealous.
>
> These powerful feelings create problems for all the partners involved and for the relationships which we would like to preserve and develop. The search for an acceptance of each other's reality and for a way not only to cope but to grow requires communication and negotiation.
>
> In this workshop we will use techniques from art therapy for portraying the "green-eyed monster," Gestalt therapy for working with our ambivalences, role-playing and psychodrama to re-enact and renegotiate the jealousy-pro-

Robert O. Blood, Ph.D., (1921-   ) and Margaret C. Blood, M.A., (1918-   ) are marriage counselors and workshop facilitators in private practice in Ann Arbor, Michigan. Bob, former associate professor of sociology at the University of Michigan, is the author of *The Family* (New York: Free Press, 1972), *Marriage* (New York: Free Press, 2nd ed., 1969), and *Husbands and Wives: The Dynamics of Family Living* (New York: Free Press, 1960). Bob and Margaret were married in 1944 and have four sons. This paper was written especially for this volume.

voking situation we are experiencing. This workshop should prove especially useful to couples and triangles who wish to deal jointly with this issue in their relationships. However, it is also open to individuals who may work with simulated partners and third parties drawn from the group. The group will be limited to ten persons.

THE PARTICIPANTS

Those who come to a jealousy workshop face a common problem. They are involved in triangular relationships which have provoked jealousy in at least one of the three persons.

The cast of characters in a triangle includes a man and woman in an ongoing primary relationship which is both sexual and affectional. They may be married to one another, living together unmarried, or simply going together. In any case they want to maintain their relationship because it has primary importance to them. The third party to the triangle is an "other wo/man" with whom one partner to the couple has a relationship of sufficient intimacy (whether sexual or affectional or both) to provoke a jealous reaction in his/her partner.

Typically the jealous person is not actively involved outside the pair-bond, so we call that person the "inactive partner" in contrast with the "active partner" who is relating to the other wo/man. Occasional couples come where each partner has outside relationships which the other partner feels threaten the primary relationship. But the symmetry of bilateral external involvement seems to be easier for most couples to live with than the asymmetry of a situation where only one partner is externally involved.

Our typical inactive partner is not only inactive in practice but has no desire to become active. Moreover, most of our inactive participants believe in sexual and affectional exclusivity as a moral principle, and are not only jealous of the active partner but judgmental as well. Some inactive partners believe intellectually in sexual/affectional freedom but find themselves reacting jealously nevertheless. In these cases, the judgmental feelings are turned against the self so that such persons carry a double burden of feeling jealous and feeling guilty about feeling jealous.

Most participants come to our workshops as primary couples, fairly evenly divided between married couples and unmarried couples. Many of the unmarried couples have such unstable relationships that their outside involvements are highly threatening. A considerable number of inactive persons come alone without their partner. A few secondary couples come (an active partner with his/her other wo/man) and even fewer whole triangles come together. Our experience shows that participants benefit most from a workshop when they come as primary couples or as whole triangles, since they can then interact and negotiate directly with one another.

THE PROGRAM: TRIANGULAR INTERACTION

1. The workshop begins with each primary couple in turn facing one another and each partner in turn stating without interruption or response his/her feelings toward the primary partner. Persons who come alone to the workshop choose someone from the group to fill in for the absent partner in such exercises. These simulated partners merely listen to the "real" person's statements, since they have no basis for responding knowledgeably. This exercise updates the partners' knowledge of where they stand with each other and reveals the strength or weakness of the core relationship.

2. Next, we form real or simulated triangles for similar baseline statements. The active partner tells his external friend how s/he feels about him/her, the inactive partner follows suits, and finally the "other wo/man" speaks to each of them about his/her feelings. As usual, only the actual role incumbents participate vocally in this exercise; the simulated incumbents merely sit in to lend reality to the situation.

3. Each "actual" person in each of these triangles "sculptures" the relationship as s/he sees it. The sculptor first places each of the other two persons in appropriate postures and then adds his/her own body to make a composite three-person portrayal of the total relationship. The sculptor then transforms this into a dynamic sculpture. For example, the active partner may move back and forth between his/her primary partner and the secondary partner. After the movement has come to a natural completion, the sculptor tells the persons he has sculpted what s/he intended by his/her portrayal, and they in turn share what it felt like to experience those positions.

4. Each member of the workshop is asked to draw a colored picture of his/her own jealousy (or, if s/he feels no personal jealousy, to portray the partner's jealousy and its effect upon him/her). Some drawings depict the conventional green-eyed monster. Others show a thundercloud with bolts of lightning, an erupting volcano, or a lovely wood full of hidden land mines. Each drawing is snown to the group with an explanation by the artist or the feeling s/he intended to convey. Using Gestalt techniques, we

ask the artist to "become" and speak from the vantage point of the objects and colors in the picture. Then we tape the pictures up on the livingroom wall and live with them for the rest of the weekend.

5. Each couple or individual is asked to decide on their highest priority issue to be worked on. This agenda item is stated to the real or simulated partner, explored until it is fully understood, and negotiated toward an agreement which will reduce the strain on the relationship. Where both partners to a relationship are present, this dialogue takes place directly between them, facilitated by the workshop leaders. Where only one partner is present, the simulated partner is first addressed by the "real" person; but then the latter exchanges places with the simulated partner so that s/he may experience and speak from the other person's vantage point. Negotiation in simulated pairs is less effective than between real partners, but nevertheless it gives the workshop member a chance to rehearse what s/he may wish to say to the real partner upon returning home.

6. Each real or simulated triangle dances a three-person creative dance to recorded music of their choice while the other members of the workshop watch. The music often has a jealousy theme. The dance provides an opportunity to express the dynamics of the triangle more extensively than in the moving sculpture, and it also gives the three persons a taste of the greater richness of movement possibilities among three persons in comparison to the conventional two.

7. Each real couple choose a third party to form a three-person group for massage. These three negotiate among themselves the kind of massages they feel comfortable giving and receiving. The diversity of behavior in this structure reflects a climate within which no one is pressured to do anything s/he does not wish to do, and, conversely, everyone is free to express his/her own wishes. Each person in each triangle is massaged simultaneously by the other two in turn. The next morning around the breakfast table, the members of the workshop share what it felt like to negotiate a level of massage which felt comfortable to each of the participants, to receive from more than one person at a time, and to join with a partner in giving to a third person.

8. Each member tells the groups what s/he has gained from the weekend and what s/he intends to do on returning home.

9. By the end of the workshop everyone feels sympathetic and supportive of one another, even though they may come out in different places in how they deal with the jealousy issue. One-to-one farewells between all individuals allow for expression of this caring feedback.

WORKSHOP OUTCOMES

Our goals are not to impose any particular outcome on the participants, but to enable them to focus their attention on the jealousy issue so that they may move beyond the impasse which so often motivates attendance at the workshop. That movement may be a change in attitudes, a new agreement on ground rules between the partners, or a shift in focus away from the triangular problem to problems in the core relationship. Changes may involve a lessening of jealousy or a recognition of its strength, an acceptance of a more open relationship, or a decision to reduce its openness. It may involve deciding to strengthen the primary relationship, or deciding to abandon it in favor of the secondary relationship, or deciding to terminate the relationship.

A common outcome is the discovery that the primary relationship is too weak to stand the strain of outside involvements. The main problem of one young couple was that the woman wanted the man to move in with her but he was unwilling to do so until she got rid of her cats to which he was allergic. His external involvements sank into the background in the face of this disagreement. A married couple with two small children discovered that their marriage was too weak to provide a secure place for both partners' external involvements. They decided to focus their attention internally by going into marriage counseling.

Negotiations between partners have led to a wide variety of outcomes. One middle-aged woman asked her husband to inform her in advance when he was going to spend the night with another woman so that she would not worry over his unexpected absence and would know where she could reach him in an emergency. A young woman secured an agreement from her partner that he would not spend the whole night with any other woman but would limit himself to early evening dates. A middle-aged woman secured a commitment from her husband that he would not have sexual intercourse with anyone else during the coming year because she had too been too upset by his outside sexual activity. Many couples have negotiated about how open they wish to be in reporting to one another about their outside experiences—wishing as often to hear nothing as to hear everything. And couples decide similarly how discreet they wish to be in letting others know about their external involvements.

For inactive individuals who come alone to a workshop, a frequent outcome has been a reduction in the asymmetry of the jealousy situation. This may take the form either of decreased jealousy on the part of the workshop participant or of increased jealousy on the part of the active partner who did not attend. One professional man had never experienced massage before, and he determined to take it home to his marriage. He also became less judgmental of his wife's friendships because of the warmth he had experienced in the workshop, and he hoped to free himself up to relate more warmly to his own friends.

A young mother who came to a workshop to deal with her resentment of her husband's desire for sexual relationships with other women telephoned him before the Saturday evening massage to find out how he felt about her participation. She discovered, to her surprise, that he was intensely jealous and did not want her to participate in that exercise. From that point on, their marriage involved bilateral instead of unilateral jealousy. They subsequently experimented with separate-but-equal outside experiences, and still later moved into marriage counseling to deal with their complex feelings about this issue.

A graduate student who had always been the outside man and never a primary partner experienced a major breakthrough as he came to feel that he could enjoy being a secondary partner for what it was worth. Previously he had always broken off his friendships as soon as he discovered his subordinate status. Now he felt that he could allow those relationships to continue and could savor whatever "goodies" came his way.

For a two-man, one-woman triangle, the outcome of the jealousy workship was to confirm the unproblematic nature of their relationships. Husband and wife reaffirmed their primary commitment to one another. The husband and the other man expressed their caring and friendship for each other. All three enjoyed their triangular dancing and massage. And the other man chose to work not on his relationship to this couple but on the jealousy he was experiencing toward a new woman friend as a result of her involvement with other men. This triangle's mutual comfortableness and their lack of internal jealousy demonstrates the wide range of responses to the issue of triangular relationships.

THE USES OF JEALOUSY WORKSHOPS

Structured exercises and professional facilitation create a space for working on painful feelings which are difficult for a couple to deal with on their own. The leaders, the group, and the structures provide a safe environment and a discipline that keeps both partners in touch with each other, avoiding the temptation to run away when the going gets rough.

Participants learn not only by working actively on their own problems but by observing the interaction of others. A jealousy workshop brings together people who are facing similar problems. Other persons express feelings similar to mine and similar to my partner's. It is easier to hear those thoughts expressed by new voices than when they are expressed by the partner with whom I am struggling. I gain perspective on myself as I observe the dialogue of others and the solutions they arrive at. The diversity of feelings and behaviors in the group helps each of us pay attention to our own selves and search for solutions which are uniquely right for us.

By dealing with our troubles openly in the group, we "come out of the closet" with what has felt like a shameful aspect of our lives. By reducing our feelings of shame and guilt, we may more easily confront the realities of our separate life journeys.

Through the workshop experience, we realize that we are not unique, weird, or crazy—but that our feelings are very human. Both the naturalness of attraction to more than one person and the naturalness of jealous feelings are dramatized by the diversity within the group and by the diversity between the two leaders of the workshop.

Most participants come to a workshop in a polarized position, defining themselves as purely jealous or as unambivalently eager for external involvement. During the workshop, the other side of each person's feelings is given attention. A jealous woman, for example, may come to appreciate the value that her husband's relationship to another woman has not only for him but the value that it may have for her as well as she comes to see the other woman as a sister instead of merely as a competitor. An active partner may become more aware of the costs that his/her external involvement has for the partner and therefore come to recognize the need to balance outside activity with a greater investment of time and energy in the primary relationship.

People often hope that the outcome of a workshop will be the complete evaporation of the inactive partner's jealousy or the complete cessation of the active partner's external involvement. Such a total about-face rarely happens. More often, both partners see that they must find some kind of middle ground between their opposing positions. Both partners tend to become less judgmental of the other's unfaithfulness or possessiveness. Both come to see that they cannot expect to control the other's behavior and attitudes entirely to their own satisfaction, but that they must search for give-and-take compromise positions. Such negotations are not painless, because neither partner gets all of what s/he wants. Reality is painful, but secrecy may be even more so as the imagination of the inactive partner runs wild, fantasizing situations remote from reality.

Some couples decide that they have been too protective of one another, holding back from dealing openly with their needs and wants for fear of hurting or blocking the other. They may decide to put more energy into struggling with the reality of their differing value systems and less into blaming and trying to control or manipulate the other. Being forced to listen to one another and to get into one another's shoes as they work together frequently reveals fantasies and fears about the other's feelings not based in reality. The hassles over this issue, the blaming, and the hurt have broken down communication and the expression of tenderness.

The confirmation of the primary partner which occurs during the workshop may lead to a realization that confirmation has been a missing ingredient in their life back home. They may decide to focus more attention on the good things they have together and on expressing their caring for one another. One couple decided that their marriage was 95% rewarding and only 5% stressful around the jealousy issue, thereby gaining perspective on the overwhelmingly solid quality of their primary relationship. The jealousy issue may be the toughest problem any couple has to face, but it yields as couples become more aware of better processes of interacting. Willingness to listen to the other's feelings, willingness to represent oneself and ask for what one wants, and willingness to deal with the reality of the present rather than the hurts of the past or fears of the future—such commitments allow couples to move forward out of their impasses.

Once couples begin to move, they can more easily arrive at ground rules for their own relationship and for their outside relationships. Since every individual is different, every couple will have different ground rules. Other people's agreements may look attractive but may not fit; so undue pressure must not be put on one partner to accept rules discovered in books, in groups, or in peer relationships.

Negotiating ground rules is the hardest task of all—and the most rewarding. Most couples experience a sense of relief from their despair when they are able to agree on anything at all in this troublesome area. Sometimes the relief lasts a long time. Sometimes the agreements themselves have to be renegotiated as one partner or both find themselves moving into new places. Each ground rule represents a mini-contract which is subject to revision when it no longer describes the position of either partner. A rule is a way of saying what each of us wants in this present moment, and where we can unite to bring this about.

Confronting the disagreements between partners is easier if the workshop is led by persons who have a primary relationship to one another and are faced with similar issues of involvement and jealousy. If their primary relationship is weak, this is threatening to the workshop participants, and the workshop material in turn is threatening to the leaders themselves. If they have resolved their problems too blithely, they may leave either the active or the inactive partners in other couples feeling unsupported.

In between these extremes, if jealousy is a live issue but under reasonable control for the facilitators, they can participate in the workshop in ways which give the other participants a feeling of personal support and a model of successful negotiation. They can do this both by demonstrating the various workshop exercises using material from their own current experience, and by participating comfortably in the work of the other workshop members, doubling for them (speaking over their shoulders) when they become tongue-tied, and helping them to articulate latent solutions to difficult dilemmas.

Jealousy workshops thus provide a place where people who are suffering from internal and interpersonal conflict over their negative reactions to a partner's external affectional/sexual involvement can deal squarely with the whole range of feelings and issues involved in living on the margin between closed and open relationships.

Synthesis:
Jealousy and Intimate
Partnership Today

In the last weeks of our work on this book, two acquaintances, neither of whom knew we were doing a book on jealousy, told us about recent experiences pertinent to the topic. Tina, a woman in her late thirties, told us she was in the process of divorcing her second husband because he did not allow her enough freedom. She would not remarry, she said, unless she could find a man who was willing to try an open marriage. "What about jealousy?" we asked. She replied: "Everybody *feels* jealous from time to time but no one need allow themselves to be *taken over* by it. Jealousy can be managed. I can handle mine and I'm looking for a man who can handle his."

Two days later, as if in answer to Tina's confident view of the matter, Nick (a divorced man in his forties) dropped by and shared this story. He had returned at the end of an evening out to the apartment of his date, a woman who had been divorced for two years. Suddenly the woman's ex-husband burst *through* a plate-glass door brandishing a straight razor. He attacked and wounded both of them. It took three peace officers and a quick-thinking neighbor to subdue the enraged ex-husband. Uncontrolled jealousy almost cost several people their lives.

These two vignettes, taken together, show us the extremes of the jealousy spectrum. Tina feels that she is ready for an open relationship and that jealousy, although it may appear, will not be able to undermine her relationships or erode her self-esteem. Nick believes that jealousy is deep within each of us, a blind instinct ready to express itself in homicidal and suicidal behavior. And they are both right.

The experience of jealousy varies enormously from age to age, from culture to culture, from couple to couple, from person to person, and within a person over time. Indeed, the "nature" of jealousy seems to have changed for large numbers of people in the United States within the conscious memory of everyone born before about 1950. Media analysis suggests that for a substantial proportion of the American middle-class (and above), especially in the young adult age group, a change of attitude toward jealousy took place in the late 1960s and early 1970s. "Normal" jealousy, which had been seen as an inevitable accompaniment of love and therefore as a support for marriage, came to be seen by some as evidence of personal insecurity and weakness in the relationship—and therefore as a threat to successful intimate partnership.

Jealousy is a malleable emotion; it comes in so many forms that people have difficulty talking about it—like the several witnesses to a robbery who cannot agree on a description of the thief. And because jealousy can be squeezed into many different shapes, it is subject to a variety of uses and abuses.

PROTECTION, COMMUNICATION, CONTROL:
USES OF JEALOUSY

One very basic and quite legitimate function of jealousy is to alert us to threats to our personal security and to the well-being of an important relationship. The jealous flash is the cognitive and psychological equivalent of the physiological system of skin receptors and nerves which protects us from bodily harm. Physical pain warns us that the security of the organism is being threatened by some physical object or force. Psychological pain (such as jealousy) warns us that our psychic security is being threatened, that a relationship upon which we depend requires attention. We ignore physical pain at our own peril; the same is true of psychological pain. The pain of jealousy is a herald; it comes to warn us that greater pain may be in store unless we attend to the relationship.

The experience of jealousy can also facilitate catharsis, the cleansing, purifying release which can reduce anxiety. To admit that one feels jealous, to acknowledge that jealousy, to experience it fully within oneself may serve to reduce distress and make destructive *expressions* of jealousy unnecessary.

Jealousy is also subject to a variety of *symbolic* uses. Expressions of jealousy—verbal and nonverbal—are a means of communicating with others. When you say, "That makes me jealous" (or when you behave in such a way as to move others to ask, "Are you jealous?"), you are employing a set of symbols, given to you by society, to express important concerns.

The language and gestures of jealousy can be employed in a variety of ways. A jealous outburst may simply be a cry for attention, a way of saying, "I am hurting! Notice me!" If no constructive use is made of such a declaration, the expressions of jealousy may become part of a masochistic pattern in which the jealous person broods over the partner's infidelities (real or imagined), demands detailed accounts of the partner's experiences with others, wallows in depression and self-pity, and seeks the sympathy of anyone who will listen to the tale of woe. This pattern is not without its hidden payoffs: It may generate feelings of self-righteousness and legitimize the decision to avoid the hard work (on oneself and on the relationship) which might reduce the jealousy. The jealous outburst can also serve as a vehicle for sadism. Jealousy gives one the right to be cruel; it seems to legitimize retaliation. Jealousy can be used to justify withdrawal from the partner or to drive an unloved partner away.

A common use of jealousy is the attempt to control the behavior of the partner and/or the third party. The message implicit in the expression of jealousy is this: "Stop what you are doing or I shall be even more miserable." This may be accompanied by threats of retaliation and/or flight.

The Beechers (1971:16), following Adler, see jealousy as rooted in feelings of inferiority, and jealous behavior as a strategy to achieve power. Typically, this strategy either fails outright *or*, if "successful," produces resentment in the manipulated partner.

The attempt to control is often accompanied by an appeal to *duty:* "You *owe* it to me to stop seeing him/her." But this ploy is of limited usefulness. As Bertrand Russell (in Bohm 1967:574) has written:

> In former days parents ruined their relations with their children by preaching love as a duty; husbands and wives still too often ruin their relations to each other by the same mistake. Love cannot be a duty, because it is not subject to the will.

Masochistic, sadistic, and manipulative uses of jealousy are often unconscious (hidden from oneself) and/or veiled (hidden from others). They may be discovered by means of honest exploration within the couple, in candid conversation with a good friend, or in jealousy workshops. In some cases, intensive psychotherapy may be required to uncover these unconscious strategies and their hidden payoffs.

Jealousy can also mark the beginning of constructive dialogue. The expression of jealousy can trigger communication which leads to clarification of needs, meanings, beliefs, and values. Such talking-through may lead to negotiations whereby the pain of jealousy is reduced and the relationship is strengthened.

Of course, "working on our jealousy" can be the occasion for more unconstructive conflict and another means by which the partners may attempt to manipulate and blame each other. Example: "Melissa, we won't be able to get *any*where with our jealousy problems until *you* do something about your low self-esteem and your fear of true intimacy and . . ." When negotiations deteriorate into name-calling, it is time to either draw back or seek outside help.

One further caution is appropriate here. The *meanings* of jealous feelings, expressions, and behaviors are not self-evident; neither are they constant from person to person or over time. Insofar as jealousy is symbolic, it is dependent upon the *inter-pretations* given to it by real people in specific situations. For this reason, explorations of jealousy and attempts to negotiate around it must proceed slowly and carefully, with each person being allowed to express him/herself fully. The tyranny of a frown or an interruption, an abuse of one's ability to analyze or articulate, can derail the best intentions. Constructive negotiations must involve listening as well as talking.

NATURE AND NURTURE: ELEMENTS OF JEALOUSY

Working constructively with jealousy begins with an adequate *understanding* of the emotion. That is why we placed consideration of the psychological mechanisms and the social patternings of jealousy *between* sections dealing with the experience and the management of jealousy.

Jealousy is a complex phenomenon; it resists every attempt to map its boundaries or chart its course. Every simplification in the service of explanation does violence to the complexity, but without such reduction we remain confused. Let us, therefore, seek to understand jealousy as having three principal elements: the physiological, the developmental, and the social.

THE PHYSIOLOGICAL ELEMENT: THE JEALOUSY FLASH

Jealousy is, at its root, an instinctoid[1] reaction to certain types of threats. In humans, as in other animals, self-protection appears to be instinctive. This is obvious in the case of the protection of the *physical* self: If we fall, we grab for support, if we are punched, we hit back or run away or cover our heads. Note well: The self-protective impulse does not tell us *how* to protect ourselves. We choose to fight, to flee, or to cover up on the basis of personal idiosyncrasies and social definitions. But we are apparently programmed to do *something* other than stand there and absorb a beating.

Similarly, our readiness to protect the *psychological* self would appear to be virtually instinctive. Again, it is self-perception and social definitions which tell us *when* to feel threatened and *how* to respond. But the psyche's general readiness to avoid pain is apparently quite "natural."

[1]We prefer the term instinc*toid* rather than instinc*tive* as a way of reminding ourselves that although humans are subject to physiological drives that are hereditary, "the choice of object and the choice of behavior must be acquired or learned in the course of the life history" (Maslow 1970:27). This is in contrast to other animals whose instinctive behaviors appear to be much more narrowly "scripted" by nature.

Jealousy may or may not be physiologically distinct from other emotions. The authors of Chapter 8 suggest that the "jealous" flash may be a very general state of physiological arousal which requires specification by means of experience and learning before we label it jealousy. Put differently: Perhaps "jealousy" is what we have been taught to call emotional upset experienced in connection with a (real or imagined) threat to our security in an important relationship. The emotional upset (although dependent upon learning and social conventions) is, at root, physiological and instinctive.

To acknowledge that jealousy has a physiological element is not to conclude that we are *determined* by our nature rather than our nurture. The instinctive dimension is but *part* of the jealousy we feel and observe. The conditions under which one feels the jealous flash and the ways in which it is expressed are profoundly influenced by personal experiences and by the norms and values of the larger society. Jealousy is *both* instinctive *and* social. As Gottschalk (in Bohm 1967:571) puts it:

> Jealousy is a natural, original, instinctive, sexual reaction which nevertheless is capable simultaneously of adapting itself to a large extent to the needs of society and of changing with them.

THE DEVELOPMENTAL ELEMENT: LEARNING TO SHARE

The general biological propensity toward jealousy is further elaborated by certain early experiences common to us all. As infants, each of us had to learn to "let go" of the mother, to share this most important love-object with the father and (typically) with siblings. We learned that henceforth we would be denied full control over and total access to those on whom we depend. These experiences were more traumatic for some of us than for others, but we *all* learned crucial lessons about jealousy in the first few months of our lives.

The key distinction between the developmental element and the social element (which follows) is this: The developmental element is what is common to us all—especially the dependency of infancy and the gradual accomodation to the loss of control of the mother. Even as the infant passes through the stages of this universal process, s/he is already beginning to *learn* about jealousy. This social learning is variable from culture to culture and from family to family. In childhood, the developmental and social elements are *both* being acquired. The two overlap and intertwine, but they are conceptually distinct. In order to understand jealousy, we must look at *both* the early experiences of dependency, loss, and adjustment that are common to us all *and* the social learning of jealousy which begins early but varies somewhat from person to person.

In a literal sense, this developmental element is part of "nurture"; it is not inborn. But it is *necessary* because of the *nature* of the human organism. Each of us was born *very dependent* upon the mother. Each of us learned to modify that dependency, to adjust to the loss of oneness with and apparent control over that most significant other. Those experiences are part of who we are.

THE SOCIAL ELEMENT: GROWING UP JEALOUS

From infancy onward, each of us *learned* about jealousy from those around us, from what we heard and saw, and from our own experiences (as interpreted through what we had learned to date). Most of this learning was informal, unstructured, and quite subtle. Gradually we acquired some beliefs, some expectations about jealousy. Each of us built up an *understanding* of jealousy which we utilize each time jealousy pops up. New experiences may change this "picture" of jealousy you carry In your head; then a "revised version" of the picture will be there to guide you the *next* time jealousy is an issue.

The process by which we learn when to be jealous, how to express jealousy, and how to react to jealousy is life-long and continuous. While no stage of the process can be shown to be wholly determinative of the propensity toward jealousy, certain steps appear to be important.

Your parents' handling of your coming to terms as an infant with the "loss" of the mother gave you your first template by which to gauge future jealousies. If you felt loved and approved of despite your "abandonment," you may have a relatively low propensity for jealousy. If you were punished for your clutching and crying out, you may have learned to repress a great deal of jealousy (and other affect). If your parents truly rejected you—beyond the necessary separating out—you may be anxious, insecure, and more susceptible to jealousy.[2]

The parents' handling of sibling rivalry contributes substantially to a person's understanding of jealousy. If you always felt that Mom liked your brother best, you may be prone to jealousy. If

---

[2] These examples are greatly simplified. In fact, the relationship between literal experience and an individual's internalized version of it is very complex and cannot be charted with precision.

your parents (and others) commented often on your sister's beauty and kidded you about your freckles, you may worry that you are not attractive and fear that your partner will leave you because of it. Even small put-downs and jests can have a devastating effect on the child or adolescent growing up in a society in which there is so much competition, comparison, and ranking.

Surely adolescence is important in the formation of one's understanding of jealousy. First experiences of sexual interest, of competition, of love, of loss, and of recovery contribute to the young person's sense of what jealousy is and how s/he must deal with it. Meanwhile, the adolescent has begun to read more widely and to view films with "adult" themes (which seems to mean: more sex, more violence, and, not incidentally, more jealousy). From these disparate bits of input, the young person forms a picture of jealousy.

For the increasing number of persons who do not marry early, young adulthood may be a time of several important love affairs, each of which may modify a person's understanding of and susceptibility to jealousy. An important relationship, whether or not it leads to marriage, introduces a new concern. Now you must learn about your *lover's* experiences, feelings, and values with regard to sexuality, fidelity, and jealousy. This is an exciting aspect of a developing relationship. Candor and trust at this point can help the partners construct a shared understanding of concerns pertinent to jealousy. If one partner imposes a set of definitions on the other or if (as is more often the case) the partners simply *assume* that they see eye-to-eye on these matters, disruptive experiences of jealousy are more likely.

Experiences of romantic love in adolescence and young adulthood re-create the near-total fascination with and dependency upon one other person which we experienced as infants. Once again, we must learn to share a most significant other with his/her other friends and interests.

In a relatively static society with low mobility and few channels of communication, "adulthood" would be a stage of life marked by little change in one's beliefs and values—especially with regard to something as basic to the personality as jealousy. But in a changing society with high mobility and elaborate, overlapping communications systems, a person might change significantly over the course of his/her adulthood. It is not unusual for adults in our culture to change careers, to convert to new religions and worldviews (or merely to abandon old ones), to adopt new political philosophies, and to experiment with new life-style options (see Lifton 1969:311f.). Adulthood is no longer a single stage in the life-cycle; it is a *sequence* of stages and phases (see Sheehy 1976) through which understandings of sex, love, fidelity, and jealousy may vary considerably.

You (and your partner) are constantly being influenced by the people around you and by the people you "meet" on television, at the movies, in books, magazines, and newspapers. New input can further alter your understanding of jealousy and/or disrupt the congruence which you and your partner once enjoyed.

To point out that jealousy is learned, and to note that it varies from culture to culture, is not to suggest that its power in a *specific* culture is thereby undone. The demands of society are external to us, but they are very powerful. A man may wish to forgive his wife's adultery, but he knows his friends will not respect him unless he beats her up. A woman may be tolerant of her husband's flirtations and then have to endure the pity of friends who would be scandalized if *their* husbands behaved similarly. A person may wish to express jealous anger but be inhibited by the expectation of disapproval from a circle of "liberated" friends.

Furthermore, societal demands are not only "out there," they are also *inside* us. We have internalized the beliefs and values of the persons and institutions around us—some consciously, some unconsciously. We cannot overturn a lifetime of learning in a minute. Sometimes our difficulty in adopting new (and seemingly desirable) attitudes is a function of deeply rooted beliefs of which we are scarcely aware.

Jealousy, then, is a complex mixture of the physiological, the developmental. and the social. It reflects a basic organismic potential which is given specificity by life-experience in a particular culture and which is energized by particular provocations.

Your jealousy, to put it simply, is a part of *you*. To reject it—to repress, deny, or condemn it—is to reject part of yourself. To look closely at your jealousy is to look closely at yourself: at your biological organism (and its needs and limits); at your life-experience so far; at everything you have learned about sex, love, marriage and the family, about good and evil, right and wrong; at the norms values of the groups within which you have lived, worked, and played; at the ethos of the whole society and the current shape of your love/hate relationship with it.

You cannot detach your jealousy from yourself and work on it objectively any more than you can do so with your arm, your heart, or your brain. To seek to understand your jealousy is to seek to *know yourself*. To seek to manage your jealousy is to seek a measure of self-control or self-mastery. Such quests are not to be undertaken lightly.

TAKING STOCK: TYPES OF JEALOUSY

The deeper understanding and the management of jealousy require an appreciation of the specific types of jealousy and of the contextual factors which amplify or mute the jealous flash. The "sorting" of jealous feelings might well begin with this question: *Does a particular experience of jealousy come from feeling excluded or from a fear of loss?* The distinction is important; it is the difference between a small problem and a large one, between the benign and the malignant.

FEELING EXCLUDED

Probably *most* jealous flashes come from feeling *left out* of an activity involving your partner and another (or others). When your partner "attends" (in whatever way) to another, his/her attention is elsewhere. When you notice that, before you process the implications or possible consequences, your first reaction is to note that they are "in," and you are "out." They are not noticing you—or, at least, not giving you as much attention as they are giving each other. You feel excluded, ignored, unappreciated. Perhaps you wish *you* could do what they are doing (whatever it is), but for reasons you don't quite understand, you can't.

This kind of experience is commonplace in our society, and dealing with it gracefully is part of the etiquette of our time—especially as women become more involved in occupational and social activities outside the home. The boss wants to dance with your wife. A woman takes more initiative in conversation with your husband than you would with a man you had just met. Your partner and a friend both discover that they *adore* Bergman's films (which you never particularly enjoyed). And so on. Such experiences trigger the jealous flash, but, typically, they do not fan it into a flame. The jealous feelings usually fade when the precipitating event is over—although one might still need to say, on the way home, "I cannot *imagine* what you and Pat could have found interesting enough to discuss for an hour."

If you find yourself troubled or upset by the "sharing" of your partner that is considered appropriate in your circle of friends, perhaps your "feeling excluded" is a symptom of an underlying fear of loss, the more serious "strain" of jealousy. If you literally cannot stand to let your partner out of your sight—and this is a condition observed among *both* the very conventional *and* some swingers—your jealousy is probably rooted in a persistent *fear* rather than in a temporary irritation.

Definitions of appropriate limits vary from one peer group to another, from one subculture to another. Behavior that is considered "friendly" in one circle may be viewed as "seductive" and "immoral" in another. What seems "proper" to my Uncle Calvin may seem "stuffy" or "cold" to Bob and Carol and Ted and Alice. We choose our values when we choose our neighbors, our workmates, our playmates, our helpmates.[3]

FEAR OF LOSS

If your jealous flash signals *more* than irritation at being temporarily excluded, it probably reflects a *fear of loss*. This is more serious, but it need not be fatal to your self-esteem or to your relationship with your partner. To treat it you must diagnose it more precisely. *Exactly what is it you are afraid you might lose*? There are several possibilities, some more serious than others.

Perhaps it is *loss of "face"* that frightens you. If your wife is vivacious in company, perhaps the guys you drink with will think you "can't keep her in line." If your husband is appreciative of attractive women, perhaps your friends will suspect that he's dissatisfied with you. If your mate is too friendly with a person of the opposite sex, perhaps others will assume that they are sexually involved. If you don't *like* the third party, if s/he seems "unworthy" of your mate's attention, the fear of loss of reputation can be especially powerful.

The fear of loss of face may be a minor problem or a major one, temporary or recurrent. It affects the way you feel about yourself and the way you present yourself to others. And these, in turn, influence your susceptibility to jealousy in the future.

But perhaps you fear *more* than loss of face; perhaps you fear that you are losing *control*—control of your spouse, control of the relationship, control of the future, control of your *self*. You cannot predict your partner's behavior. You are reluctant to voice complaints because you don't know how s/he will react. You are unsure of the motives of the third party. Your anxiety breeds tension which corrodes your relationship.

[3]Popular awareness of this variation is reflected in the bit of folk sociology which says that when two couples ride in one car, the seating arrangement will vary as follows: Working-class persons sit one couple in the front seat, the other in back. Middle-class couples regroup so that the men sit in front, the women in the back. The rich swap mates for the drive; each man sits next to the other's wife.

The fear of loss of control is rooted in insecurity and is a specific form of a neurosis that is quite general in our time. As we lose control of other sectors of our lives—or discover that we never really *had* control—we wish all the more to be secure in our intimate relationships and family life. If things are chaotic at work, if the crime rate is going up, if political life is a tragi-comedy with a cast of criminals and incompetents, it becomes all the more important to keep things together at home.

The most serious jealousy is the jealousy which is *fear of loss of the partner*—and of all the love and affection, support and services s/he provides. This can be a terrifying feeling. To *lose* your partner may be to lose your history, your identity, your means of support, your housekeeper, your home, your children (or someone to help you rear them), perhaps even your reason for living. Not surprisingly, you become anxious and defensive. You assume—although this is questionable—that if you lose him/her it will be to another woman/man, so you view others with suspicion and fear. Such behaviors make you less attractive to your mate, and, perhaps, less entitled to consideration from the point of view of the third party. Thus jealousy begets aloofness and scorn, which deepen the fear that is at the root of the jealousy.

CONTEXTUAL FACTORS

The jealousy you feel—no matter of what type—is shaped in part by certain background features. One of these is your mood. When you feel good about yourself, you are less likely to feel jealous. When you are depressed and dissatisfied with yourself, you are more susceptible to jealousy. When you feel secure in your relationship, jealousy is less apt to be a problem. When you are unhappy or unsure about the relationship, you will be more fearful.

Your feelings about the third party are important too. If you like him/her and consider him/her a "worthy" friend for your partner, their affectionate hugs may not bother you. If you dislike him/her, the same gesture may constitute an offense.

The amount of felt jealousy is not only person-specific; it is also *role*-specific. For example: Among those experimenting with postmonogamous life-styles, we have observed that a person's lover is more apt to be jealous of *another lover* than of the spouse. Jealousy arises when the *particular* relationship we have with another appears to be threatened.

Timing is important, too. If you feel you do not have enough time with your partner, you are more apt to feel jealous of his/her new interests. Friendships and activities which inconvenience the partner or disrupt agreed-upon routines are more apt to evoke jealousy than similar involvements which are thoughtfully planned.

STRATEGIES: WORKING WITH JEALOUSY

The actual steps you take to manage your jealousy will depend upon what you learn from taking stock (determining the *type* of jealousy you are feeling, noting the contribution of your mood, locating important contextual factors) *and* upon your own sense of the kind of work you want to do on your relationship. As we suggested in the Introduction to this volume, the active orientation takes several forms. Some couples wish to *enrich* their marriages without questioning traditional sex-role expectations and definitions of fidelity. Others seek to *remodel* marriage; they "renegotiate" roles and expectations in response to the women's movement, the human potential movement, and the popular self-help literature. Still others attempt to *revolutionize* their intimate partnerships. This may involve experimentation with consensual relationships (sexual and/or emotional) outside the pair bond.

Some nondefensive strategies for dealing with jealousy are useful in all types of intimate partnerships. Others may be suitable only for remodeling or revolutionizing relationships. You should employ only those strategies which are congenial with your history, your present relationship, and your realistic hopes for the future.

Each of the suggestions which follow builds upon the ones that come before; that is, the strategies are cumulative. The enrichment strategies are basic to *all* attempts to work with jealousy. The remodeling strategies facilitate the kind of renegotiations which are increasingly common in partnerships touched by the human potential movement and the women's movement. The final cluster of strategies will be of value only to those who wish to experiment with sexual and/or emotional involvements outside of the primary relationship.

MARRIAGE ENRICHMENT

If you are interested in enriching your relationship, in preserving its structure but improving its quality, begin with a close look at yourself. The clues to understanding jealousy are in you. (Your quickness to blame others is a psychic defense; try to penetrate it.)

Jealousy seems to be closely tied with how you feel about yourself. The first step in understanding *your* jealousy is to explore your own feelings.

- How do you feel when you feel jealous?
- How would you *like* to feel?
- Why are you choosing to deal with these feelings now?
- How do you feel about yourself in general? About your body? About sex?

Each experience of jealousy reminds a person of his/her incompleteness, of the tendency to depend on another for a wholeness which can only be achieved within. The reduction of jealousy is served by the development of personal wholeness.[4] If you see yourself as incomplete without your mate, if you cannot imagine living without him/her, you will be more susceptible to jealousy. Similarly, success in working with your jealousy will make you feel more autonomous, less dependent.

It is through developing a sense of his/her own value and personhood that the child moves beyond his dependency on the mother and thus learns to manage his jealousy of her. The same process must be repeated in the intimate partnerships of adulthood. The best antidote against recurrent jealousy is growth toward autonomy. Autonomy is not isolation nor is it aloofness; autonomy is self-direction, the ability to guide one's own life and to prosper outside of any particular relationship. This kind of personal strength can make a person more attractive to the partner (thus strengthening the relationship) *and* less susceptible to feelings of insecurity (thus reducing jealousy).

Sometimes experiences of jealousy can catalyze self-improvement and expressions of appreciation which strengthen an intimate partnership. Anxious competition exacerbates jealousy, but sometimes "little jealousies" can trigger the small escalation of affect that peps up a relationship and heightens the partners' appreciation of one another.

You may wish to go beyond self-analysis and self-improvement. Perhaps you can open up communication with your mate on issues having to do with jealousy. Talking is a form of contact, so it is often better than being silent and therefore out of touch. Talking is less disruptive than flight, less destructive than violence. Therefore, you ought to try to substitute talking for these less constructive behaviors.

[4] Maslow (1970:195) notes, in passing, an absence of jealousy in "self-actualizing persons."

You may wish to begin by talking about *past* experiences of jealousy; sometimes we can learn a great deal from a "replay" of an event which no longer carries high emotional valence. Discuss your expectations and hopes for the future. Be specific about what you expect from one another. What kinds of behaviors are O.K.? Which are taboo?

When experiences of jealousy come up, try talking about them. Use the jealous flash as a catalyst for learning about yourself and your relationship. Clarify boundaries so as to minimize jealousy in the future. Reaffirm your commitment to one another. Focus on the strengths of your relationship; you'll probably find that these greatly outweigh the bad feelings of the moment.

But perhaps not. You may discover that the "jealousy problem" is part of a larger pattern of distrust, deception, and manipulation which surfaces in many sectors of your life together. You may find out something you would rather not know; you may disrupt a symbiotic relationship which, despite its flaws, you do not want to lose. "Talking it through" serves to heighten awareness and diffuse power: You will learn things you did not know and you will be "more equal" as the less articulate, less powerful partner learns to express him/herself more effectively.

In your talking-through and in your interpretations of your mate's behavior afterward, remember that fantasies are not subject to the will. It is, therefore, counterproductive to demand that your mate promise not to *imagine* doing things s/he has promised not to do. Fantasies and dreams seem to have a "safety valve" effect, diffusing erotic energy which might otherwise seek a specific person as its object. "Innocent flirtations" (as defined by your personal history and social context) probably function in this same way. It is unrealistic and counterproductive to demand of one's mate the complete suppression of affect for others.

Candid discussion of important issues in marriage has been beneficial for large numbers of couples in very conventional marriages as well as in more experimental forms of partnership. But this course ought not be cavalierly chosen simply because others have chosen it. It is no panacea and it is not without its risks. Talking things through will be most constructive:

- if *both* of you want to do it,
- if both of you will *listen* as well as talk, and
- if both of you are willing to *follow through* on thorny items rather than retreating into wounded silence.

Monitor your process; evaluate it both from your own personal perspective *and* in dialogue with your partner. Be ready to revise your plans if it appears that the communication you desire will disrupt the relationship profoundly. Very often, because of old wounds and bad habits, the more candid style must be developed slowly rather than adopted all at once.

Sometimes working with a marriage counselor or in a group setting can smooth and speed constructive interaction between partners—but, again, this can happen only if both are committed to this course.

REMODELING MARRIAGE

Candid communication in an atmosphere of trust is *useful* in marriage enrichment, but it is quite *essential* for those who seek to remodel marriage in accord with the pervasive revolutions of morals and manners of the last decade and a half. The accelerating integration of women into all sectors of the society, the new candor with which people express their sexuality and sensuality, and the various let-it-all-hang-out schools of interpersonal relations have inspired and facilitated reappraisal of certain taken-for-granted aspects of marital life for millions of people (especially young adults, especially in the upper-middle class). Implicit and explicit renegotiations of sex-role expectations are under way throughout the land. Many women are demanding more freedom to control their own lives; they are becoming more assertive in their relationship with men. Standards of appropriate sexual behavior are changing, leaving many married persons confused about their own needs and values—and those of their partners. Some contemporary marriages are marked by small revolts against the ideology of "togetherness." The ethos of candor (itself a response to high mobility and the fragmentation of traditional forms of family and community) requires that we work with problems we previously ignored.

If you are in the process of remodeling your partnership and jealousy becomes an issue, straight talking is in order. Set aside uninterrupted time and space. Discuss particular persons and situations, but don't limit yourself to that. Get into your needs and limits, your beliefs and values. Seek congruence—but don't be upset if you discover discrepancies.

Tell your partner what kinds of behaviors and what kind of people are most apt to trigger your jealousy and learn the same from him/her. Talk about what you would both do—or hope you'd do—in various hypothetical situations. Find out what your partner expects of you *and* take responsibility for making sure that s/he knows what *your* expectations are. A great deal of felt jealousy is a function of misunderstanding and bad timing. Many couples find that jealousy is reduced by honest expression of feelings and needs and by negotiations of new limits.

Good communication can reduce jealousy but cannot eradicate it. You will still feel the jealous flash. But all we have discovered about the social-learning element of jealousy suggests that you might have considerable latitude with regard to how you interpret and react to the experience which triggered the flash. Consider these two possible responses to a situation in which a man first notices that his wife is interested in another:

1. His interest in her confirms my suspicion that he is "on the make." (I never did trust him.) Her interest in him shows that she is dissatisfied with me. He's quite attractive; I guess she's grown tired of me. And he's so attentive to her, so appreciative. I guess I've come to take her for granted. No wonder she's so turned on by his little courtesies. They want to go to the opera together; I feel left out. I wonder what other excuses they'll find to spend time together. Maybe she'll take time away from me to be with him. Maybe I'll have to cook dinner and take care of the kids while she's off at the "opera." If I can't count on my own wife, what the hell *can* I count on?

2. His interest in her confirms her attractiveness. I'm proud of her. Her interest in him shows that she is alert and alive. I'm glad for that. An "inert" partner, no matter how "secure" the relationship, is a bad deal. He's like me in some ways so I am affirmed by her choice of him. He's different from me in some ways—suggesting that she has some needs that I don't meet. I must consider these carefully and try to find out if there might be ways of doing a better job of meeting her needs. *But* I realize that I cannot meet *all* of her interpersonal needs without violation of my own autonomy (if at all), so I must work to become *glad* that she has other friends who can fulfill her as I do not—and would rather not. (Thank God she's found someone who *wants* to go to the opera with her.) I want to be reassured that our relationship means as much to her as it does to me, but I won't demand that she renounce all others in order to demonstrate that to me.

It is your life-experience, your social learning, which determines which of these reactions seems most "natural" to you. Most of us have been programmed with some version of the first script. Perhaps it would be possible to change ourselves so that the second response would become more likely. Try it. Look for positive ways of interpreting your mate's interest in others. If your primary relationship is secure, if you are honest with each other, if you respect the boundaries you've agreed upon, then the non-defensive reaction may feel right to you.

If you can authentically respond in this way, *do*. This kind of reaction reduces anxieties all around and it often strengthens the relationship as well. *But,* if you cannot bring yourself to interpret the situation in this way, don't pretend. You cannot blame your partner for being insensitive to your needs unless you tell him/her what they are.

NEW FORMS OF INTIMATE PARTNERSHIP

Unless you can imagine being comfortable with some version of script number two, you probably ought not consider the radical alternative of opening your relationship to sexual and/or emotional experiences with others. Toward the end of their influential book *Open Marriage*, Nena and George O'Neill (1972:257f.) speak of "new possibilities for additional relationships" and of the joy of "comradeship with others of the opposite sex beside your mate." *But,* you ask, what about *sexual* relationships and comradeship?

> We are not recommending outside sex, but we are not saying it should be avoided, either. The choice is entirely up to you, and can be made only upon your own knowledge of the degree to which you have achieved, within your marriage, the trust, identity, and open communication necessary to the eradication of jealousy. Outside sexual experiences when they are in the context of a meaningful relationship may be rewarding and beneficial to an open marriage. But such relationships are not necessarily an integral part of open marriage. It is another option that you may or may not choose to explore. . . .
> To have an extramarital affair without first developing yourself to the point where you are ready, and your mate is ready, for such a step could be detrimental to the possibility of developing a true open marriage.

We agree. You ought not experiment with consensual extramarital relationships because it's fashionable or in order to prove you've got a great marriage. And such experiments are *not* what you need if your relationship is shaky or your sex life is problematic. Be honest with yourself; many "open marriage" agreements are (conscious or unconscious) strategies for ending the marriage and/or for smoothing the transition to the next relationship.

If, despite the obvious risks, you and your partner do open your relationships to outside experiences, here are some strategies which others have found useful. Build trust during an initial monogamous period. Give yourself time and space to get to know each other. Form a solid, satisfying connection *before* opening the relationship. Even if you've largely transcended your jealousy in one relationship, you will still probably need to go through an initial monogamous period with a new mate. Intimacy and trust in the primary relationship are the best shield against insecurity and jealousy.

Some apparently successful open relationships are the result of negotiating the freer arrangement *before* a particular third party was on the scene: *pre-need* thinking, imagining, talking. An additional strain is placed on negotiations which begin only after someone has become involved with another. If possible, draw your limits and formulate your rules *before* outside relationships are begun. Be suspicious of new rules inspired by new passions.

Protect your limits. Structure outside activities so as to protect (and symbolize) the primacy of your partnership. Don't allow romantic impulses to disrupt routines your partner (and children) count on.

Develop "ground rules" which are acceptable to both of you. Be specific. Change the rules only when you are ready for something else. Don't push or pressure your partner; make sure that you are not pushed or pressured. Avoid legalistic and manipulative uses of your rules. When ground rules are fairly negotiated and constructively employed, they focus attention on the primary relationship (rather than being seen as a means to some extra-marital end) and they increase your feeling of being in control. As you live by the rules you have worked out together, you come to trust each other more and you get better at formulating guidelines which serve both your needs.

Here are some ground rules which others experimenting with postmonogamous life-styles have found useful. You will note that some of these contradict others. That is because needs and values vary from couple to couple. Use this list as a resource for the development of guidelines that are right for you and your partner.

- If there is ever a conflict between the needs of the primary and secondary relationships, the primary relationship gets the benefit of the doubt.
- Don't get sexually or emotionally involved without checking with me first.
- Do what you will but don't tell me about it. And make sure the children and the neighbors don't find out.
- Outside experiences are all right but emotional involvements are taboo. Keep it light.
- Outside sexual experiences are all right but only with people you really care about.
- Only if I like the other person.
- Only if the other person is someone I don't know and won't meet.

- Only with single people.
- Only with people who are happily married and honest with their spouses.
- Only if I'm similarly involved.
- When one of us is out of town, we both do what we like.
- Not too often. (Be specific.)
- Tuesday night off. Each of us is entitled to some private time and space to spend as we will.
- I agree to wait a month before getting involved with _____ so we can work through some of the implications of this new relationship.

If outside relationships are not to undermine your partnership, you must find ways of minimizing the *competition* which seems so "natural" [5] under the circumstances. If the situation is defined as competition, we expect that someone will "win" and someone will "lose." This zero-sum perception activates the fear of loss: loss of control (which is dizzying), loss of the partner (which would be devastating). If the person with whom your partner is involved sees him/herself as a rival and acts that way, you may be drawn into a competitive relationship with that person even if you approach the encounter noncompetitively.

Here are some ways others have sought to minimize competitiveness:

- Make certain the third party understands that you and your partner have an open relationship which allows what is happening.
- Let the third party know that you don't see him/her as a rival—but avoid the condescension which suggests that this person is not *worthy* of competition with you.
- Perhaps the three of you could enjoy spending time together. If so, you are less apt to become a victim of your own fantasies, more apt to understand what your mate enjoys and appreciates about the other person.
- Watch out for competition *between you and your partner*. The need to "keep things even" can turn an "open relationship" into a seductive game in which other human beings are seen only as notches on the bedpost.

---

[5]*Natural* is in quotation marks to remind us that whatever physiological propensity toward competition we have within us, it is through social learning that we acquire a repertoire of appropriate outlets for that propensity and a framework within which to interpret the competitive behaviors of others. Like jealousy, competitiveness has an instinctive root, but only life among others teaches us when and how to express it.

THE ONGOING MANAGEMENT OF JEALOUSY

As long as human beings need affection, there will be some jealousy; it probably cannot be completely eradicated. Even if you are relatively successful in working with your jealousy—and no matter what type of partnership you have or hope for—*jealousy will recur*. Don't be surprised when this happens. Remember: The jealous flash is a natural response; you'll feel it every time an important relationship appears to be threatened. When this happens, don't congratulate yourself—but don't condemn yourself either. Your jealousy is neither proof of love nor evidence of personal failure. It is a signal which tells you to attend to your relationship—and to yourself.

Persons who feel that they are making some progress in managing jealousy are even more likely to deny jealous feelings, especially if they (and their friends) view jealousy as evidence of personal failure. David Riesman (personal correspondence, 1975) sums it up like this:

> I think the notion. . . that low self-esteem can be a catalyst for jealous feelings is a good one—though high self-esteem may be a catalyst among the "enlightened" further to suppress the jealousy one is not supposed to have.

The ongoing management of jealousy requires that one draw the fine line between repression and denial on the one hand and *considerate restraint* on the other. You ought not *hide* your jealousy, but you *should* try to express your jealousy as constructively as possible. This might involve postponing a confrontation until you've "cooled off," or until you've returned home where constructive discussion is more likely. Sometimes such a delay permits one to forget the provocation altogether, or, at least, to "put it in perspective" so that it is robbed of its power to disrupt.

Just as you might consciously hold back the urge to throw up so as not to disrupt a party and soil the carpet, so also you might postpone an expression of jealousy for the sake of a relationship which might be unnecessarily shaken by an immediate and angry response. The vomiting reflex is nature's way of clearing the body of harmful substances; jealousy, at its root, is an instinctoid self-protective reaction in the face of a threat. Just as you ought not repeatedly and persistently fight back a powerful urge to throw up, so also you ought not repeatedly and persistently suppress your

Jealousy. But if you delay your jealous response, or if you consciously soften an expression of jealousy out of concern for the partner and the relationship, the constructive management of jealousy becomes more likely.

Much more has been written about the feeling and management of one's *own* jealousy than about the jealousy that one *provokes* in others. Yet surely the provocation of jealousy is an important factor, one worthy of the thoughtful attention of those who would seek to "manage" jealousy. Indeed, perhaps one element of an internally consistent effort to control one's own jealousy should be an attempt to provoke as little jealousy as possible (in your mate and in others). Jealousy is dialectical: If you want to feel less jealousy, provoke less jealousy.

Jealousy is dialectical. By this we mean: Every aspect of an experience of jealousy is simultaneously an effect (of previous experiences of jealousy) and a cause (of jealousies yet to come). This is scary; it means that every new expression of jealousy can set off a "chain reaction." But this same dialectical property means that every aspect of the experience of jealousy is—at least potentially—a point at which the chain can be broken.

PROSPECTS: THE FUTURE OF JEALOUSY

Spinoza does not include jealousy in his comrehensive listing of emotions (or passions). Neither do Aristotle, Locke, or James. *Envy* is sometimes listed, but jealousy is not (Adler 1952:417). Perhaps this is because those philosophers who sought to catalogue the emotions realized that jealousy is not a single emotion. It is, rather, a social construction which employs *several* emotions (such as love, hatred, fear, pride, anger, and lust) in accordance with the norms and values of specific human groups.

Jealousy, as we have seen, is structured by the groups, the institutions, and the communities in which we live. Changes in the shape of these groups, changes in the values within a society, bring about changes in the experience, the expression, and the interpretation of jealousy.

Jealousy is, by nature, a boundary-maintaining device. As the prevailing understanding of marriage changes, new boundaries are drawn. As a result, some jealous behaviors become obsolete—and, in all probability, new forms of jealousy will be generated to protect the new boundaries. Kingsley Davis (1936:400) reminds us that the forms jealousy takes vary with the needs of the human groups within which it is experienced.

Where exclusive possession of an individual's entire love is customary, jealousy will demand that exclusiveness. Where love is divided it will be divided according to some scheme, and jealousy will reinforce the division.

The institution of marriage is changing in contemporary American society. So too are the expectations people bring to intimate partnerships. All people do not feel all the changes; there are substantial variations by age, by region, by class, and by sub-culture. But there are three major trends which, in one manifestation or another, have touched most of us—and affected the ways we experience, express, and interpret jealousy. These are: (1) the liberalization of sexual mores, (2) the erosion of the "together-ness" motif, and (3) the shift toward more equitable, more "symmetrical" female/male relationships. These three mutually reinforcing trends, although conceptually distinct, are profoundly intermingled in real life. In recent years, all of these changes have been especially important for women who, in turn, have been im-portant catalysts of the changes. Our discussion of these issues will necessarily be sketchy, and, at a few points, speculative.

SEX AFTER THE "SEXUAL REVOLUTION"

The revaluation of sexual jealousy now in progress is part of the larger ongoing revaluation of human sexuality which began early in the twentieth century and which was dramatically accelerated in the 1960s. The three age-old deterrents of freer sexual expression were *detection* (the fear of strong parental or community disapproval), *infection* (the fear of venereal diseases), and *conception* (the fear of unwanted pregnancy and the commitments that usually entailed). These were reinforced by various "double-standards" favoring the male and by socialization which sought to make males and females as *different* from one another as possible.[6]

The concern about detection has ebbed because of the auto-mobile, the anonymity of urban life, the secularization of religious institutions, and the tolerance of diversity required in a pluralistic society in which the popular media tell everyone what is going on everywhere. Modern antibiotics, sex education, and the increasing availability of nonjudgmental medical personnel offer the promise of controlling venereal diseases even as the population become

[6] That is, our socialization has tended to enhance and reinforce (rather than to minimize) the natural differences between males and females. For example, we typically encourage boys—who are bigger and stronger by nature—to eat a lot, to play sports, and to lift weights.

more active sexually. (VD is still a problem but, wisely or unwisely, increasing numbers of people behave as though it were not.)

The introduction of the oral contraceptive in the early 1960s and the more liberal abortion laws of the late 1960s and early 1970s have all but eradicated fear of unwanted pregnancy as a deterrent of sexual activity for very large segments of the population. As a result, women are more enthusiastic about sex—both in and outside of marriage.

The Pill made it possible to separate sex from babymaking. Gradually, people became aware that sex had two, perhaps three distinct aspects: the procreational, the relational, and the recreational. Sex was not *only* for making babies; it was also a means of strengthening the relationship between marriage partners. Thus, nonprocreational sex was enlisted as an agent of the "togetherness" the American family sought in the 1950s and 1960s. Even the voices of moral and marital convention (many clergymen, the *Reader's Digest*, "Dear Abby" and *The Total Woman*) came to insist that good sex makes for a good marriage.

Some people went still farther with the new latitude granted by the Pill and the legitimization of sexual pleasure it catalyzed. Some used nonprocreational sex as a way of getting to know several people of the opposite sex before (or instead of) settling down with one. Since extensive premarital sex makes extramarital sex more likely,[7] we should not be surprised to discover that the present generation of young marrieds—the first to enjoy the new, liberal *pre*marital sex ethic—are more interested in and open about sex *outside* of marriage. For many today, the new toleration of extramarital sex smooths the transition from one one-and-only to another. Others claim that they can have outside sexual friendships and experiences which enhance (or, at least, do not damage) their primary relationships. It is too soon to know whether or not these nonmonogamous partnerships will be viable life-styles for more than a very few. *But* any increase in the toleration of extramarital sex requires a redrawing of boundaries and some redefinition of jealousy.

In the 1960s and 1970s, then, the old sex ethic was *joined* (not replaced) by a "new morality," or, more precisely, by a whole *range* of new moralities, new *mores*, new patterns of sexual feelings and behaviors. In many sectors the new was the more permissive, the more experimental. Throughout the society, people grew more tolerant of the sexual values and styles of others. And toleration

[7] In the Kinsey study (1953:427) 29 per cent of the females with histories of premarital coitus had had extramarital coitus by the time they were interviewed. Only 13 per cent of those who were virgins till marriage had engaged in extramarital intercourse.

begat more experimentation, which reinforced the permissiveness, which demanded more toleration—and so on. The boundaries of appropriate sexual behavior have moved and are moving for many persons and groups in this society. Thus, jealousy, a natural boundary-maintaining device, is changing in order to protect the new boundaries.

THE EROSION OF THE "TOGETHERNESS" MOTIF

The ideology of "togetherness" emerged just after World War II as a reaction to the new affluence and mobility which threatened to tear the American family apart. The 1950s gave us slogans such as, "The family that plays (or prays) together, stays together." The back yard barbecue with Dad as chef, family outings, and activities husband and wife could do together were prescribed as palliatives for families feeling the strains of speed, novelty, impermanence, and upward mobility.

Apparently the pendulum has now swung the other way. The divorce rate is high and rising. Census Bureau statistics show that the number of single-parent families in the United States has risen sharply since 1965. More and more people are *choosing* to be single—at least for a substantial segment of their lives (Stein 1976). Many recent divorcees are deciding to live (or relive) the single life before (or instead of) rushing back into marriage. New institutions catering to single adults are proliferating.

The growing popularity of the single life may be enhanced by economic and occupational considerations. The nuclear family (a man, a woman, and their children) fits the needs of the modern industrial system better than did the extended family (the nuclear family plus relatives and, sometimes, hired help, boarders, etc.). The nuclear family is more portable, more modular. It facilitates the mobility and the interchangability required of those who prosper in the technological society (see Goode 1963). Does it not follow that the forms of the "family" which would be even *more* compatible with the needs of the industrial system are: (1) the child-free couple (often also a dual-career couple), and (2) the single adult whose intimate life is, by design, a series of temporary relationships and/or partnerships? If priests and nuns give up marriage for their religious vocations, might not some persons decide against marriage for the sake of a personally meaningful secular career—especially in a world grown more tolerant of meaningful friendships and sexual intimacy outside of marriage?

Another economic factor deserves mention in this context. Contrary to the conventional wisdom, two *cannot* live as cheaply as one.

But, assuming a given level of physical comfort, the single life is more expensive *per person* than living in pairs. Thus one factor which inhibits the choice of a single life-style (and which often halts the drift toward divorce) is the economic factor. Affluence reinforces the trend toward singlehood as a life choice. Put differently: Up to a point, a society gets as many one-adult households as it can afford.

Even within many contemporary marriages, there is a concern that there be "spaces in the togetherness." Personal autonomy is considered a legitimate goal for many married persons. Marriage partners are naming and claiming their "right" to some privacy and solitude (Myers and Leggitt 1975). Jealousy of the partner's time spent alone can be as much of a problem as jealousy of time spent with another. This "jealousy of solitude" will probably become more common and more troublesome as married Americans seek to strike workable balances between the "togetherness" that smothers and the "autonomy" which is sometimes a euphemism for "nothing left to lose."

THE QUEST FOR SYMMETRY

The recent emphasis of the women's liberation movement on equity in marriage is part of a longer, more pervasive trend away from traditional patterns of complementary marriage (in which the characters and activities of husband and wife were expected to be different and complement one another). In "symmetrical marriage," it is expected that husband and wife will have relatively *similar* characteristics and activities. (See Gorer 1971, and Young and Willmott 1974).

Many contemporary marriages have as their ideal an equitable balance of power. It is no longer assumed that father knows best. Several contributors to this collection suggested that fairness in a relationship minimizes jealousy. Both the various prevailing double-standards which favor males *and* the "women's prerogatives" which they have called forth in reaction make jealousy more likely. As couples work toward a healthy balance of power in relationships, they simultaneously reduce the likelihood of jealousy and develop the kind of good communication which serves the management of jealousy when it appears.

As the partner comes to be seen less and less as *property*, jealous behavior in defense of the partner will seem less and less appropriate (see Bernard, Chapter 13). As spouses give up control over the partner such as was common 20 years ago, there will be less need for the boundary-maintaining jealous reactions which then seemed "normal."

It seems reasonable to expect that behavior and values relevant to sex and marriage will continue to change over time. (It will take some time for us to integrate changes already in progress.) This means that the understanding and management of jealousy will require that you "keep up" with your partnership (and the needs, values, and expectations you and your mate bring to it) *and* with the social pressures on it.

JEALOUSY AS A SOCIAL PROBLEM

If equitable power relations in intimate partnerships help to minimize jealousy, perhaps more equitable power relations in the community and the society would have the same effect. Margaret Mead (see Chapter 10) says that jealousy will be least problematic in "the least stratified society, the one which has the fewest social, racial, or religious classes, [and] which has the strongest tendency to stress only *humanity*." And, Mead adds, if women have been "the jealous sex," it is only because, throughout history, they have been the *insecure* sex. As women achieve social, economic, and legal independence, they will perhaps be less susceptible to the jealousies which have traditionally afflicted them. (It will be interesting to see whether or not such "liberated women" will also become *more* susceptible to the forms of jealousy previously associated with men.)

The jealousy felt by an individual is correlated with particular familial and cultural forms. Jealousy is aggravated by the worship of a jealous, monotheistic God, by the ideal of life-long monogamous marriage, and by the demand for a monocentric, rational and repressed personality (see Downing, Chapter 6). Insofar as any of these symbols loses power in the culture, jealousy may become less powerful in the person. *But* these symbols are not without their payoffs—some obvious, some hidden. Perhaps the jealousy and other "discontents" they require of us are part of the necessary cost of the benefits of civilized existence. Jealousy management in the person, and the reduction of jealousy via new familial and social designs, must be approached with an appreciation of this complexity and interconnectedness.

Those aspects of social experience which set off and exacerbate feelings of jealousy are beyond us in some ways, *but* they are built up, elaborated, extended, and validated by individual compliance. As Philip Slater (1975:176) reminds us:

> People are the nerve endings of social systems. If they are stupid enough stoically to bear the pain such a system inflicts upon them, the system will go right on inflicting it.

Today's children are tomorrow's adults. Even now, we are socializing the next generation, a generation which most of us will actually meet as adults later in our own lives. Those who rear and educate children profoundly affect their individual propensities for jealousy. Indeed, we are all continuously socializing one another. Approval of jealous rage makes its reappearance more likely. A constructive alternative, once introduced, may be shared with others—and jealousy may thereby be reduced in several relationships.

The relationship between self and society is dialectical, but it is not an equal relationship. The individual sends out ripples and gets back waves. That is, the impact of society on each of us is greater than our impact on it. Nevertheless, each of us has some voice in the kind of family, the kind of community, the kind of society we shall have. It is society and its institutions which have, in large measure, made us what we are; but it is individuals, working in concert, who will change institutions and thus make society what it will become.

Appendices

The appendices consist of four articles on jealousy by Gordon Clanton that were published after the first edition of this book (1977). Appendix I was included in the second edition (1986). The other three are new to this third edition (1997).

You may wish to read the appendices first, starting with Appendix IV, and then return to the beginning of the book. These articles concisely summarize many of the main points of the book. They update some issues and summarize more recent research.

The appendices further develop the sociological approach to the study of jealousy and other emotions that was introduced in the first edition. This approach utilizes historical and cross-cultural research, functional analysis, conflict theory, the sociology of knowledge, and empirical assessment.

The comparative materials reveal the diversity of jealousy. Functional analysis reveals the hidden social usefulness of jealousy: In all societies, jealousy protects marriage (and other valued relationships) from adultery (and other threats), thus helping to preserve social order. Conflict theory reveals the economic and political implications of jealousy — and draws attention to power differences within couples. The sociology of knowledge reveals that an experience of jealousy depends on deeply learned beliefs, which are built up through interaction with others and which reflect the social context in which they are formed. Preliminary empirical research suggests that jealousy is *not* strongly associated with mental illness, early childhood conflicts, or low-self-esteem.

The sociological approach developed here incorporates the findings of cognitive social psychology, utilizes some psychoanalytic concepts, and carries some implications for psychotherapy, counseling, and self-understanding.

Appendix I, "Frontiers of Jealousy Research," argues that the jealousy felt by an individual is shaped by relationship issues, by social institutions, by society and culture.

Appendix II, "Jealousy in American Culture, 1945-1985," shows how and why jealousy has changed since mid-century — and it challenges the popular notion that jealousy is caused mostly by low self-esteem.

Appendix III, "Developmental Correlates of Jealousy," challenges the widespread assumption that adult jealousy is associated with early childhood conflicts or mental illness.

Appendix IV, "A Sociology of Jealousy," reveals the hidden usefulness of jealousy and summarizes many of the main points of this book.

Frontiers of Jealousy Research

Gordon Clanton

Although jealousy has been a topic of imaginative literature and philosophy from the beginnings of Western civilization, the scientific study of jealousy is in its infancy. It is, however, alive and growing. This issue of *Alternative Lifestyles* presents recent social science research on jealousy. This introductory essay offers a brief history of the study of jealousy by social science, thus providing a context in which to interpret the five articles that follow. Some of the major unanswered questions in jealousy research are then posed and the partial answers offered by the articles in this issue are summarized and interpreted. Attention is also given to the limits of what we know and some directions for future research and theorizing are proposed. Along the way, comment is offered on some implications of what we are learning about jealousy for improving relationships, for

This article served as the introduction to a special issue on jealousy of the journal *Alternative Lifestyles* (now *Journal of Family and Economic Issues*), Vol. 4: No. 3, August 1981.

therapy, self-understanding, and personal growth, and for understanding alternative lifestyles.

Jealousy may be defined as a protective reaction to a perceived threat (especially adultery) to a valued relationship (especially marriage) or to its quality. This working definition appears to be in harmony with the several definitions stated or implied in the articles in this issue. The protective reaction can involve thoughts, feelings, and/or actions. Although jealous behaviors sometimes damage relationships, the *intention* of jealousy is the protection of the relationship and/or the protection of the ego of the threatened partner. Adult jealousy typically results when a person believes that a marriage or romantic relationship is threatened by a real or imagined rival.

One other preliminary matter: Because of the importance of jealousy in love relationships and because of the importance of love relationships in our culture and in our lives, persons other than social scientists are likely to read the articles that follow. Some will come seeking prescriptions for personal problems or scientific proof-texts to support personal choices already made. These articles offer neither. Social science seeks to describe and explain human behavior. While most researchers hope that their findings will be put to good use by others, the application and especially the therapeutic application of social science findings is not a simple matter. Bits of scientific knowledge do not automatically produce self-knowledge. Furthermore, the conclusions reported in this issue are provisional. Therefore, while these articles may be of interest and value to readers with personal problems, they ought not be read for advice, prescriptions, or cures.

HISTORY OF JEALOUSY RESEARCH

When Lynn Smith and I set out in 1974 to bring together the best social scientific literature for our book *Jealousy* (Clanton and Smith, 1977), we found very little. Apart from the psychoanalytic tradition, there was almost no psychological literature on jealousy. Finding no experimental or quantitative research, we commissioned Elaine Hatfield and Ellen Berscheid to sum up what experimental social psychology had learned about jealousy. Although neither knew of empirical studies of jealousy, both reported results from other pertinent studies — including Schachter's well-known anger/euphoria experiments and various studies of romantic attraction — and both made imaginative suggestions of hypotheses that might be tested in future research. To summarize: As *Jealousy* went to press in 1977, there was very little psychological literature on jealousy and virtually no experimental or quantitative research in print.

Sociologists and anthropologists had not done much better. Kingsley Davis published the classic sociological analysis of jealousy in 1936 and later used it in his influential textbook to demonstrate the explanatory power of sociology as a distinctive science. Jealousy, Davis argued, is shaped by prevailing marriage rules. Its social function, its purpose, is the protection of pair bonds valued by the group. A 1931 article by Margaret Mead called attention to the cross-cultural variability of jealousy, but neither she nor any other anthropologist has given us a systematic account of jealousy in many cultures. We included the Davis and Mead articles in our anthology, but we found no real follow-up in the sociological or anthropoiogical literatures except for one article by Jessie Bernard. We commissioned two additional articles on jealousy in contemporary American society. Robert Whitehurst offered an overview of ways in which North American attitudes and values contribute to jealousy, and Brian Gilmartin used data from his study of one hundred swinging couples and one hundred nonswinging couples to show that learned belief systems influence the experience of jealousy. I utilized and extended some of these ideas in the Synthesis at the end of our book, but much work remains to be done on the sociology of jealousy and other emotions.

A symposium on jealousy was part of the annual meeting of the American Psychological Association in San Francisco in August 1977. Four articles were presented in a well-attended session chaired by Harold Sigall of the University of Maryland. Robert G. Bringle reported findings to support an understanding of jealousy as a disposition or personality characteristic. Gregory L. White proposed that jealousy is influenced by the relative power of the two persons in a relationship, the person with less power typically admitting to more jealousy. Ralph B. Hupka argued that jealousy is culturally determined and offered evidence of this from the ethnographic literature. (Revised and expanded versions of these three papers are included in this issue.) Jeff B. Bryson (San Diego State University) reported small group experiments that suggest that an unattractive rival might provoke more jealousy than an attractive one (Shettel-Neuber et al., 1978). He also found some differences between the ways men and women manage jealousy: Men are more apt to blame the partner and to try to protect their own self-esteem while women are more likely to blame themselves and to try to save the relationship. I was invited to comment on the papers and to interpret them in a sociological framework.

Five articles on different aspects of jealousy are included in this issue. The three articles with roots going back to the 1977 APA symposium contain many implications for alternative lifestyles, as well as for more conventional forms of intimate partnership. Two other articles are included here that describe and interpret specific alternative lifestyles. Bram Buunk examines sexually open marriages in the Netherlands. Ayala Pines and Elliott Aronson describe a utopian community whose members claim that a new form of group marriage has eliminated jealousy.

ISSUES IN JEALOUSY RESEARCH

The research reported in this issue may be considered as partial answers to four key questions about jealousy:

1. What personal characteristics are associated with jealousy? (Bringle)
2. What properties of relationships make jealousy more or less likely? (White)
3. How is jealousy influenced by culture? (Hupka)
4. How is jealousy experienced and managed in alternative lifestyles? (Buunk, Pines and Aronson)

The articles look at jealousy from three levels: the personal (Bringle), the interpersonal (White), and the cultural (Hupka) or subcultural (Buunk, Pines and Aronson). Because jealousy, like most emotions, is influenced by social situations and by social learning, an adequate explanation of jealousy will have to take into account the general influence of social forces (including time, place, class, education, religion), as well as the specific mechanisms of the private feeling.

WHAT PERSONAL CHARACTERISTICS
ARE ASSOCIATED WITH JEALOUSY?

Robert G. Bringle offers the case for viewing jealousy as a disposition or personality trait. He summarizes research with college student samples that shows that persons who are self-deprecating and dogmatic and who view themselves as unhappy, anxious, and externally controlled also report that they are relatively more likely to experience jealousy in 20 hypothetical jealousy-provoking situations. The correlations are moderate. No significant difference was found between males and females.

As Bringle notes, correlation does not establish causation. These findings cannot tell us whether these personality characteristics cause the self-report of jealousy or if the view of oneself as jealous causes the personality characteristics.

Elsewhere (Clanton and Smith, 1977: 13-46; see also Appendix II) I have shown that beliefs and attitudes about jealousy have shifted substantially in the United States in recent decades. Prior to about 1966, most people viewed jealousy as a natural evidence of love and as good for marriage. Beginning in the late 1960s, many people have come to see jealousy as evidence of a defect in the personality of the jealous person (such as low self-esteem) and as bad for relationships. This shift was most noticeable among the young, the more affluent, and the better educated. Thus, we should not be surprised if contemporary college students (who are young, whose parents are relatively affluent, and who are — one hopes — in the process of getting educated) associate their potential for experiencing and expressing jealousy with their personal weaknesses rather than with their personal strengths. Had we been able to ask these questions of the parents of these students back in the 1950s or early 1960s when they were in college, we might have obtained a very different picture of jealousy as a disposition. Indeed, I would anticipate that older persons, rural persons, and/or religious persons would be less likely than the younger, urban, and secular to view jealousy as a defect and less likely, therefore, to exhibit the association of jealousy with various personality defects.

Culture shapes our evaluations of our emotions and thereby, to some degree, shapes our emotions. If questionnaires are to tap this dimension, longitudinal and cross-cultural comparisons will be required.

If we lose sight of the influence of culture on the experience, the expressions, and the evaluation of jealousy, we are more inclined to stereotype and stigmatize the person who expresses or admits jealousy. Telling a person that he or she is "dispositionally jealous" may reinforce a self-understanding of himself or herself as profoundly and irretrievably jealous. It may be therapeutically useful to remind people that jealousy is related to a lifetime of learning and that it is not, therefore, easily unlearned or relearned. A view of jealousy as a disposition or character trait may inhibit the kind of relearning that can minimize destructive jealousy in a person or a relationship. Furthermore, if the jealous person is stigmatized as dogmatic, unhappy, and anxious, he or she will probably be reluctant to express felt jealousy, but this does not guarantee that the jealousy will be wiped out or managed more constructively.

One further problem attends this type of research. The conclusions depend entirely on self-report in response to 20 hypothetical situations. Respondents are not asked what they would do or say; they are asked how *jealous* they would be. To pose the questions this way is to assume: (1) that everyone knows what jealousy is (when, in fact, different people have different definitions of it), (2) that people always know when they are jealous (when, in fact, they may be jealous and not be aware of it), (3) that people always tell the truth about their feelings (when, in fact, they often lie about them), and (4) that people will respond as they say they would when presented with a hypothetical situation (when, in fact, people often respond very differently). These assumptions make possible a methodological shortcut, but they also place limits on the usefulness and generalizability of the findings. A measure of the self-report of jealousy is not necessarily a good measure of jealousy.

For now we may say that Bringle has shown that in four small samples of college students persons who were self-deprecating and dissatisfied with their lives were more likely to report that they would be jealous in a series of hypothetical situations. Note that the researcher assumes that these situations will provoke jealousy in at least some people. Furthermore, after judging most personal and interpersonal approaches to jealousy management to be unproductive, Bringle concludes that one of the most effective ways of minimizing jealousy is to avoid the situations likely to evoke it. Thus, Bringle acknowledges the importance of the social situation. But he also challenges those whose analysis of jealousy is primarily situational to take into account the wide range of personal reactions to a given situation and to consider the personal characteristics that correlate with a jealous self-report. This emphasis points to the usefulness of carefully studying the processes by which we are socialized into our emotional habits and patterns.

WHAT PROPERTIES OF RELATIONSHIPS MAKE JEALOUSY MORE OR LESS LIKELY?

Gregory L. White presents evidence from survey research to suggest that the more involved person in a relationship is more likely to report jealousy. Similarly, the partner less likely to quickly establish a new relationship (if the present one ends) is more likely to report jealousy. Following Thibaut and Kelley, White views this more involved person with fewer options as the less powerful partner. It is the less powerful person in a relationship who is more likely to admit being jealous. Like Bringle, White finds no strong gender differences in the self-report of jealousy.

White's conclusions are based on questionnaire responses of 150 couples, mostly undergraduates at UCLA. About one-fifth were casual daters. About half were serious daters. Less than one-third were cohabiting, engaged, or married. The modal relationship was 18 months old. Only 61 percent agreed in their relative ratings of involvement.

Jealousy was measured by six self-report items such as, "In general, how jealous a person do you think you are?" Five of the six items include a form of the word "jealousy" — as though the definition of jealousy and its valuation by the respondent were unproblematic.

As I suggested above, the self-report of jealousy is an unreliable measure. Consider the case of Glenn, a young man I know. When another man asked Glenn's date to dance with him, Glenn punched the guy out. When a bystander suggested that he was a very jealous fellow, Glenn growled, "I wasn't jealous. I was pissed!" By relabeling his jealousy as anger, he was able to deny it. And if he responded to White's six-item jealousy scale, he would score very unjealous. Semantical difficulties and the apparent complexity of jealousy require that we devise more sophisticated and subtle measures of it.

The apparent good news in White's article is that there is a near-certain way of assuring that you will never feel jealous in a romantic relationship: Just be sure you are never more involved with (or committed to) another than he or she is with you. Likewise, be sure that you always have a spare lover standing by to leap to if the present relationship ends. The bad news, of course, is that these "cures" might be worse than the "disease." Obviously, if both members of a couple are trying to underbid the other in commitment, if both are busily developing "back-up" relationships, both partners are less likely to find satisfaction in the relationship over time. These data, then, suggest that one could reduce jealousy by reducing love — but since the function of jealousy is the protection of love, that would probably be counterproductive in the long run.

White's article makes us aware of the influence on jealousy of power differences in a relationship. It appears that high power is negatively correlated with self-reports of jealousy and that low power is positively correlated with self-reports of jealousy. Perhaps future research will be able to tell us more about relationships in which power is equal or almost equal. As White reports, Hill, Rubin, and Peplau found that unequally involved partners were more than twice as likely to break up in two years than the equally involved. If a sharp power difference produces one person prone to jealousy and one relatively free of it, perhaps a low power difference would make serious jealousy less likely in both partners — at least in those relationships in which relative equality is seen as desirable and in which such issues are discussed rather than ignored.

HOW IS JEALOUSY INFLUENCED BY CULTURE?

Historical and cross-cultural evidence supports Kingsley Davis's conclusion that the function of jealousy is the same in all societies — the protection of valued relationships, especially marriage and relationships leading to marriage, from adultery and other forms of betrayal. Western history reveals that jealousy has also protected other kinds of valued relationships as well. In classical Greek culture, jealousy protected the homoerotic relationships of men. In the Middle Ages, jealousy protected the tender, extramarital flirtations of Roman Catholic lords and ladies whose ideal was to love "pure and chaste from afar." Following the Protestant Reformation, jealousy protected Puritan marriage, a new kind of man-woman relationship that attempted for the first time to combine sex, love, and companionship in marriage. The Protestant Reformation and the Industrial Revolution weakened the ancient custom of arranged marriage and encouraged the modern practice of choosing one's own mate on the basis of love.

In every culture people form valued relationships in accordance with prevailing norms. Jealousy protects whatever kinds of relationships cultures teach people to value (Davis, 1936). Thus, while jealousy has a universal function — the protection of relationships in which the community has a stake — the specific jealous behaviors vary enormously across cultures because of the great diversity of human beliefs about (a) what constitutes a valued relationship, (b) what constitutes a threat to such a relationship, and (c) what one ought to do to protect a threatened relationship.

This diversity is revealed and explored in Ralph Hupka's review of ethnographic materials. Culture, he argues, influences an individual's interpretation of an event as threatening or not threatening to a valued relationship. Similarly, culture prescribes behaviors designed to protect the relationship by preventing the intrusions of the rival, punishing an aberrant mate and/or the rival, compensating an aggrieved mate, restoring one's standing in the eyes of others, and so forth.

Jealousy, Hupka concludes, is learned from culture — and it is learned differently in different cultures. For example, in the case of a man who finds that his wife has been sexually involved with a neighbor, a particular culture (or subculture) may prescribe one or more of several responses: killing the spouse and/or the rival with the approval of the community; fighting the rival until one combatant is seriously wounded or killed; mock combat supervised by friends and relatives of the rivals so that neither is likely to be seriously wounded or killed; loud, abusive arguing; a debate or formal insult match; a drum match or other musical competition; and others.[1] In fact, most cultures provide several possible solutions so that a jealous person may choose a reaction that fits his or her disposition.

Hupka concludes that the word jealousy refers to a situation characterized by the potential or actual loss of a loved one to a real or imagined rival. Such a situation has meaning only in the context of culture. Jealous behaviors are learned from culture as aspects of prevailing religious, moral, and economic values.

HOW IS JEALOUSY EXPERIENCED AND MANAGED IN ALTERNATIVE LIFESTYLES?

In the small, simple societies that Hupka surveyed, there is typically a high degree of consensus regarding sexual rules and gender roles. Large industrial societies are pluralistic; there is considerable variety in the forms of intimate association. If a Zuni woman suspects that her husband has been sexual with another, the wife has a culturally prescribed way of communicating her displeasure to her husband and to the community: She dumps the unwashed laundry out in front of their dwelling. An American wife with similar suspicions has not been provided with a culturally prescribed response. Her pluralistic culture allows considerable latitude. Similarly, she and her husband have considerable freedom to develop their marriage according to their own ground rules. These explicit and implicit rules may differ from the ground rules of other couples — and they often differ from the ground rules of one's parents or parents-in-law. In other words, modern industrial societies allow considerable diversity in intimate partnership. This toleration of variety makes alternative lifestyles possible.

Alternative lifestyles may be viewed as experiments. If we can temporarily suspend the moral judgments, the skepticism, and the envy that nontraditional forms often evoke, we shall learn more about the range and limits of human possibility. As important as it is to learn from one's own experience, it is also important to be able to learn from the experiences of others. (Consider how long you would last if the only way you could learn that being hit by a speeding truck is very bad for your health was from your own experience.) The last two articles in this issue investigate two nontraditional lifestyles: open marriage in the Netherlands and a utopian group marriage commune in San Francisco.

Open Marriage in the Netherlands

Perhaps the most intriguing feature of Bram Buunk's study of sexually open marriage in Holland is the sample — 125 men and 125 women, all of whom were or had been in a sexually open marriage in which one or both partners had had extramarital sexual experience. They are sexually liberal but most are not "swingers"; fewer than one-fifth have had three or more experiences of "mate exchange." This is significant because so much of the research literature on sexually open marriages is about swingers (probably because they are relatively easier to find and more willing to be interviewed than persons experimenting with other forms of sexually open marriage). Swingers may or may not be representative of other sexually liberal people. Perhaps Buunk's article will stimulate others to study sexually liberal but nonswinging persons and couples.

Because Buunk's sample is older and much more sexually liberal than Bringle's college student sample, we should expect some differences in the respective findings of these two studies. In contrast to Bringle, Buunk finds self-esteem and dependency to be only weakly related to jealousy, if at all. (Jealousy was positively correlated with neuroticism, which reflects general anxiety, and with low marital satisfaction for men but not for women.) Unlike Bringle and White, Buunk found women to be more jealous than men — and more likely than men to say that jealousy was reduced by good communication.

Perhaps the most significant finding in Buunk's study is that in most experiences of jealousy, feeling excluded is more important than fear of loss. In other words, threats to one's happiness or self-esteem in connection with a valued relationship are likely to produce more experiences of something called "jealousy" than the fear that one might actually lose the relationship. Thus, the prevention and management of jealousy depend not only on the preservation of the relationship but also on the *quality* of the relationship, especially with regard to the personal needs each partner meets through it.

Group Marriage in San Francisco

The last article in this issue reports on another alternative lifestyle — a utopian group marriage in that crucible of lifestyle experimentation, San Francisco. Ayala Pines and Elliot Aronson administered their jealousy inventory to the nine women and six men who make up Kerista Village and compared their responses with those of 87 Americans and 17 Israelis. The Keristans see themselves as a family unit with sexual intimacy occurring equally between all members of the other gender but with no sexual involvement outside the group.

Not surprisingly, the Keristans report less jealousy than the Americans and the Israelis. What is surprising is the unanimity of their responses. The Keristans report that, without exception, they feel no jealousy in connection with their multiple sexual and emotional relationships with each other. Similarly, they report that, without reservation, they trust each other not to become sexually or emotionally involved outside the group. On nearly all pertinent questions, the standard deviations were zero.

Significantly, there was no difference between the three samples in their self-reports of jealousy during childhood, adolescence, and young adulthood. It is only since they joined Kerista Village that its members report the complete absence of jealousy. Thus we note with interest certain features of their community life.

In some ways they are very conventional, even conservative. They do not become sexually involved with each other until they have made a mutual commitment to "a current intention of a lifetime involvement." They have two young children; they plan to have more (and to rear them communally). They are faithful to each other in their own way, having extended "the limits of a twosome to include fifteen people," as one member put it. Indeed, their contract with each other requires that all the adults be equally "in love" with all the adult members of the other gender. The community's norms are embedded in and supported by an elaborate system of beliefs, rituals, and slogans. The Keristans have constructed their own economic system and their own religion — complete with holidays, rituals, and a hip, black, female deity who wears sneakers. Members give themselves new names after entering the community, as do persons in many cultures who have made important religious commitments. Their goals and beliefs are set out in the Kerista Village Handbook. They also publish a magazine and a newspaper and conduct seminars. They use television and comic books to spread their utopian ideology. All these structures and activities help to build up and to sustain the shared understandings that hold this group together. It is this shared picture of reality that makes possible the unanimous claim of the Keristans that they feel no jealousy and are certain that they will feel none in the future. In his penetrating study of the formation and maintenance of the sustaining ideology of a counterculture commune, Bennett Berger (1981) reminds us that to call attention to the social causes and social functions of ideas and of ideologies need not necessarily involve the attempt to discredit or impugn them. After all, all knowledge is socially grounded. Everything we know was learned from others for some group purpose. To understand what people do and say — including their responses to questionnaires — we must find out what they know, what they believe to be true. And to account for what they know, we must ask (a) from whom and (b) for what group purpose they learned it.

The Keristans share an elaborate and carefully nurtured picture or reality. From whom have they learned it? Much of it they have made up together; they have learned it from each other (with some borrowing from the cultural storehouse) whereas most of us received our views of such matters from a culture that already existed when we were born. For what group purpose have the Keristans acquired their worldview? It enhances their solidarity as a group. It helps them hang together in the face of the very different picture of reality offered by the dominant culture. Their unusual pattern of responses to the jealousy inventory is a byproduct (not a primary goal) of the values and routines that bind the Keristans together. Likewise, a more conventional person's responses will be shaped by what he or she has learned from others about the protection of valued relationships in the face of perceived threats. Our parents and other role models teach us how to feel jealous when they teach us how to love and how to protect love.

CONCLUSION

Considered together, the articles in this issue reveal the complexity of jealousy and warn us against reducing jealousy to "nothing but" proof of love (as was fashionable as recently as the early 1960s) or to "nothing but" insecurity or low self-esteem (as is currently fashionable). If jealousy is the way we protect valued relationships in the face of perceived threats, we should expect jealousy to be as complex as everything we know — everything we have learned — about (a) what constitutes a valued relationship, (b) what constitutes a threat to such a relationship, and (c) what one ought to do to protect a threatened relationship.

From this it follows that one might reduce or manage painful jealousy by relearning and/or reframing in each of these areas. For example, one might (a) revise an unrealistic picture of what the valued relationship must be like and/or (b) discover that some perceived threats to the relationship are not really threats after all and/or (c) learn constructive ways of expressing concern and of protecting and nurturing the relationship so that destructive jealous responses become less likely. Perhaps this last area is the key: If we find positive, constructive ways of protecting valued relationships, we prevent and reduce painful jealousy.

Of course, the bits of knowledge on which jealousy depends are deeply learned and may not, therefore, be easily unlearned and relearned. Change is most likely when supported by persuasive new information and by a community of persons who share the new orientation one seeks to cultivate.

NOTE

1. Of course, in a few cultures (e.g., the Toda) and subcultures (e.g., contemporary "swingers" and practitioners of sexually open marriage), a man who finds that his wife has been sexually involved with a neighbor may not interpret this as a threat to his relationship with his wife, provided that the extramarital involvement conformed to the cultural or subcultural norms governing such matters. In the absence of a perceived threat to a valued relationship or to its quality, there would be no jealousy.

Jealousy in American Culture, 1945-1985

Gordon Clanton

EMOTIONS IN SOCIOLOGICAL PERSPECTIVE

Emotions are social as well as psychological phenomena. Emotions are responses to situations interpreted on the basis of previous social learning. They reflect the norms, attitudes, and values of groups as well as individuals. They are useful and dangerous for groups as well as individuals. These and other *social* aspects of emotions are the subject matter of the sociology of emotions. Until recently, sociology has had little to say about emotions despite their obvious importance in human affairs. Emotions have social dimensions. It is the business of sociology to explore them.

Emotions are shaped by society. Private experiences of emotion are embedded in history, in culture, in social structure. Not only our feelings but also our feelings about

This article was published in *The Sociology of Emotions: Original Essays and Research Papers*, edited by David D. Franks and E. Doyle McCarthy (Greenwich, CT: JAI Press, 1989).

258

our feelings are shaped by psychological, philosophical, and theological frameworks that are institutionalized in social life. Thus, patterns of emotional experience change in response to changes in society and culture. A powerful illustration of this principle is found in the evolution over the last four decades of the experience of jealousy.

For present purposes, *jealousy may be defined as a protective reaction to a perceived threat to a valued relationship or to its quality.* The protective reaction can involve thoughts, feelings, or actions. Although jealous behavior sometimes damages relationships, jealousy always *intends* the protection of the relationship and/or the protection of the ego of the threatened partner. Adult jealousy typically results when one believes that a romantic relationship is threatened by a real or imaginary rival. As Goffman (1967) notes about embarrassment, jealousy is not an irrational impulse breaking through socially prescribed behavior but part of this orderly behavior itself.

An analysis of articles in popular magazines reveals that the experience, expression, interpretation, and treatment of jealousy have changed substantially in the United States since World War II. Before about 1970, much jealousy was seen by many people as proof of love. Since 1970, jealousy has been seen by many people as a personal defect rooted in low self-esteem. Applying the sociology of knowledge to this patterning of human emotion, this article summarizes these changes, explores their social causes and effects, and suggests some implications for clinical practice and for self-understanding.

JEALOUSY IN POPULAR MAGAZINES

The popular media of a society can serve as an imprecise but useful barometer of the interests and concerns of the populations served by the media in question. Seeking to understand how jealousy has been viewed in the United States since World War II, I used the *Readers' Guide to Periodical Literature* to identify every article on jealousy published from 1945 to 1985 in the magazines indexed. The *Readers' Guide* is a cumulative index to general interest periodicals published in the United States. Thus, it provides a wide cross-section of publications sufficient for identification of trends. The *Readers' Guide*, which currently lists almost 200 periodicals, is arranged so that one can look up the subject of jealousy and find out which magazines included articles on this topic for a given time period. The *Readers' Guide* does not index fiction by subject so this survey included only non-fiction treatments of jealousy.

In addition to articles on adult jealousy in romantic relationships and in marriage, the entries for "Jealousy" typically include articles on sibling rivalry and other family jealousies as well as miscellaneous advice columns and other short items in which jealousy is one of several issues discussed. It is not always possible to tell from the title just what the article is about. Similarly, it is not always possible to classify articles as representing the "old" or "new" view of jealousy summarized later in this article.

If one considers only major articles on adult jealousy, one finds about one article per year from 1945 through the late 1950s and about two per year in the early 1960s. Almost nothing was published about adult jealousy from 1966 to 1972. From 1973 through 1978 there were, once again, about two articles per year. Since 1978, the average number of articles has increased to about five per year. To summarize: Except for the period from 1966 to 1972 when almost nothing was published about jealousy, the number of articles on jealousy in the magazines indexed in the *Readers' Guide* increased about five-fold over the four decades surveyed — with most of the increase occurring since 1978.

It should be noted that the survey was not intended to generate a precise or systematic survey of the contents of the approximately eighty articles published and reviewed. Rather, the intention was to read the articles in order to identify axial shifts taking place over the decades in people's views of jealousy, their evaluation of jealousy, and its social significance. For this reason, this report will highlight those specific articles that best communicate the "old" and "new" views of jealousy during the post-World War II period.

Over the forty-year span surveyed an interesting shift has occurred in the relative numbers of articles on adult jealousy as opposed to sibling rivalry and other jealousies among family members. Prior to 1966, articles on sibling rivalry and other family jealousies were more numerous than articles on adult jealousy in romantic relationships and in marriage. Since 1970, however, among the articles indexed under "Jealousy" in the *Readers' Guide*, those on adult jealousy have outnumbered articles on family jealousies by roughly six to one. Over this period, articles on sibling rivalry continued to appear and to be filed under "Siblings" or "Sibling rivalry." Apparently, however, fewer and fewer of these articles used the word "jealousy" in their titles. As a result, they are not indexed under "Jealousy." Thus, it appears that prior to 1966, the word "jealousy" was commonly used with reference to both adult jealousy and sibling rivalry. Since about 1970, the word "jealousy" has been used primarily with reference to adult jealousy in romantic relationships and marriage.

Another subtle shift in the connotations of the word "jealousy" is revealed by these data. Prior to 1966, most articles about adult jealousy focused on relatively innocent *flirtations*, for example, what to do if, at a party, your mate spends most of the evening in animated conversation with an attractive member of the other gender. Since about 1970, many articles on adult jealousy are about the threat of real sexual adventures and affairs, for example, what to do if your mate betrays you sexually or proposes an "open marriage."

Canvassing all the listed articles on jealousy over the forty-year period, one notes that the great bulk of them appeared in magazines oriented toward women readers. This pattern suggests that women have more interest in jealousy and other emotions than men.

JEALOUSY AS PROOF OF LOVE: 1945-1965

From the end of World War II until the late 1960s, virtually all of the articles in popular magazines said that a certain amount of jealousy was natural, proof of love, and good for marriage. The reader (typically a woman) was advised to keep her jealous feelings "under control" and to avoid the "unreasonable" jealousy that is marked by suspicion, hostility, accusations, and threats. The woman was told to avoid situations that might make her husband jealous but to interpret *his* expressions of jealousy as evidence of love.[1]   If jealousy threatened the stability of the marriage, the reader was advised to seek professional help.

Representative of this approach was a short piece in *McCall's* magazine (May 1962) by David R. Mace, a well-known marriage counselor and author. The article, titled "Two Faces of Jealousy," hinged on the distinction between normal and abnormal (or pathological) jealousy and moved from the assumption that the differences between the two were self-evident and nonproblematic. Normal jealousy, according to Mace, "is the instinct that flashes a warning when the exclusiveness of marriage is threatened. . . . Normal jealousy is a protective instinct that has saved many a marriage. Abnormal jealousy is a destructive obsession and often requires professional treatment." In this article, no attention was given to the possibility that definitions of "normal" and "abnormal" jealousy might vary from time to time, from place to place, and from couple to couple.

Judith Viorst's March 1970 Redbook article, "Confessions of a Jealous Wife," summed up the view of jealousy that had prevailed in the middle sectors of American society until about that time. Jealousy was approved and defended as a normal accompaniment of love. Some conventional strategies for coping with jealousy were discussed, including sarcasm, violence, and trying to make the spouse jealous. What Viorst refers to as the "civilized" response and the open marriage approach were ruled out. The author concluded that nothing really works. Jealousy is inevitable: "A man who wasn't attractive to other women, a man who wasn't alive enough to enjoy other women, a man who was incapable of making me jealous, would never be the kind of man I'd love."

Although it appeared in 1970, Viorst's "Confessions" represented the "old view" of jealousy, which was taken-for-granted in the 1950s and early 1960s. Nearly all articles on adult jealousy in popular magazines prior to 1970 reflected this point of view: Jealousy is natural; it is proof of love; it is good for marriage. Although the possibility of pathological jealousy was acknowledged and warned against, the focus was on little episodes of "normal" jealousy that show love is alive and need not threaten the quality of the relationship. After 1970, this "old view" of jealousy largely disappeared from the popular media for more than a decade.

JEALOUSY AS A PERSONAL DEFECT: 1970-1980

The magazines listed in the *Readers' Guide* and the popular media in general were largely silent about jealousy from 1966 to 1972. This is surprising in light of the fact that the same period produced an explosion of popular writing on sex, love, relationships, and personal growth. Perhaps the prevailing view of jealousy was changing so fast that writers and editors were unsure how to characterize it.

By about 1970, a new view of jealousy was taking root in a substantial and influential minority of Americans. Magazine articles began to question the appropriateness of jealous feelings in love relationships. Many people no longer assumed that jealousy is evidence of love. For the first time guilt about jealousy became an issue for large numbers of people.

According to the emerging view, jealousy was not natural; it was learned. Jealousy was no longer seen as proof of love;

it was, rather, evidence of a defect such as low self-esteem or the inability to trust. Thus, jealousy was not seen as good for relationships; it was bad for them. From this it followed that one could and should seek to eradicate every trace of jealousy from one's personality. Various prescriptions for achieving this were offered by therapists, gurus, and advice-givers.

Typical of magazine articles espousing the "new view" of jealousy was "Taming the Green-eyed Monster" by veteran writer Norman Lobsenz. Like the article by Judith Viorst previously discussed, the Lobsenz article also appeared in *Redbook* — exactly five years later (March 1975). Its thrust and tone, however, were quite different. Lobsenz cited psychologists and sociologists who suggested that jealousy was becoming outdated as society moved into an era of "liberated" relationships between men and women. He recounted the experiences of several young couples who tried to minimize jealousy in their marriages. He described how he overcame his own moment of jealousy when, at a party, his wife spent most of the evening in animated conversation with a good-looking man: "Once I realized that my wife's conversation with someone else took nothing away from me, . . . I also realized that there was no reason for jealousy." As with most articles reflecting the "new view," little attention was given to situations in which there really is a threat to the relationship and, therefore, a reason for jealousy. The semantics of the "new view" lead us to lose sight of appropriate jealousies rooted in real threats to valued relationships.

Lobsenz acknowledged that the would-be "liberated" are sometimes troubled by unexpected jealous feelings, which are all the more painful because these people are convinced that they ought not feel jealous. But even here, he is suggesting that it is desirable to be completely without jealousy. Reading such an article, one could easily believe that only defective people with poor reality-testing ever feel jealousy.

Lobsenz found the roots of jealousy in self-doubt and lack of self-esteem. He was confident that we can learn from our experiences of jealousy and that we can constructively redirect our jealous energy. This article offered an optimistic, rational, and one might say, a masculine counterpart to the treatments of jealousy published before 1970.

Not all articles advocating the new "liberated" view of jealousy were so optimistic. In the *Village Voice* (October 18, 1973), Karen Durbin observed that jealousy is "well on the way to becoming the New Sin of the liberated generation." In her own counter-cultural milieu with its emphasis on radical politics and women's liberation, possessiveness in love relationships was criticized as "emotional imperialism." Thus, Durbin tried to be liberated and felt guilty when she became jealous. For her and for others she knew, "The energy required for all that coping was too much, and I fled." All jealousy, Durbin concluded, is a cry of pain. It "will probably be with us as long as sex remains an expression of love and as long as love remains the most effective means (apart from religion) of assuaging our essential isolation." Durbin's article and her TV talk show appearances were much discussed in New York City and elsewhere. No doubt, many of the would-be liberated were relieved to hear a voice from the left suggesting it might sometimes be all right to feel jealous.

As different as they are in outcome and mood, the underlying assumptions about jealousy that characterize the articles by Lobsenz and Durbin are very similar. Both reflect the "new view" of jealousy as (1) a learned behavior that can and should be unlearned, (2) rooted in the personal defects of the jealous person, and (3) bad for relationships and for one's soul.

The change in the understanding of jealousy was accompanied by semantical shifts — changes in language that reflected new beliefs. Whereas in the 1950s the word "jealousy" often was used to describe normal and possibly beneficial feelings and behaviors, by the early 1970s the word increasingly was used primarily with reference to inappropriate, unconstructive, and even pathological reactions such as suspiciousness, paranoia, and violence. In the common speech of the l970s, the jealous person was usually characterized as unduly possessive, insecure, and suffering from low self-esteem.2

Of course, many people continued to hold onto the idea that some jealousy is appropriate and constructive, even as the popular media increasingly focused on its inappropriate manifestations. *McCall's*, for example, bucked the trend with a May 1974 article titled "In Defense of Jealousy." The United States is a pluralistic society. Amid rapid social change, old styles are *joined*, not replaced, by new styles. As a result, the number of styles is always increasing. Among more conventional people, "jealousy" continued to refer primarily to little misunderstandings and flirtations. For these people, a little jealousy continued to be seen as proof of love. Among those with more liberal views of sexual rules and gender roles, "jealousy" had to do with the possibility of greater personal freedom including, for some, levels of sexual freedom previously seen as incompatible with marriage. For these people, jealousy came to be associated with low self-esteem, poor reality-testing, inappropriate possessiveness, and unconstructive behavior. Given the demographics of the magazines in which the "new view" articles were published, it appears that the new view of jealousy was found more among the affluent than the poor, more among the better-educated than the less-well-educated, and more among the urban and the suburban than the rural.3

SOCIOLOGY OF KNOWLEDGE AND SOCIOLOGY OF EMOTIONS

Although some social scientists and helping professionals are among the advocates of the "new view" of jealousy, it is not the business of sociology to approve one of these interpretations as truer or better than the other. The rather more modest goal of sociology is to describe the change and to explain it by locating its social causes and social effects.

The search for the social roots and social functions of information, ideas, and opinions is the work of the sociology of knowledge. Early work in this field looked for the social sources of "big ideas" such as political philosophies and religions — often with the goal of discrediting the ideas and beliefs of others by pointing to their social causes.

In a major theoretical advance, Peter L. Berger and Thomas Luckmann (1966) proposed that the sociology of knowledge could and should be employed to analyze everything that people "know," everything they believe to be true. In other words, the many "small ideas" — the attitudes, beliefs, and values that make up one's picture of reality — are socially constructed and can be analyzed in terms of the social processes that gave rise to them.

To call attention to the social causes and social functions of ideas and attitudes need not necessarily involve the attempt to discredit or impugn them (Berger, 1981). All knowledge is socially grounded. My beliefs, no less than my opponents beliefs, are shaped by social forces. Thus, regarding this or that belief pertaining to an emotion such as jealousy, the sociology of knowledge asks not "Is this true?" but rather "Where did this idea come from?" and "How and why has it changed over time?"

This article is an exercise in the sociology of knowledge. We are searching for the social roots of the knowledge — the attitudes, beliefs, and values — on which the experience and interpretation of jealousy depend. In other words, we are looking for the social sources of the changing fashions in jealousy summarized above, namely, the shift from seeing jealousy as proof of love to seeing jealousy as a defect rooted in low self-esteem.

The experience and expression of emotions depend on what one "knows," what one believes to be true. Jealousy, as previously noted, is a protective reaction to a perceived threat to a valued relationship or to its quality. Thus, the experience and expression of jealousy depend on what one knows about (1) what constitutes a valued relationship (i.e., its boundaries and rules), (2) what constitutes a threat to the relationship or to its quality, and (3) what one ought to do to protect a threatened relationship. Jealousy and other emotions can be analyzed in terms of the social causes that give rise to the substantive beliefs and norms on which they depend.

Jealousy, in other words, is a consequence of social organization and will vary as forms of social organization vary. For example, swingers do not view sexual exclusiveness as a necessary condition for a happy marriage and so appear to be without jealousy in situations which would make most people jealous (see Gilmartin, Chapter 14). Similarly, people in other cultures get jealous in situations in which we do not (and vice-versa) because of cultural variations in definitions of relationship boundaries, threats, and protective strategies (see Mead, Chapter 10; Hupka, 1981).

SOCIAL SOURCES OF THE NEW VIEW OF JEALOUSY

The new view of jealousy that arose in the late 1960s and peaked in the early 1970s was a by-product of a larger shift in the shape of love relationships in the United States. The 1950s and early 1960s were characterized by an emphasis on relationship commitment or "togetherness." There was almost no talk about personal freedom in marriage. The "sexual revolution" and the women's movement were not yet topics of conversation. In such a time, jealousy was seen as a natural proof of love and as good for marriage.

In contrast, in the late 1960s and early 1970s, many individuals sought to enhance personal freedom in relationships, often at the cost of the forms of commitment characteristic of earlier times. Cohabitation became much more common. Women demanded fairness. The divorce rate rose. The media reported on nude beaches, communes, and gay pride. A book titled *Open Marriage* topped the best sellers list for over a year in 1972. For more on these trends, see Gagnon (1977), Swidler (1980), and Clanton (1984).

As a result of these and other manifestations of concern for more personal freedom in love relationships, jealousy came to be viewed by many as a personal defect. If one emphasizes freedom in relationships, one will see much jealousy as inappropriate and undesirable.

The quest for more personal freedom in love relationships and in marriage was part of a larger trend in favor of more freedom, more experimentation, and a more positive view of pleasure. These qualities often are associated with the youthful counter-culture of the late 1960s but, in fact, various manifestations of these themes diffused through the whole culture in the 1970s and 1980s. Although flowers and beads are less fashionable now than they were in the late 1960s, the counter-cultural view of jealousy as a defect remains quite strong today — even though the rhetoric of the 1980s and 1990s includes a certain amount of backlash against 1960s themes and values.

A longer view of history, amplified by cross-cultural comparisons, reveals that jealousy functions to protect love and other forms of valued relationships (Davis, 1936).[4] In every culture people form valued relationships in accordance with prevailing norms. Jealousy protects whatever kinds of relationships cultures teach people to value. Specific jealous behaviors vary enormously across cultures because of the great diversity of human beliefs about relationship boundaries, threats, and protection. The experience and the interpretation of jealousy change as beliefs about these matters change.

To summarize: The sexual conservatism of the period before about 1965 produced a relatively positive view of jealousy while the liberalization of the late 1960s and early

1970s produced a negative appraisal of jealousy.[5] Today many people still hold some version of the late 1960s view that jealousy is a personal detect. At the same time, "commitment" seems to be making something of a comeback. One hears less talk than before about freedom, adventure, and open marriage. Insofar as fear of AIDS and other developments make North American culture somewhat more conservative about sex, jealousy will, to some degree, be "rehabilitated" and more generally approved.

IMPLICATIONS FOR THERAPY AND SELF-HELP

A sociological view of jealousy can facilitate better self-understanding and more effective therapy. Although full discussion of these matters is not possible in the space available, I shall attempt briefly to illustrate that awareness of social forces can (1) enhance understanding of the contemporary experience of jealousy and (2) provide a basis for a critique of the fashionable but misleading view of jealousy as caused by low self- esteem.

Jealousy Today

The emphasis on personal freedom in relationships and the related view of jealousy as a personal defect peaked in the early 1970s. Since then, Americans have been integrating the new input of the late 1960s and recovering some of the concern about commitment and "togetherness" that characterized earlier times. In the United States today one finds adherents of both views of jealousy. As noted above, the "new view" that jealousy is evidence of personal defects remains very strong. But many contemporary people are skeptical of a too simple emphasis on either commitment or freedom. For more and more individuals and couples, the stated goal is to strike a balance between commitment and freedom in love relationships (Swidler, 1980).

Such a balance is not easy to achieve. American society is increasingly pluralistic. This means that husband and wife are more likely than in the past to have different values in connection with issues that bear on relationship quality. As a result, the management of jealousy will increasingly depend on good communication between partners of their personal needs and values and on honest negotiations where their respective needs and values are incongruent (Margolin, 1981). Such negotiations are not easy to achieve because most individuals in most relationships are reluctant to give up any power or advantage they hold.

C. Wright Mills (1959) reminded us that biography is embedded in history. Self-understanding often is enhanced by considering one's life against the backdrop of the events of one's time. The recent historical shift from an emphasis on commitment to an emphasis on freedom to an emphasis on balancing the two is analogous to the sequence of personal experience for most individuals. In the life-cycle of the developing person, attention first is given to the establishment of a committed relationship. Later there may emerge a concern for personal freedom in the context of commitment. Still later, perhaps following a break-up or divorce, many individuals rediscover the importance of commitment and seek to achieve a workable balance of commitment and freedom. Striking such a balance is the challenge of our time, especially for middle-aged individuals whose young adulthood coincided with the culture's emphasis on the personal freedom which, in the words of songwriter Kris Kristofferson, was sometimes "just another word for nothing left to lose."

Individuals who are aware of the cultural shifts described in this article may better understand important changes in their own lives. They will be less likely to adopt uncritically the still-fashionable view that jealousy is a personal defect. They will be more likely to look for the roots of jealousy in relationship dysfunctions rather than in intrapsychic disturbances. They will seek a balance of commitment and freedom rather than focus exclusively on one or the other. They will attempt to negotiate that balance rather than adopt some standard external to the couple or imposed by the partner. Awareness of the social forces does not guarantee that we shall find easy answers to complex personal questions, but, without such awareness, we are at the mercy of fads and fashions that may be harmful to us and to our love relationships.

Jealousy and Self-esteem

Today it is fashionable to assume that low self-esteem is a major cause of jealousy and that raising one's self-esteem is a good way to reduce or "cure" jealousy. The sociology of knowledge encourages a search for the social roots of this assumption.

Explanations of jealousy as evidence of low self-esteem are part of the larger tendency in the 1970s and 1980s to view a wide range of personal failures and problems as caused by low self-esteem. This view is widely taken for granted by both helping professionals and lay people. It is, nevertheless, erroneous and dangerous. In fact, one may have high self-esteem in general but still be uncertain and vulnerable in some situations. One may have high self-esteem but still experience jealousy if a valued relationship appears to be threatened.

Although it enjoys the status of a "scientific" principle of great therapeutic usefulness, the notion that emotional upsets are caused by low self-esteem is, in fact, an erroneous extension of the commonsense principle that success is associated with self-confidence and with liking oneself and that failure is associated with lack of self-confidence and not liking oneself (i. e., low self-esteem). Explanations of human behavior often assert that low self-esteem causes failure but it is at least as true that *failure causes low self-esteem* (or, that the relationship is reciprocal).   Thus, most statements in the popular psychological literature about the relationship between low self-esteem and various personal failures or inadequacies are, at best, circular and, at worst, backward. That is, such statements either say nothing beyond the truism that successful people feel better about themselves than do failures, or, worse: they actually invert the causal relationship and view low self-esteem as the cause of failure when, in fact, failure is more often the cause of lowered self-esteem.

Leaving aside the methodological problems that characterize many of the studies of jealousy and self-esteem (see Appendix I), several kinds of evidence suggest that, despite wide-spread opinion to the contrary, low self-esteem is *not* the principal cause of jealousy.

1. Cross-cultural surveys reveal that low self-esteem plays little or no role in explanations of jealousy in various cultures (Hupka, 1981). In all cultures, jealousy is provoked by perceived violations of marriage rules, by real events in the social world, not by personal defects in isolated individuals (Davis, 1936).

2. The "low self-esteem" explanation for jealousy is not found in the popular media in the United States before about 1970. If it were a timeless truth, you would expect somebody to write about it earlier.

3. Empirical research has not found a consistent correlation between low self-esteem and jealousy. David J. Kosins (1983: 75f.) reviews the literature and finds five studies that report modest correlations and five more that find no significant correlation. Gary L. Hansen (1985: 263) cites one study that finds a negative relationship between self-esteem and jealousy for both men and women, one that finds this relationship only for men, and three that find no relationship between the two variables. In his own research, Hansen (1985: 267) finds low self-esteem to be associated with jealousy for females but not for males. To summarize: Empirical research has not demonstrated a consistent correlation between jealousy and low self-esteem.

Furthermore, most studies do not address at all the question of causation.

4. The Kosins (1983) study finds no statistically significant relationship between jealousy and several developmental variables including childhood conflicts with siblings, separations and losses during childhood, harshness of parental discipline, quality of early parent-child relations, and emotional support from peers in childhood. Furthermore, there was no significant difference in the intensity of jealousy reported by college students (representing the "normal" or nonclinical population), psychotherapy outpatients, and a small sample of psychiatric inpatients. These surprising findings suggest that most jealousy is not best viewed as an emotional disorder rooted in the psychological deficiencies of the jealous person. (For further discussion, see Appendix III.)

5. Those who assume that low self-esteem causes jealousy (rather than the other way around) are also likely to assume that low self-esteem causes delinquent behavior in young people. Contrary to this expectation, John D. McCarthy and Dean R. Hoge (1984) found that the effect of self-esteem on subsequent delinquent behavior is negligible. Instead, they found consistent but weak negative effects of delinquent behavior on subsequent self-esteem. In other words, low self-esteem does not cause delinquency but delinquency has some tendency to lower self-esteem. The "common-sense" assumption of causal direction is backward. Furthermore, it is reasonable to assume that delinquent behavior sometimes raises self-esteem for persons who can find no other route to "success." At the very minimum, this study challenges the assumption that low self-esteem is responsible for problematic behavior including jealousy.

With these bits of evidence before us, we can re-evaluate the widespread belief that low self-esteem is the principal cause of jealousy.[6] Reflecting this viewpoint, a psychotherapist recently told me, "I have never had a jealous patient who was not also suffering from low self esteem." She was puzzled when I asked her which caused which. Like many others, she *assumed* that the low self-esteem caused the jealousy. It is at least as plausible that the jealousy caused the low self-esteem. That is, individuals' experiences of jealousy resulted in their feeling less good about themselves, a tendency encouraged by the "new view," which sees jealousy as a personal defect.[7]

If, as I have suggested, low self-esteem is more often an *effect* than a cause of jealousy, then one cannot reasonably hope to reduce jealousy by artificially pumping up one's self-esteem. To the contrary, one would need to find ways of reducing jealousy in order to raise self-esteem. The focus on raising self-esteem might actually divert attention away from the kind of work on one's jealousy that would be necessary if self-esteem is to be raised. As Gayla Margolin (1981) has noted, jealousy is an interactional problem more often than it is an individual problem. Jealousy is often a reflection of larger issues of relationship satisfaction and dissatisfaction.

CONCLUSION

This article, an exercise in the sociology of emotions and the sociology of knowledge, has argued that the experience, the expression, the interpretation, and the treatment of jealousy change as society and culture change. Since about 1970, jealousy has been seen by many as a personal defect rooted in low self-esteem. Awareness of the social roots of this shift illuminates the contemporary experience of jealousy and calls into question the still-fashionable view of jealousy as a useless emotion that grows out of low self-esteem.

NOTES

1. Accounts of such efforts suggest the necessity of "emotion work," active attempts to manage our emotions by evoking desirable ones and suppressing undesirable ones. For discussion see Hochschild (1983) and Thoits (1984).

2. Three of the magazine articles discussed in this article — those authored by Judith Viorst, Norman M. Lobsenz, and Karen Durbin — are reproduced and discussed in Part I of this book.

3. *Psychology Today* magazine has published five articles on jealousy, beginning with an excerpt (March 1977) from the 1977 Prentice-Hall edition of this book. These articles were research-oriented and so did not explicitly advocate either the "old" or the "new" view of jealousy. They do, nevertheless, reflect the movement of popular opinion toward the "liberated" view of jealousy. As evidence of this, the *Psychology Today* editors gave the excerpt from our book the "new view" title "The Self-inflicted Pain of Jealousy" — thus suggesting, as the book did not, that jealousy is a personal problem we bring on ourselves.

4. The analysis offered here is consistent with that of Kingsley Davis in his 1936 article "Jealousy and Sexual Property" but I have deliberately avoided the metaphor of *property*, because contemporary connotations of the term "property" distract from Davis' point and from mine. One need not view one's mate as property (in the contemporary pejorative sense of the word) in order to feel jealous. The Davis article is about rules of sexual access (especially marriage rules) and their impact on the experience of jealousy. The article is *not* a trendy condemnation of the double standard or of the practice of "treating one's mate like property." Beware the semantical shifts of fifty years.

5. Cross-cultural surveys (see Mead, Chapter 10; Hupka, 1981) confirm that, in general, societies with relatively restrictive sexual norms provide more occasions for jealousy and value it more highly than societies with more permissive norms. Insofar as the norms encourage freedom in relationships, many jealous behaviors will be seen as inappropriate and undesirable.

6. Our use of the term *cause* or *causal* is not meant to imply either a mechanical or one-way or stimulus-response relationship between a person's experiences of jealousy and of low self-

esteem. As used here, cause means that jealous feelings can often *precede* a person's view of himself or herself as an inferior or inadequate person (especially when jealousy is de-valued by current norms). It also means that it is reasonable to assume that jealousy evokes feelings of inferiority.

7. As Ellis and Weinstein (1986) point out, after the intrusive episode that provokes the jealousy, one can no longer take for granted the partner's commitment. This undercuts one's sense of self. The jealous person must be on guard against threats to self as well as against the possible loss of the partner. Similarly, Buunk and Bringle (1986) conclude that the experience of jealousy results in loss of self-esteem.

Developmental Correlates of Jealousy

Gordon Clanton and David J. Kosins

Conventional wisdom assumes, as do many approaches to clinical psychology, that early conflicts with parents and siblings make one more likely to experience intense jealousy in adult relationships. Our research fails to support this assumption. We found no statistically significant relationships between the self-report of jealousy and several developmental variables — namely, childhood conflicts with siblings, separations and losses during childhood, harshness of parental discipline, quality of early parent-child relations, and emotional support from peers in childhood. Furthermore, there was no significant difference in the intensity of jealousy reported by college students (representing the "normal" or nonclinical population), psychotherapy outpatients, and a small group of psychiatric inpatients. These findings suggest that jealousy is *not* best viewed primarily as an emotional disorder and that

This article was published in *The Psychology of Jealousy and Envy*, edited by Peter Salovey (New York: Guilford Press, 1991).

therapists treating clients with jealousy problems ought *not* assume that jealousy is always rooted in disrupted attachment history and early sibling conflicts. Additional discussion relates adult jealousy to social desirability, demographic variables, and family constellation.

The purpose of the study reported here was to examine the relationship between adult jealousy and a number of developmental variables. Despite much speculation, no empirical literature on adult jealousy prior to this research had assessed the impact of developmental correlates. Furthermore, previous research had studied *either* pathologically jealous cases *or* jealousy in a normal sample (usually college students). The present study set out to compare results across three samples: (1) college students, representing a "normal" or nonclinical population; (2) psychotherapy outpatients; and (3) psychiatric inpatients.

For present purposes, jealousy may be defined as a protective reaction to a perceived threat to a valued relationship or to its quality. The protective reaction can involve thoughts, feelings, and/or actions. Although jealous behaviors sometimes damage relationships, the *intention* of jealousy is the protection of the relationship and/or the protection of the ego of the threatened partner. Adult jealousy typically results when one believes that a romantic relationship is threatened by a real or imaginary rival.

We tested the psychoanalytic speculation that early sibling conflicts may increase the intensity of jealousy in adult romantic relationships (Freud, 1922/1955; Reik, 1945; Schmideberg,1953). We also measured the relationship between adult jealousy and several developmental variables central to the attachment theory of John Bowlby (1969, 1973, 1980). Psychoanalytic formulations are notoriously difficult to test empirically, but Bowlby's work has resulted in instruments to measure disrupted attachment history. Such instruments were employed in this research. We acknowledge that we have not

devised an empirical test of psychoanalytic theory. Our goal
was much more modest.

Bowlby postulated that ill-formed or disrupted
attachment with early caretakers often results in the
condition of "anxious attachment." The anxiously-attached
person remains "excessively sensitive to the possibility of
separation or loss of love" (Bowlby, 1973: 238) throughout
the lifespan. Attachment theory suggests that individuals
whose affectional bonds with primary caretakers have been
disrupted would be especially susceptible to adult jealousy.
As Bowlby (1979: 142) put it:

> A man who during childhood was frequently threatened
> with abandonment can easily attribute such   intentions
> to his wife. He will then misinterpret things she says or
> does in terms of such intent, and then take whatever
> action he thinks would best meet the situation he
> believes to exist.   Misunderstanding and conflict must
> follow.

On the basis of Bowlby's concept of anxious attachment,
one would expect that a disrupted attachment history would
increase vulnerability to adult jealousy by heightening
perception of threat. In particular, intensity of adult
jealousy was hypothesized to covary positively with number
of separations and losses during childhood and harshness of
parental discipline, and to covary negatively with quality of
parent-child relations and degree of emotional support from
peers during childhood.

This study was an unusual collaboration between a
psychologist and a sociologist — two investigators guided by
different theoretical frameworks, but agreeing on how to test
hypotheses of interest to both. As the research was
undertaken, the psychologist (Kosins) anticipated that adult
jealousy would correlate with disrupted attachment history
and formed his hypotheses accordingly. The sociologist
(Clanton) anticipated that the correlations would be weak or

nonexistent, thus supporting the null hypothesis. As we shall see, the psychological hypotheses were not supported by the results. A sociological perspective will inform the discussion of why the hypotheses were not supported.

METHOD

The subjects in this study were 86 men and 165 women between the ages of 18 and 50, representing three separate voluntary populations: 85 undergraduate students enrolled in introductory psychology classes; 129 nonpsychotic, nonsociopathic psychotherapy outpatients; and 37 nonpsychotic, nonsociopathic psychiatric inpatients living on open wards of two private psychiatric hospitals. Table 1 presents more detailed demographic information on this sample.

The inpatient sample was later dropped from the hypothesis testing because of an insufficient number of males in this group; this left 77 men and 137 women in the sample. After the data of several participants who reported their ages as over 50 were excluded, only nine male subjects remained in the inpatient group. Deleting subjects with missing data further reduced the inpatient group to a size judged inadequate for inclusion in the analysis. Answers to many questions raised by this research must await its replication with a study that includes a larger sample of male inpatients.

Six self-report instruments were employed:

1. The dependent variable, intensity of jealousy, was assessed by the Romantic Relationship Scale (RRS), developed in a pilot study for this investigation (Kosins, 1983). It is described below.

2. The Sibling Relationship Scale (SRS), adapted from Cattell (1953), measured degree of early sibling conflict, including early rivalry, envy, and jealousy among siblings, as well as parental comparisons and favoritism that might foster such feelings.

TABLE 1. Demographic Characteristics of the Research Sample

Characteristic	College students Males (n = 30)	College students Females (n = 55)	Outpatients Males (n = 47)	Outpatients Females (n = 82)	Inpatients Males (n = 9)	Inpatients Females (n = 28)	Total (n = 251)
Age							
M	25.2	25.3	32.6	31.5	36.6	34.7	30.12
SD	7.9	7.6	7.5	6.9	9.8	7.4	8.27
Education (years)							
M	13.2	12.9	14.5	14.4	12.4	12.8	13.7
SD	1.4	1.1	2.5	2.2	2.4	2.4	2.1
Marital status (%)							
Never married	66.7	56.4	30.4	30.5	11.1	8.0	37.7
Married	20.0	27.3	37.0	40.2	77.8	68.0	38.5
Divorced	10.0	7.3	26.1	22.0	—	16.0	16.6
Separated	3.3	9.0	6.5	6.1	11.1	4.0	6.5
Widowed	—	—	—	1.2	—	4.0	.8
Annual income (%)							
Less than $10,000	25.0	23.1	8.7	13.6	11.1	—	14.5
$10,000-$19,999	10.7	26.9	34.8	30.9	—	20.8	26.3
$20,000-$29,999	32.1	23.1	21.7	13.6	66.7	41.7	24.2
$30,000-$39,999	7.1	11.5	13.0	22.2	11.1	16.7	15.4
$40,000-$49,999	10.7	7.7	4.3	6.2	—	4.2	6.3
$50,000 or more	14.3	7.7	17.4	13.6	11.1	16.7	13.3

Race (%)							
Caucasian	78.6	74.1	86.7	97.6	88.9	69.6	85.1
Hispanic	3.6	14.8	11.1	2.4	11.1	17.4	8.7
Black	3.6	1.9	—	—	—	13.0	2.1
Oriental	10.7	7.4	—	—	—	—	2.9
Other	3.6	1.9	2.2	—	—	—	1.2
Religion							
Protestant	35.7	40.7	39.1	38.3	37.5	29.2	37.8
Catholic	25.0	29.6	21.7	23.5	25.0	62.5	28.6
Jewish	—	1.9	2.2	3.7	—	—	2.1
Atheist/agnostic	10.7	3.7	28.3	16.0	25.0	—	13.7
Other	28.6	24.1	8.7	18.5	12.5	8.3	17.8

Note. Missing cases for these variables are as follows: education, 4; marital status, 4; income, 11; race, 10; religion, 10.

3. The Attachment History Questionnaire (AHQ), based on the work of Kessler and Pottharst (1982), assessed number of separations and losses during childhood (AHQ1); harshness of parental discipline, including threats of abandonment (AHQ2); quality of parent-child relations (AHQ3); and quality of peer relations in childhood (AHQ4). The AHQ asks about hospitalizations and boarding school, family conflict and dissolution, parental support and criticism, types of punishment, and relationships with friends while still living with one's parents.

4. A demographic questionnaire was used to collect background data.

5. The Edwards Social Desirability Scale (Edwards, 1957) was administered to identify the extent to which the social desirability response set biased self-report on the variables under study.

6. Finally, subjects were given the Interpersonal Relationship Scale (IRS) (Hupka and Rusch, 1977), a measure of jealousy and envy previously used in several research studies (Hupka and Bachelor, 1979; Rosmarin, Chambless, and LaPointe, 1979). This was included to generate an index of convergent validity of the RRS.[2]

Our jealousy measure, the Romantic Relationship Scale (RRS), presented subjects with 15 hypothetical situations that might produce jealousy (e.g., "At a party, your partner hugs another man/woman," and "Your partner tells you he/she is sexually attracted to a mutual friend of yours"). Respondents were asked to indicate on a 5-point Likert scale how they would feel: "very pleased," "pleased," "neutral," "displeased," or "very displeased." In addition, subjects were asked to indicate on a 5-point Likert scale the extent to which they agreed or disagreed with 13 statements such as "I frequently check up to see if my partner has been where he/she says he/she has been," and "I often worry that I'll lose my partner to another man/woman." Whereas some jealousy measures assess reaction to betrayal or relationship loss, we sought to include a range of situations in which the threat was more ambiguous and the outcome more dependent on the interpretation of the individual. See the Appendix for the full text of the RRS.

Because jealousy is viewed pejoratively by many people, the development of the RRS, our jealousy measure, included numerous steps to reduce distortion from participants' trying to answer in socially desirable ways. One such step was to avoid the use of the word "jealousy" in the instrument.[3] The RRS in this study had adequate internal consistency (coefficient alpha $= .90$) and test-retest reliability ($r = .82$, $p < .001$) established over a 2-week interval. The convergent validity coefficient with the IRS (Hupka & Rusch, 1977) was .69 ($p < .001$). See Kosins (1983: 112-122) for a more thorough discussion of construct and content validity of the RRS and the other scales.

Procedures for data collection differed for each subject group. The college students completed the batteries in class. The outpatients received the packets from one of 57 participating psychotherapists and mailed them to the principal investigator (Kosins). The inpatients completed their packets during their regular community meetings. For each group, all data gathered remained anonymous.

Treatment of the data involved multiple-regression analyses, with five predictor variables (corresponding to the five hypotheses described above) and one outcome variable (the intensity of adult jealousy). Four control variables were also included in the regression model: group membership, gender, the interaction of group and gender, and social desirability as measured by the Edwards Scale. We then tried to identify the degree to which the predictor variables were associated with adult jealousy, after taking into account the control variables.

RESULTS

Neither sibling conflict during childhood nor any of the four hypothesized attributes of attachment history was associated with adult jealousy, after controlling for group membership, gender, the interaction of group and gender, and social desirability. No statistically significant relationships were found between the predictor variables and the outcome variable, adult jealousy (see Table 2).

Confirming our sense that the self-report of jealousy is distorted by the desire to deny personal experience of what is perceived as a negative emotion, the Edwards Social Desirability Scale was the variable most strongly associated with jealousy in this study (see Table 3). Those people with low scores on the Edwards Scale obtained higher scores on the RRS, F (1, 136) = 6.51, p = .012. In other words, the less a person tended to give socially desirable responses in self-description, the more jealousy he or she admitted. Put differently, the willingness to admit one's weaknesses correlated more strongly with the self-report of jealousy than did any other variable considered in this study. This finding suggests that jealousy is very hard to assess by self-report, no matter how subtle the instrument.

It is important to remember that most of the scales social scientists use to measure jealousy are in fact measures of the ability to acknowledge and the willingness to disclose jealousy. In a time when jealousy in widely viewed in pejorative terms, we should not be surprised by the finding of Bringle (1981) that college students who were self-deprecating and dissatisfied with their lives were more likely to report that they would be jealous in a series of hypothetical jealousy-provoking situations. This finding does not demonstrate that jealous people are necessarily self-deprecating and dissatisfied with themselves. It does suggest, however, that people who are more willing to admit to dissatisfaction with themselves are also more likely to admit to jealousy.

TABLE 2. Partial *F* Tests for Prediction of RRS from SRS and AHQ, Controlling for Group, Gender, Group X Gender, and Edwards Scores

Source	SS	df	MS	F	p
SRS	10.82	1	10.82	0.07	.799
AHQ1	85.28	1	85.28	0.51	.475
AHQ2	16.24	1	16.24	0.10	.755
AHQ3	162.25	1	162.25	0.98	.325
AHQ4	245.56	1	245.56	1.48	.226
SRS and AHQ1-AHQ4	538.91	5	107.78	0.65	.663
Residual	22,608.82	136	166.24		

Note. The impatient group was excluded from this analysis. RRS, Romantic Relationship Scale, a measure of jealousy; SRS, Sibling Relationship Scale; AHQ, Attachment History Questionnaire (AHQ1, separations and losses during childhood; AHQ2, harshness of parental discipline, threats of abandonment; AHQ3, quality of parent-child relations; AHQ4, quality of peer relations in childhood).

TABLE 3. The Full Model for the Prediction of RRS Scores from Group Membership, Gender, the Edwards Covariate, and the Five Predictors

Variable	Raw score coefficient	Standard error of coefficient	Beta
Constant	108.09		
Group	2.19	2.90	.08
Gender	—4.47	2.89	—.16
Group X gender	—0.93	4.66	—.02
Edwards	—0.49	0.19	—.24
SRS	0.03	0.11	.02
AHQ1	—0.23	0.32	—.06
AHQ2	—0.02	0.07	—.04
AHQ3	0.08	0.08	.10
AHQ4	0.17	0.14	.12

$$\text{Standard error of estimate} = 12.89$$
$$\text{Multiple } R = .37$$
$$\text{Multiple } R^2 = .14$$

RRS, Romantic Relationship Scale, a measure of jealousy; SRS, Sibling Relationship Scale; AHQ, Attachment History Questionnaire (AHQ1, separations and losses during childhood; AHQ2, harshness of parental discipline, threats of abandonment; AHQ3, quality of parent-child relations; AHQ4, quality of peer relations in childhood).

With regard to gender differences, no significant differences between men and women were noted when they were compared directly. However, in all three subject groups, there was a tendency for women to respond with more jealousy than men to the hypothetical situations presented by both the RRS and the IRS. In addition, women in each group scored slightly lower than their male counterparts on the Edwards Scale. When social desirability and other control and independent variables were included in the full model regression analysis, the contribution of gender was still significant, with higher jealousy scores for women. Given the strong relationship between self-reported jealousy and the social desirability response set noted above, the tendency in this study for women to report more jealousy than men may reflect women's greater willingness to disclose negative experiences and feelings (Jourard, 1964).

A supplemental analysis found no relationship between adult jealousy and subjects' reports of whether or not their partners had ever been unfaithful. However, subjects who reported never having a sexual affair during their current relationship scored significantly higher on the jealousy measure than subjects who had experienced sex with others. In other words, fidelity was associated with increased jealousy over one's partner. (For further discussion of these results, see Kosins, 1983: 195-197.)

Apart from gender, discussed above, none of the demographic variables (age, marital status, length of relationship, race, religion, income, and educational level) was found to correlate significantly with scores on the RRS. Birth order, age spacing, and family size were found to have no significant relationship to the intensity of adult jealousy, even though early research demonstrated associations between family constellation and *childhood* jealousy (e.g., Foster, 1927; Ross, 1931; Sewall, 1930). Thus, individuals may compensate in adulthood for early experiences that might otherwise influence the development of adult jealousy.

Although the small number of valid questionnaires required that we drop the inpatient group from the hypothesis testing, our findings in this connection are at once provocative and congruent with other outcomes of this study. Contrary to what many would expect, the small inpatient group scored no higher on the jealousy measure than did the "normal" college students. This finding constitutes provisional, circumstantial evidence that jealousy may be no more prevalent in clinical populations (inpatient as well as outpatient) than in nonclinical populations (represented by the student group). (An exception may be the presence of pathological or delusional jealousy in patients with paranoid disorders. Such patients were not included in this study.) If psychiatric inpatients are no more jealous than "normal" people, doubt is cast on the widespread assumption that jealousy usually grows out of some psychological defect. Certainly this matter is worthy of further research.

DISCUSSION

Although the developmental hypotheses tested here were not supported by the data,[4] this study is useful precisely because it provides *an empirical basis for questioning the widespread view that jealousy is a psychological defect rooted in early experience.* The hypothesized relationship between jealousy and disrupted attachment history might well be found in a sample of pathologically jealous subjects, such as individuals with paranoid disorders or prisoners convicted of "crimes of passion." In our less pathological samples, however, jealousy did not correlate with disrupted relationships with parents, siblings, and peers during childhood.

The surprising finding of the null hypothesis supports the sociological view that a great deal of jealousy is nonpathological, indeed, functional behavior. The universal social function of jealousy is the protection of marriage and other valued relationships (Davis, 1936). In every culture, people marry and form other valued relationships in accordance with prevailing norms. Jealousy protects whatever kinds of relationships cultures teach people to value. Specific jealous behaviors vary enormously across cultures (Hupka, 1981) because of the great diversity of human beliefs concerning (1) what constitutes a valued relationship, (2) what constitutes a threat to such a relationship, and (3) what one ought to do to protect a threatened relationship. Across cultures, jealousy is a protective reaction to a perceived threat to a valued relationship or to its quality.

The general social usefulness of jealousy is easily overlooked in contemporary American culture, because the word "jealousy" is used primarily to describe inappropriate and unconstructive expressions of the emotion. Beginning in the late 1960s, the growing emphasis on personal freedom and self-actualization in love relationships led to a devaluation of jealousy and to a greater readiness to see jealousy as a personal defect rooted in low self-esteem (see Appendix II). The sexual conservatism and the emphasis on "togetherness" in the period before 1965 produced a relatively positive view of jealousy. The liberalization of the late 1960s and 1970s produced a generally negative appraisal of jealousy. Insofar as norms encourage personal freedom in relationships, many jealous behaviors will be seen as inappropriate and undesirable. The view that jealousy is evidence of personal defects has persisted through the 1980s and 1990s, obscuring the fact that many jealous behaviors are appropriate and constructive ways of protecting valued relationships from real threats.

Awareness of the social usefulness of jealousy helps explain why this study found no relationship between adult jealousy and disrupted attachment history as theories based on the work of Freud or Bowlby would lead one to expect. If jealousy were a pathological condition, then most jealous adults probably would report disrupted attachment histories (conflict with parents and siblings, fear of abandonment, etc.). However, if much jealousy were actually functional and most jealous individuals were "normal," jealous adults would be no more likely than other "normal" people to report disrupted attachment histories. The failure of this study to find a relationship between adult jealousy and disrupted attachment history supports the view that jealousy is useful to individuals, couples, and groups. Because most jealousy is not pathological, jealous adults ought not to be expected to report disrupted attachment histories.

The findings of this study suggest that therapists working with clients who express concerns regarding jealousy would do well to focus on etiological factors other than attachment history and early sibling relations. Other antecedent conditions that affect the experience of jealousy and that may provide the therapist with useful clues include social, cultural, and subcultural influences; situational and environmental factors; the personality characteristics of the individual; and the nature of current and previous romantic relationships (cf. Bringle & Williams, 1979). In general, therapists should give more attention to *context* and to socially constructed *meanings*, rather than focusing on jealous *behaviors* per se. Jealousy is more often an interactional problem of a couple rather than a personality defect of an individual. Very often, jealousy is a sign that something is wrong with the *relationship* rather than with one of the partners (Margolin, 1981).

Because of the wide range of clients' attitudes and values regarding relationship boundaries, threats to relationships, and protective strategies, it is difficult for therapists to determine objectively whether a particular expression of jealousy is appropriate or inappropriate, constructive or destructive. Therapists' judgments in such matters often reflect their own values and lifestyle choices, as well as the widespread but erroneous belief that all jealousy is inappropriate and destructive.

To summarize: This study challenges the widespread assumption that adult jealousy is correlated with disrupted attachment history. It thereby calls into question the common practice of viewing jealousy primarily as an emotional disorder. Given the counter-intuitive findings, however, further research will be needed to substantiate the results.

NOTES

1. This article is based on the Ph.D. dissertation of David J. Kosins submitted to the California School of Professional Psychology, San Diego. Gordon Clanton, a sociologist at San Diego State University, served on the committee that supervised the dissertation.

2. The IRS uses the word "jealousy" in all but a few of its items. Factors assessed include (a) threat to exclusive companionship, (b) self-deprecation/ envy, (c) dependency, (d) sexual possessiveness, (e) competition and vindictiveness, and (f) trust.

3. Self-report instruments that ask how "jealous" one is or how "jealous" one would be in a hypothetical situation are of limited usefulness. To pose the questions this way is to assume (a) that everyone knows what jealousy is (when, in fact, different people have different definitions of it); (b) that people always know when they are jealous (when, in fact, they may be jealous and not be aware of it); and (c) that people always tell the truth about their feelings (when, in fact, they often relabel or even lie about them). Although these assumptions make possible a methodological shortcut, they also place limits on the usefulness and generalizability of the findings. A measure of the self-report of "jealousy" is not necessarily a good measure of jealousy (cf. Bringle, 1982: 1). In our one use of the word "jealousy," our questionnaire eliciting background information asked: "In comparison to other people, how jealous of a person do you think you are?" Respondents indicated their responses along a 5-point Likert scale from "much less" to "much more." Our jealousy measure, the RRS, showed a significant positive correlation ($r = .62$, $p < .01$) with these self-ratings of jealousy.

4. For a discussion of methodological problems and limitations of the research design, see Kosins (1983: 171-184). Attention is given to social desirability response set, problems associated with self-report and retrospective reporting, instrument reactivity, missing data, biased administration, nonrandom sampling, and the limitations of correlational research.

APPENDIX: THE ROMANTIC RELATIONSHIP SCALE

This is the female form of the jealousy measure (RRS) used in this study. The male form substitutes the words "man" for "woman," "male" for "female," "he" for "she," "him" for "her," and "boyfriend" for "girlfriend."

Part I: Instructions

Below are some situations in which you may have been involved. Please rate how you would feel if you were confronted with the situation by circling the appropriate number. Do not answer in terms of how you think you *should* feel, but rather how you would *actually* feel. Answer as if you were in a serious relationship. If you have not been involved in a particular situation, then *imagine* how you would feel in that situation and reply to the item accordingly. Be sure to answer each item — even if you have to guess. Your first reaction to the item is what matters. There is no time limit, but work quickly. There are no right or wrong answers.

Scale of how you would *actually* feel:
  1 — Very pleased
  2 — Pleased
  3 — Neutral
  4 — Displeased
  5 — Very displeased

1. At a party, your partner dances with another woman.   1 2 3 4 5

2. Your partner comments to you on how attractive another woman is.   1 2 3 4 5

3. Another woman kisses your partner on the cheek at a New Year's party.   1 2 3 4 5

4. You see a picture in your partner's wallet of a woman he used to date.   1 2 3 4 5

5. At a party, your partner hugs another woman.   1 2 3 4 5

6. Someone flirts with your partner.   1 2 3 4 5

7. Your partner sees an old girlfriend and responds   1 2 3 4 5
   with a great deal of happiness.
8. Your partner pays more attention to another   1 2 3 4 5
   woman besides you at a party.
9. You hear your partner enjoying a conversation   1 2 3 4 5
   with another woman on the telephone. When he
   sees you he hangs up.
10. At a party, your partner disappears for a long   1 2 3 4 5
    period of time.
11. Your partner flirts with another woman.   1 2 3 4 5

12. Your partner goes to a bar several evenings   1 2 3 4 5
    without you.
13. Your partner tells you he is sexually attracted   1 2 3 4 5
    to a mutual friend of yours.
14. Your partner receives a letter from a former   1 2 3 4 5
    lover and refuses to tell you what it says.
15. At a party, your partner passionately kisses   1 2 3 4 5
    a woman you do not know.

Part II: Instructions

Below you will find a list of statements. After reading each statement, circle the appropriate number to indicate how true the statement is for you. As before, answer as though you were in a serious romantic relationship. Say how you would *actually* feel, not how you think you *should* feel. Be sure to answer each one.

Scale of how you would *actually* feel:
  1 — Strongly disagree
  2 — Disagree
  3 — Neutral
  4 — Agree
  5 — Strongly agree

1. If my partner admired another woman, I would   1 2 3 4 5
   feel irritated.
2. I wouldn't worry or become suspicious if a   1 2 3 4 5
   female stranger called my partner.

3. I frequently check up to see if my partner has been where he says he has been.　　1 2 3 4 5

4. I wouldn't mind if my partner were accidentally to call me by the wrong name.　　1 2 3 4 5

5. I seldom worry about where my partner is or what he is doing with his time.　　1 2 3 4 5

6. I like to find fault with my partner's former girlfriends.　　1 2 3 4 5

7. If I thought that my partner was interested in another woman, I would get very upset.　　1 2 3 4 5

8. I feel inferior when my partner talks to an attractive stranger.　　1 2 3 4 5

9. I often worry that I'll lose my partner to another woman.　　1 2 3 4 5

10. It wouldn't bother me if my partner flirted with another woman.　　1 2 3 4 5

11. If my partner becomes close to another woman, I feel happy for him.　　1 2 3 4 5

12. If I thought my partner was seeing another lover, I would feel angry or hurt.　　1 2 3 4 5

13. If my partner went out with another woman, I would get intensely upset.　　1 2 3 4 5

A Sociology of Jealousy

Gordon Clanton

This paper sums up more than 20 years of research and reflection on jealousy. A chronological account of this work is followed by a thematic summary of the findings and some discussion of the relationship between sociology and psychology. Sociological analysis shows that jealousy and other emotions are shaped by social situations, social processes, and social forces. Micro-sociology reveals that jealousy is learned. Jealousy reflects the life experience of the individual. Meso-sociology reveals that jealousy is socially useful, indeed, indispensable to social order. Jealousy reflects the institution of marriage and the prohibition of adultery. Macro-sociology reveals that jealousy is shaped by society and culture. Jealousy reflects the history and the values of a people — and the relevant values vary from time to time and place to place. In the United States, for example, a new and more negative view of jealousy emerged after about 1970 as a result of the sexual revolution and the women's movement.

This article was published in the *International Journal of Sociology and Social Policy*, Vol. 16: No. 9/10, 1996.

LOOKING AT JEALOUSY SOCIOLOGICALLY

Since graduate school, I have been interested in the dramatic changes in matters of sex, love, marriage, and the family that began in the 1960s (see Clanton and Downing, 1975; Clanton, 1984). As Brigitte and Peter Berger (1984) later noted, Americans have been involved since the 1960s in a cultural war over the family — a vociferous and value-loaded debate over the history, the present condition, the prospects, and the human and societal value of the family. Americans are sharply divided over issues such as birth control, abortion, sex education, unmarried cohabitation, single parents, and homosexuality.

I approached the broader issue of family and social change by focusing on jealousy, an emotion that becomes especially salient when sexual norms and gender roles are in flux. Although jealousy may be experienced in many types of relationships including sibling rivalry and jealousy of non-sexual friends, the focus of this research is the adult jealousy that arises in romantic relationships and in marriage.

For present purposes, jealousy may be defined as a protective reaction to a perceived threat (especially adultery) to a valued relationship (especially marriage) or to its quality. The protective reaction can involve thoughts, feelings, and/or actions. Although jealous behaviors sometimes damage relationships, the *intention* of jealousy is the protection of the relationship and/or the protection of the ego of the threatened partner. Adult jealousy typically results when a person believes that a marriage or romantic relationship is threatened by a real or imagined rival.

Social Aspects of Jealousy

The recent history of jealousy in the United States reveals that jealousy changes as society changes. Prior to the late 1960s, the prevailing view of marriage emphasized commitment and "togetherness," so jealousy (within appropriate limits) was widely viewed as a natural emotion, as evidence of love, and as good for marriage. Women's magazines told readers that they should be flattered if their husbands were a little jealous. Beginning in the late 1960s, as the sexual revolution and the women's movement introduced a new concern with personal freedom and "personal space," jealousy came to be viewed by many as a learned emotion, as evidence of some personal defect such as "low self-esteem," and as bad for marriage and other intimate relationships. By the early 1970s, women's magazines reflected the new view of jealousy as a useless emotion that is out of place in a world of "liberated" relationships. Changes in society and culture produced changes in the private emotional life of individuals (Clanton and Smith, 1977; Clanton, 1989).

In our 1977 book *Jealousy*, psychologist Lynn Smith and I assembled an integrated anthology of writings on jealousy by sociologists, anthropologists, psychologists, and psychotherapists. Contributors include Kingsley Davis (on the social function of jealousy), Margaret Mead (on its cross-cultural variability), Jessie Bernard (on recent changes in jealousy), and Robert Whitehurst (on jealousy and American values). The book also includes chapters on various psychological approaches to jealousy, including psychoanalysis, cognitive social psychology, and rational-emotive therapy. The book closes with a synthesis of these materials and with a provisional statement of a sociology of jealousy that draws attention to the situations in which jealousy arises, the social learning by which it is shaped, the social institutions in which it is embedded, and the society and culture that it reflects.

Utilizing the recent history of jealousy as reflected in women's magazines and employing the sociology of knowledge developed by Peter Berger and Thomas Luckmann (1966), we argued that jealousy is a socially-constructed emotion that changes to reflect changes in marriage rules, the adultery taboo, and gender roles. Following Kingsley Davis (1936), we argued that jealousy is not useless, but rather serves the social function of protecting marriage and relationships leading to marriage, thereby contributing to social order. We defined jealousy as a protective reaction to a perceived threat to a valued relationship or to its quality (Clanton and Smith, 1986: vi, 239). And we noted that the universal protective function of jealousy is easily overlooked in a culture in which the new view of jealousy as a personal defect remains strong and, indeed, has become a staple of popular psychology.

Following publication of the book on jealousy, I developed one of the first courses in the sociology of emotions. Since 1977, more than 4,000 students have taken Love, Jealousy, and Envy. The course includes a historical analysis of sex, love, marriage, and family in Western culture; a sociological social psychology of jealousy; and an exploration of the political implications of envy. The course introduces students to a wide range of historical and comparative materials and to diverse theoretical perspectives as it demonstrates the influence of social forces on the private emotions of individuals. Teaching a course on love, jealousy, and envy affords me contact with students who share their personal experiences, observations, clippings from the media, hunches, and theories. For accounts of the course, see Clanton (1985, 1986, and 1987).

Collaborating with several psychologists, I edited a special issue on jealousy for the journal *Alternative Lifestyles* (4:3, August 1981), later renamed the *Journal of Family and Economic Issues*. My introduction, "Frontiers of Jealousy Research" (Clanton, 1981), included a brief history of social science research on jealousy, an integrative summary of the five articles in the special issue, and some suggestions for further research. The articles confirmed the importance of social learning, social institutions, culture, and social structure. Gregory L. White showed that the perception that oneself is relatively more involved than one's partner tends to increase jealousy, thus suggesting that the balance of power in a relationship may be more important in the production of jealousy than the low self-esteem of an individual (see also White and Mullen, 1989). Ralph B. Hupka used ethnographic literature to show that jealousy arises in situations characterized by the potential loss of one's mate to a real or imagined rival, thus suggesting that jealousy is learned from culture as individuals internalize prevailing religious, moral, and economic values. Two studies of sexually liberal subcultures (by Bram Buunk in the Netherlands and by Ayala Pines and Elliot Aronson in San Francisco) revealed that the reduction of jealousy in contexts of sexual permissiveness requires the construction and maintenance of alternate worldviews and community rituals (see also Pines, 1992).

Jealousy and Self-esteem: A Misunderstood Relationship

Following the publication in 1986 of a new edition of *Jealousy*, I updated and expanded the historical analysis of jealousy in the late 20th century, challenging the popular notion that jealousy is best understood as a result of "low self-esteem" or other psychological deficiencies in the jealous person (Clanton, 1989). Although jealousy may be exacerbated by the personal weaknesses and pathologies of individuals, sociological analysis suggests that most jealousy is best understood as a *relationship* problem that requires the attention of both members of the couple.

Although sociology is not a clinical method, the sociological study of emotions has clinical implications. Sociological analysis suggests that the reduction of painful jealousy may depend more on negotiation *between* the partners than on the eradication of some weakness in one partner. If professional help is sought, marriage counseling or relationship therapy may be more helpful than individual psychotherapy. By focusing so narrowly on the individual, psychotherapy sometimes exacerbates relationship problems.   Helping professionals who work with jealous couples should give more attention to the social forces bearing upon them, especially the life-cycle of the couple, their economic circumstances, and the changing cultural environment, especially ongoing changes in women's roles.

In 1982 David Kosins, a student at California School for Professional Psychology in San Diego, asked me to join the committee supervising his doctoral dissertation.   He tested the psychoanalytic speculation that early conflicts with parents and siblings make an individual more likely to experience intense jealousy in adult relationships.   To David's surprise, but as I anticipated, the research found *no* statistically-significant relationships between a subtle measure of jealousy and several developmental variables including childhood conflicts with siblings, separations and losses during childhood, harshness of parental discipline, quality of early parent-child relations, and emotional support from peers in childhood.   Furthermore, there was no significant difference in the intensity of jealousy reported by college students (representing the "normal" or nonclinical population), psychotherapy outpatients, and a small group of psychiatric inpatients.   These findings suggest that jealousy is *not* best viewed primarily as an emotional disorder and that therapists treating clients with jealousy problems ought *not* assume that jealousy always is rooted in disrupted attachment history and early sibling conflicts (see Kosins, 1983; Clanton and Kosins, 1991).   Although this study is a modest one and further research is needed, these findings call into question the popular view that all or most jealousy is caused by personal deficiencies such as low self-esteem.

Jealousy and Power: A Neglected Relationship

The work with David Kosins confirmed my growing sense that the key to understanding jealousy is not the low self-esteem of the jealous individual (a psychological fact) but rather the imbalance of power within the couple (a social fact). I devised the "Relationship Assessment Scale" (see Appendix) to measure power differences in love relationships such as dating, cohabitation, engagement, and marriage. Partners respond separately and without consultation to ten questions such as: Who makes more money? Who has more professional prestige? Who loves the other more? Who would find a new partner quicker if you broke up? Who desires sex with the other more? Who is more articulate, more persuasive? In most relationships, one partner will be more powerful in some areas and the other, in others.

My theory predicts that the greater the imbalance of power within the couple, the greater the likelihood of problems with jealousy. Conversely, the more equal the balance of power, the less jealousy. This suggests that movement toward equality of power in a relationship may be useful for preventing and reducing painful jealousy.

Within a couple, the less powerful partner is more likely to become jealous. Insofar as women are less powerful than men, they are likely to appear more jealous. The societal trend in the direction of greater gender equality probably has the effect of reducing jealousy generally, especially among women. This reduction in women's jealousy is reflected in higher divorce rates (which leveled off around 1980) and higher rates of unmarried mothers (which are still going up). Since the 1960s, women have been less likely than their mothers zealously and jealously to protect their relationships with men, less likely to forgive betrayal, less likely to tolerate excessive possessiveness and the double standard, and less likely to sacrifice for the sake of the marriage.

TEN DANGEROUS MISCONCEPTIONS ABOUT JEALOUSY

Much of what sociology reveals about jealousy contrasts sharply with American conventional wisdom and popular psychology since about 1970. It is useful to summarize the sociological findings so as to challenge *ten dangerous misconceptions about jealousy* that are widespread in late 20th century American culture. These misunderstandings threaten the happiness and well-being of those who hold them, and thus have implications for education, marriage, law, psychotherapy, and self-understanding — as well as for further development of the sociology of emotions. What we feel (emotions) depends on what we know (beliefs).

The Social Usefulness of Jealousy

1. It is widely believed that jealousy is a useless emotion. In fact, jealousy often is useful to individuals, to couples, to community and society. The largely overlooked social function of jealousy is the protection of love, marriage, and other valued relationships. By protecting marriage, jealousy contributes to solidarity and social order (Davis, 1936). Jealousy may be defined as a protective reaction to a perceived threat (especially adultery) to a valued relationship (especially marriage or a relationship that leads to marriage) or to its quality (Clanton 1981:260).

The usefulness of jealousy is easily overlooked in our culture because of the readiness to assume that jealousy is always a bad thing and that the jealous person is overly sensitive and probably suffering from "low self-esteem." The sexual revolution of the 1960s and 1970s encouraged the negative view of jealousy that now prevails in the United States. Most Americans today use the word "jealousy" only to describe inappropriate and unconstructive jealousy. Thus we are left with no word for constructive behavior that protects a marriage or other love relationship from a real threat.   We find it difficult to conceive of constructive jealousy.

The usefulness of appropriate and constructive jealousy is revealed in this example: A husband and wife are driving home from a party, and she says, "You spent a long time talking with Matilda tonight.   She's very pretty and I felt left out."   He says, "I'm sorry.   I didn't mean to neglect you.   Next time that happens, you should just come over and join the conversation."   She says, "Thank you, darling."   They hold hands the rest of the way home.   Their marriage is strengthened by this experience.   And the preservation of marriage contributes to the stability of the community and society.

If, in the preceding example, the wife had shrilly accused the husband of infidelity and the husband had responded with angry demands for his "personal space" and suggestions that his wife's jealousy is caused by her "low self-esteem," they may have fallen into a more general conflict.   Their marriage would be weakened by this experience.   Perhaps they would divorce.   And a high divorce rate weakens social solidarity.

Jealousy and Envy

2.   It is widely believed that jealousy and envy are the same emotion.   In fact, although jealousy and envy often are mixed together in real life, they are responses to quite different situations. Jealousy always involves an attempt to protect a valued relationship (especially marriage) from a perceived threat (especially adultery).   Envy is resentment toward someone who has some desirable object or quality that one does not have and cannot get.   Envy, in other words, is hostility toward superiors, a negative feeling toward someone who is better off.   Envy is *not* the wish for the object or advantage that provoked the envy.   Rather, envy is the much darker wish that the superior would *lose* the object or advantage.   Envy is the pleasure, the malicious joy, that is felt when the superior fails or suffers.   The envious person

rarely resorts to violence against the superior and rarely seeks to seize or to win the desired object. The most common expression of envy is gossip. Recall, for example, the deprecating labels your high school peers used to describe the student with the best grades ("teacher's pet" and worse), the best football player ("dumb jock"), and the beauty queen ("stuck up"). Any quality or achievement that provokes admiration also is likely to provoke some envy. These include wealth, status, power, fame, success, talent, good grades, good looks, and popularity.

Because envy is a completely negative emotion, it usually is repressed, denied, disguised, and relabeled. To admit straightforwardly to envy is to declare oneself to be inferior to another and hostile toward that person (or class of persons) because of that inferiority. Envy often is mislabeled as "jealousy," thus making it less likely that we shall understand it and deal with it constructively. Conversely, jealousy is almost never mislabeled as "envy." This suggests that envy is more negative, more shameful, and more deeply repressed than jealousy.

Although a full account of envy is beyond the scope of this paper, brief discussion of some social aspects of envy may be useful for illustrating the sociological approach to emotions and demonstrating the importance of the meso- and macro-level social forces that are omitted from many discussions of emotions. Here I draw upon and extend the work of Scheler (1912/1961), Schoeck (1966/1970), Foster (1972), and Lyman (1978).

Envy, paradoxically, both threatens and helps to preserve social order. Envy threatens social order by stimulating interpersonal hostility that might lead to conflict, by inhibiting innovation and accumulation of wealth that are necessary for prosperity, and by stirring the have-nots to revolution that overthrows the existing order. Thus, the management of envy is a universal social problem. All societies prohibit envy; all moral systems condemn it. In hunting and gathering societies, everyone remains poor because of the fear of being envied. In agricultural and industrial societies, various rationalizations of inequality are employed to reduce envy. The Greeks explained success in terms of luck; the Roman Catholics, in terms of the will of God; the Protestants, in terms of the work ethic. All three rationalizations are commonly used to reduce envy in contemporary American society.

The management of envy is inescapably political. Conservatives and reactionaries (defenders of capitalism) see inequality as inevitable and prescribe class segregation, emulation, and rationalizations of inequality in order to reduce envy. For the right, the chief concern is that the rich and talented should not be held back by the envy of the poor masses. Progressives and democratic socialists (critics of capitalism) see inequality as resulting from unfairness and prescribe progressive taxation in order to reduce the inequality that is at the root of envy. For the left, the chief concern is that the envy of the have-nots should be sufficient to fuel demand for reform. While the right seeks to ignore, conceal, or explain away some of the differences that provoke envy, the left seeks to publicize and ultimately to reduce those differences.

Envy also helps to preserve social order. The social usefulness of envy lies primarily in its contribution to social control. Fear of being envied is one motive for conformity to necessary norms: We conform rather than be hated for our non-conformity by those who do conform. Fear of being envied protects private property: One motive for reporting a car thief is the envious feeling that "he has no more right to that car than I do." Fear of being envied encourages fairness: We are less likely to cheat or to take a favor from a judge because we know that we would be hated and perhaps reported to authorities by those who did not cheat or receive favors. Furthermore, some envy can be turned into emulation of those who are more successful; this, presumably, would increase productivity, thus benefitting both the individual and the group. In all but a few cases, however, it is not possible for the non-rich to become rich simply by "working harder." By exaggerating the payoff for hard work, the capitalist prescription that envy be converted into emulation helps to rationalize and preserve existing inequalities.

Envy, then, is double-edged. It is necessary to society because it inhibits dangerous deviance, but it also threatens society, especially by inhibiting innovation and productivity. The goal of envy-management in society is that there should be enough envy to discourage the violation of important norms but no so much envy as to hold back the most talented individuals.

Learning to be Jealous

3. It is widely believed that jealousy is an instinctive biological reaction that humans share with lower animals. People often tell me about the jealousy of pets, suggesting thereby that human jealousy is all or mostly "instinctive." In fact, adult jealousy in humans is learned as other things are learned — through modeling, practice, and feedback. Jealousy is learned as individuals internalize marriage rules, the adultery taboo, and strategies for the protection of threatened relationships. Because these arrangements vary across cultures, jealousy is learned differently in different times and places. Monogamous and polygamous cultures produce different patterns of jealousy. Extramarital sexual activities that provoke intense jealousy in most Americans may provoke little or no reported jealousy among the wife-lending Eskimos, the sexually permissive Todas, or the contemporary swingers — assuming that the ground rules of each culture or sub-culture were honored.

The Psychology of Jealousy

4. It is widely believed that jealousy is usually a personal problem, rooted in the inadequacies of the jealous individual. In fact, jealousy is usually a *relationship* problem. Its solution requires the involvement of both partners. The unit of analysis should be the couple, not the individual. Attention should be devoted to communication and negotiation. Most jealousy problems that require professional help call for couple therapy or marital counseling rather than individual psychotherapy (see Margolin, 1981). Furthermore, when an individual enters private psychotherapy because of relationship problems, divorce is a likely outcome — especially if the therapist also is divorced and remarried.

5. It is widely believed that all or most jealousy results from low self-esteem in the jealous individual. In fact, although low self-esteem can exacerbate jealousy, most jealousy results from an *imbalance of power* between the partners (Clanton, 1989). Thus, movement toward equality of power within a relationship may reduce the potential for jealousy.

Sociological analysis calls into question the popular tendency to explain most human failure and pain as caused by "low self-esteem" and treatable by "raising self-esteem." Such explanations are circular at best and misleading at worst (Clanton, 1989). If an experience of jealousy routinely causes low self-esteem, how can low self-esteem be the principal cause of jealousy? If an experience of jealousy reflects a relationship problem, how can the jealousy be reduced solely through the enlargement of the self-esteem of one individual? And how could one hope to increase self-esteem, if stuck in the low-power position in a marriage or romantic relationship? In fact, low power is often the cause of low self-esteem. As Durkheim noted, whenever a social fact is explained in terms of a psychological fact, we can be certain the explanation is false. (For a thoughtful sociological analysis of popular self-help movements, see Irvine, 1995.)

6. It is widely believed that women are more jealous than men. In fact, there is no consistent evidence to indicate that either gender is more jealous than the other (Clanton and Smith, 1986). Women, however, are more willing to acknowledge jealousy (and to blame themselves for the problem) while men are more likely to deny or relabel jealousy (and to blame the woman and others for the problem). Ironically, one of the few things on which men and women apparently agree is that the woman is to blame for most relationship problems.

Women's greater willingness to admit to jealousy is consistent with women's greater willingness to talk honestly about feelings and to take responsibility for how a relationship is going. Kosins (1983) found that women's slightly higher scores on a measure of jealousy were roughly proportional to women's lower scores on a measure of social desirability. In other words, women appear slightly more jealous because men are more likely to give answers that make themselves look good.

7. It is widely believed that adult jealousy is rooted in disrupted attachment history and the emotional conflicts of the early years. In fact, adult jealousy shows no strong association with early conflicts (Clanton and Kosins, 1991). Experiences of romantic love and loss of love in adolescence and young adulthood probably are more important than early childhood experiences in contributing to a propensity toward adult jealousy.

8. It is widely believed that jealousy is associated with neurosis or mental illness. In fact, a comparison of patients in a mental hospital, psychotherapy outpatients, and a control group (neither hospitalized nor in therapy) found no significant differences in the amount and intensity of jealousy (Clanton and Kosins, 1991). The view of jealousy as rooted simply in a psychological weakness of the jealous person is a reflection of the negative view of jealousy that emerged at the time of the sexual revolution.

Managing Jealousy

9. It is widely believed that jealousy should be repressed and denied. Indeed, repression and denial of negative emotions is characteristic of American, English, and other Northern European Protestant cultures. In fact, jealousy should be acknowledged, expressed, and analyzed in the context of negotiations aimed at improving relationship quality. The denial of jealousy is no guarantee that it is absent.

10. It is widely believed that an individual's goal should be the complete eradication of jealousy. When I ask my students how much jealousy they want to have at the end of the course, they all say *None*. In fact, one's goal ought to be *appropriate* jealousy, *constructively* expressed. We should attempt to minimize inappropriate jealousy and destructive expressions of jealousy. But the complete absence of jealousy sometimes reflects indifference. As Kris Kristofferson warned, sometimes "freedom's just another word for nothing left to lose."

SOCIOLOGY AND PSYCHOLOGY

Sociological analysis challenges some elements of the psychological view of jealousy that prevails in the "therapeutic culture" in which we live. Sociological consideration of jealousy and other emotions draws attention to the influence of society and culture on the private emotions of individuals and to the hidden social usefulness of emotions. The sociological view tends to de-stigmatize the jealous individual and to break the cycle of blaming the victim, which is encouraged by the widespread but erroneous view that jealousy is caused primarily by the personal inadequacies (especially the low self-esteem) of the jealous person. Sociology should be included in the education of psychotherapists as an antidote to the tendency of clinicians to focus too narrowly on the early experiences and the inner life of the individual and on the dysfunctional aspects of jealousy and other emotions.

Sociological analysis shows that jealousy and other emotions are shaped by social processes and social forces. Micro-sociology reveals that jealousy is learned as other things are learned, through modeling, practice, and feedback. Jealousy reflects the life experience of the individual. Meso-sociology reveals that jealousy is socially useful, indeed, indispensable to social order. Jealousy reflects the institution of marriage and the prohibition of adultery. Macro-sociology reveals that jealousy is shaped by society and culture. Jealousy reflects the history and the values of a people — and the relevant values vary from time to time and place to place.

This analysis of jealousy is intended to demonstrate the usefulness of the sociology of emotions and to provide a framework for the sociological study of other emotions, feelings, and attitudes. The sociology of emotions is the sociology of the subjective and so, inescapably, overlaps with the sociology of knowledge and the sociology of values. As Durkheim (1897/1951) sought to demonstrate the power of sociology by explaining the solitary act of suicide in terms of the influence of group membership, I have followed Davis (1936) in seeking to demonstrate the power of sociology by explaining the private emotion of jealousy in terms of the influence of social learning, social institutions, society and culture.

APPENDIX: THE RELATIONSHIP ASSESSMENT SCALE

Instructions: Partners respond separately and without consultation — and before reading any of the information below the questions. Answer the questions with one of these three responses: (a) self, (b) partner, or (c) equal.

  1. Who has more professional prestige?
  2. Who earns the higher income?
  3. Who loves the other more?
  4. Who would find a new partner quicker if you broke up?
  5. Who gets more attention from persons of the other gender?
  6. Who desires sex with the other more?
  7. Who is more verbal, more articulate, more persuasive?
  8. Who is more likely to leave the relationship?
  9. Who has more close friends of the same gender?
  10. (a) If you have children: Who is closer to your children?
       (b) If you do not have children: Who wants children more?

Scoring: These questions provide a rough measure of power differences in love relationships such as dating, cohabitation, engagement, and marriage. In each case, the person named has more power than the other except for questions 3, 6, and 10 (b). The person thus designated as more powerful on more questions has more total power than the other. In most relationships, one partner will be more powerful in some areas and the other, in others. A common pattern in some troubled relationships is that the man is more powerful in the areas probed by questions 1, 2, 3, 4, 5, 7, and 8, while the woman has more power in the areas assessed by questions 6, 9, and 10 — with the result that the woman may withhold sex or use her relationship with the children in order to gain other kinds of power.

Further exercises: After you have looked at the scores resulting from your own answers, you may wish to compare your responses with those of your partner and to discuss differences of perception. It also may be useful to construct a *joint* assessment of the power balance in your relationship by including only those answers on which you agreed.

Jealousy and power: Jealousy and other relationship problems often are rooted *not* in the low self-esteem of an individual (a psychological fact) but rather in an *imbalance of power* in the *relationship* (a social fact). Low self-esteem may exacerbate jealousy, but it is not the cause of all jealousy as is commonly believed.   Furthermore, low self-esteem often is caused by low power.   To understand and manage jealousy, we must shift the focus away from the low self-esteem of the jealous individual (as in most psychotherapy) and give more attention to power differences *between* the partners (as in marriage counseling or relationship therapy).

Bibliography

Adler, Alfred. *Understanding Human Nature*. London: George Allen and Unwin, Ltd., 1928.

Adler, Mortimer J., ed. *The Great Ideas: A Syntopicon of Great Books of the Western World. Vol. 1.* Chicago: Encylopaedia Britannica, 1952.

Ankles, Thomas M. *A Study of Jealousy as Differentiated from Envy.* Boston: Bruce Humphries, 1939.

Arnold, Magda B. *Emotion and Personality: Vol. 1. Psychological Aspects.* New York: Columbia University Press, 1960.

Averill, James R. "Autonomic Response Patterns during Sadness and Mirth." *Psychophysiology* 5 (1969): 299-414.

Ax, A. F. "The Physiological Differentiation between Fear and Anger in Humans." *Psychosomatic Medicine* 15 (1953): 433-442.

Bach, George R., and Wyden, Peter. *The Intimate Enemy: How to Fight Fair in Love and Marriage.* New York: Avon, 1970 (c. 1968).

Balint, Michael, et al. *Focal Psychotherapy: An Example of Applied Psychoanalysis.* Philadelphia: Lippincott, 1972.

Beauvoir, Simone de. "The Question of Fidelity." *Harper's Magazine* 219 (November 1964).

Beecher, M., and Beecher, W. *The Mark of Cain: An Anatomy of Jealousy.* New York: Harper and Row, 1971.

Berger, Bennett M. *The Survival of a Counterculture.* Berkeley: University of California Press, 1981.

Berger, Brigitte, and Berger, Peter L. *The War Over the Family: Capturing the Middle Ground.* New York: Anchor/Doubleday, 1984.

Berger, Peter L., and Luckmann, Thomas. *The Social Construction of Reality: A Treatise in the Sociology of Knowledge.* Garden City, NY: Anchor/Doubleday, 1966.

Bernard, Jessie. "Infidelity: A Moral or Social Question." In J. H. Masserman, ed. *Science and Psychoanalysis.* Vol. 16. New York: Grune and Stratton, 1969, 99-126. Reprinted in Smith and Smith, eds. *Beyond Monogamy,* 1974.

_____. "No News, but New Ideas." In Paul Bohannan, ed. *Divorce and After.* New York: Doubleday, 1970, 3-28.

_____. "Jealousy in Marriage." *Medical Aspects of Human Sexuality* 5(1971): 200-215.

_____. *The Future of Marriage.* New York: Bantam, 1973 (c. 1972).

Bettleheim, Bruno. *Children of the Dream.* New York: Macmillan, 1969.

Blau, Peter M. *Exchange and Power in Social Life.* New York: John Wiley and Sons, 1967.

Bohm, Ewald. "Is Jealousy Controllable?" *International Journal of Sexology* (February 1952).

_____. "Jealousy." In Albert Ellis and Albert Abarbanel, eds. *Encyclopedia of Sexual Behavior.* New York: Hawthorne Books, 1967: 567-574.

Borel, J. *Les Psychoses Passionelles.* Paris, 1952.

Bowlby, J. *Attachment and Loss: Vol. 1. Attachment.* New York: Basic Books, 1969.

_____. *Attachment and Loss: Vol. 2. Separation.* New York: Basic Books, 1973.

_____. *The Making and Breaking of Affectional Bonds.* London: Tavistock, 1979.

_____. *Attachment and Loss: Vol. 3. Loss.* New York: Basic Books, 1980.

Briffault, Robert. *The Mothers: A Study of the Origins of Sentiments and Institutions.* Vol. 2. New York: Macmillan, 1927.

Bringle, Robert G. "Conceptualizing Jealousy as a Disposition." *Alternative Lifestyles* 4(1981): 3, 274-290.

_____. *Preliminary Report on the Revised Self-Report Jealousy Scale.* Unpublished manuscript, Indiana University-Purdue University at Indianapolis, 1982.

Bringle, Robert G., and Williams, L. J. "Parental-offspring Similarity on Jealousy and Related Personality Dimensions." *Motivation and Emotion* 3(1979): 265-286.

Brown, Barbara B. *New Mind, New Body: Bio-Feedback: New Directions for the Mind.* New York: Harper & Row, 1974.

Buunk, Bram, and Bringle, Robert G. "Jealousy in Love Relationships." In Steve Duck and Daniel Perlman, eds. *Marital Relationships.* Beverly Hills, CA: Sage, 1986.

Byrne, Don. "Attitudes and Attraction." In Leonard Berkowitz, ed. *Advances in Experimental Social Psychology* 4(1969): 35-89.

Cannon, W. B. *Bodily Changes in Pain, Hunger, Fear, and Rage.* 2nd ed. New York: Appleton, 1929.

Casler, L. "This Thing Called Love is Pathological." *Psychology Today* (December 1969): 18-20, 74-76.

Cattell, R. B. *A Guide to Mental Testing* (3rd ed.). London: University of London Press, 1953.

Chekhov, Anton P. *Uncle Vanya.* in *Chekhov: The Major Plays.* New York: Signet Classic, 1964.

Clanton, Gordon. "Frontiers of Jealousy Research." *Alternative Lifestyles* 4(1981): 3, 259-273. (In this book, Appendix I.)

_____. "Social Forces and the Changing Family." In Lester A. Kirkendall and Arthur E. Gravatt, eds. *Marriage and Family in the Year 2020.* Buffalo, NY: Prometheus Press, 1984.

_____. "Love, Jealousy, and Envy: A Course in the Sociology of Emotions." *ASA Teaching Newsletter* 10(1985): 4.

_____. "Teaching Sociology of Emotions." *Sociology of Emotions Newsletter* 1(1986):1, p. 4.

_____. "A Historical Sociology of Sex and Love." *Teaching Sociology* 15(1987): 307-311.

_____. "Jealousy in American Culture, 1945-1985: Reflections from Popular Culture." In David D. Franks and E. Doyle McCarthy, eds. *The Sociology of Emotions* (pp. 179-193). Greenwich, CT: JAI Press, 1989. (In this book, Appendix II.)

_____. "A Sociology of Jealousy." *International Journal of Sociology and Social Policy* 16(1996): 9/10, 171-189. (In this book, Appendix IV.)

Clanton, Gordon, and Downing, Chris, eds. *Face to Face to Face: An Experiment in Intimacy.* New York: Dutton, 1975. Paperback, New York: Ballantine, 1976.

Clanton, Gordon, and David J. Kosins. "Developmental Correlates of Jealousy." In Peter Salovey, ed. *The Psychology of Jealousy and Envy.* New York: Guilford Press, 1991. (In this book, Appendix III.)

Clanton, Gordon, and Smith, Lynn G., eds. *Jealousy.* Englewood Cliffs, NJ: Prentice-Hall, 1977.

_____. *Jealousy.* 2nd ed. Lanham, MD: University Press of America, 1986.

Comfort, Alex. "Sexuality in a Zero Growth Society." In Smith and Smith, eds. *Beyond Monogamy,* 1974.

Constantine, Larry. "Personal Growth in Multiperson Marriages." *Radical Therapist* 2(1971): 1.

Constantine, Larry L., and Constantine, Joan M. *Group Marriage: A Study of Contemporary Multilateral Marriage.* New York: Macmillan, 1973.

Corzine, William L. "The Phenomenon of Jealousy: A Theoretical and Empirical Analysis." Unpublished Ph.D. dissertation, United States International University, San Diego, 1974.

Darwin, Charles. *Descent of Man.* Vol. 2. London: 1888.

_____. *The Expression of the Emotions in Man and Animals.* Chicago: University of Chicago Press, 1965.

Davis, Kingsley. "Jealousy and Sexual Property." *Social Forces* 14 (1936): 395-405. (In this book, Chapter 11.)

Davitz, J. R. *The Language of Emotions.* New York: Academic Press, 1969.

Dell, Floyd. *Love in Greenwich Village.* New York: George H. Doran, 1926.

Dion, K. L., and Dion, K. K. "Correlates of Romantic Love." *Journal of Consulting and Clinical Psychology* 41(1973): 1, 51-56.

Duffy, E. *Activation and Behavior.* New York: Wiley, 1962.

Duhl, F. I., Kantor, D., and Duhl, B. S. "Learning, Space, and Action in Family Therapy: A Primer of Sculpture." In D. A. Bloch, ed. *Techniques of Family Psychotherapy: A Primer.* New York: Grune & Stratton, 1974.

Durkheim, Emile. *Suicide: A Study in Sociology.* Glencoe, IL: Free Press of Glencoe, 1951 (c. 1897).

Durrell, L. *Justine.* New York: Pocket Books, 1957.

East, N. *Society and the Criminal.* London: H.M.S.O., 1949, 53-280.

Edwards, A. L. *The Social Desirability Variable in Personality Assessment Research.* New York: Dryden Press, 1957.

Ellis, Albert. *The American Sexual Tragedy*. New York: Grove Press, 1962 (1st ed. c. 1954).

Ellis, Carolyn, and Weinstein, Eugene. "Jealousy and the Social Psychology of Emotional Experience." *Journal of Personal and Social Relationships* 3(1985): 3.

Ellis, Havelock. *Studies in the Psychology of Sex*. New York: Random House, 1936.

Erikson, Erik H. *Childhood and Society*. 2nd ed. New York: W. W. Norton, 1963.

Farrell, Warren. *The Liberated Man*. New York: Bantam, 1974.

Fei, Jack, and Berscheid, Ellen. "Perceived Dependency and Insecurity in Heterosexual Relationships." Unpublished manuscript, 1976.

Fenichel, Otto. *The Psychoanalytic Theory of Neurosis*. London: Routledge and Kegan Paul, 1955.

Ford, Clellan, S., and Beach, Frank A. *Patterns of Sexual Behavior*. New York: Harper & Row, 1951.

Forel, A. *Die Sexuelle Frage*. Munchen: Ernst Reinhardt, 1931.

Foster, George M. "The Anatomy of Envy: A Study in Symbolic Behavior." *Current Anthropology* 13 (1972): 2, 165-186.

Foster, S. "A Study of the Personality Makeup and Social Setting of Fifty Jealous Children." *Mental Hygiene* 10(1927): 61-69.

Francoeur, Anna K., and Francoeur, Robert T. "A Biology of Jealousy: Variety vs. Territory?" *Hot and Cool Sex: Cultures in Conflict*. New York: Harcourt Brace, Jovanovich, 1974.

Frazer, James George. *Totemism and Exogamy*. London: Dawsons of Pall Mall, 1968 (c. 1910).

French, J. R. P., Jr., and Raven, B. "The Bases of Social Power." In D. Cartwright, ed. *Studies in Social Power*. Ann Arbor, MI: Institute for Social Research, 1959, 150-157.

Freud, Sigmund. "Some Neurotic Mechanisms in Jealousy, Paranoia and Homosexuality" (1922). In J. Strachey, ed. and trans. *The Standard Edition of the Complete Psychological Works of Sigmund Freud* (Vol. 18, pp. 221-232). London: Hogarth Press, 1955.

_____. "Certain Neurotic Mechanisms in Jealousy, Paranoia and Homosexuality" (1922). In *Collected Papers*. Vol. 2. New York: Basic Books, 1959. Reprinted in Philip Rieff, ed. *Sexuality and the Psychology of Love*. New York: Collier, 1963.

Funkenstein, D. H., King, S. H., and Drolette, M. E. *Mastery of Stress*. Cambridge, MA: Harvard University Press, 1957.

Gagnon, John H. *Human Sexualities.* Glenview, IL: Scott-Foresman, 1977.

Gesell, Arnold L. "Jealousy." *The American Journal of Psychology* XVII (1906): 4, 437-496.

Gilmartin, Brian G. "Jealousy among the Swingers." In Gordon Clanton and Lynn G. Smith, eds. *Jealousy.* Englewood Cliffs, NJ: Prentice-Hall, 1977. (In this book, Chapter 14.)

Giradoux, J. *Amphitryon 38.* Adapt. S. N. Behrman. New York: Random House, 1938.

Goffman, Erving. "Embarrassment and Social Organization." In his *Interaction Ritual.* Garden City, NY: Doubleday, 1967.

Goode, William J. *World Revolution and Family Patterns.* New York: Free Press, 1963.

Gordon, Thomas. *Parent Effectiveness Training.* New York: Peter H. Wyden, 1970.

Gorer, Geoffrey. *Sex and Marriage in England Today.* New York: Humanities Press, 1971.

Gottschalk, Helmuth. *Skinsygens Problemer (Problems of Jealousy).* Copenhagen: Fremad, 1936.

Hansen, Gary L. "Perceived Threats and Marital Jealousy." *Social Psychology Quarterly* 48(1985): 3, 262-268.

Hatfield, Tom. *Sandstone Experience.* New York: Crown, 1975.

Hochschild, Arlie Russell. *The Managed Heart: Commercialization of Human Feeling.* Berkeley: University of California Press, 1983.

Hohmann, G. W. "The Effect of Dysfunctions of the Autonomic Nervous System on Experienced Feelings and Emotions." Paper read at Conference on Emotions and Feelings at New School for Social Research, New York, 1962.

Homans, George. *Social Behavior: Its Elementary Forms.* New York: Harcourt Brace & World, 1961.

Hunt, Morton, M. *The Natural History of Love.* New York: Grove Press, 1959.

Hupka, Ralph B. "Cultural Determinants of Jealousy." *Alternative Lifestyles* 4(1981): 3, 310-356.

Hupka, Ralph B., and Bachelor, B. "Validation of a Scale to Measure Romantic Jealousy." Paper presented at the meeting of the Western Psychological Association, San Diego, 1979.

Hupka, Ralph B., and Rusch, P. A. "Development and Validation of a Scale to Measure Romantic Jealousy." Paper presented at the meeting of the Western Psychological Association, Seattle, 1977.

Irvine, Leslie J. "Codependency and Recovery: Gender, Self, and Emotions in Popular Self-Help." *Symbolic Interaction* 18(1995): 2, 145-163.

James, William. *Psychology*. New York: Dover, 1951.

_____. *The Principles of Psychology*. Chicago: Encyclopaedia Britannica, 1952.

Jones, Ernest. "Jealousy." *Revue Francaise de Psychanalyse*. Tome III (1929).

Jourard, Sidney M. *The Transparent Self*. Princeton, NJ: Van Nostrand, 1964.

Kamiya, Joe, et al., eds. *Biofeedback and Self-Control*. Chicago: Aldine, 1971.

Kammeyer, Kenneth C. W., ed. *Confronting the Issues: Sex Roles, Marriage and the Family*. Boston: Allyn and Bacon, 1975.

Kardiner, Abraham.*The Individual and His Society*. New York: Columbia University Press, 1939.

Kessler, R. P., and Pottharst, K. "An Instrument for Measuring Affectional Bonding: The Attachment History Questionnaire." Unpublished manuscript, California School for Professional Psychology, Los Angeles, 1982.

Kinkade, Kathleen. *A Walden Two Experiment: The First Five Years of Twin Oaks Community*. New York: William Morris, 1972.

Kinsey, Alfred C., et al. *Sexual Behavior in the Human Male*. Philadelphia: W. B. Saunders, 1948.

_____. *Sexual Behavior in the Human Female*. Philadelphia: W. B. Saunders, 1953.

Klein, M., and Riviere, J. *Love, Hate, and Repatriation*. London: Hogarth Press, 1953.

Kosins, David J. *Developmental Correlates of Sexual Jealousy*. Doctoral dissertation, California School for Professional Psychology, San Diego, 1983.

Lacey, J. I. "Somatic Response Patterning and Stress: Some Revisions of Activation Theory." In M. H. Appley and R. Trumbull, eds. *Psychological Stress*. New York: Appleton, 1967.

Lagache, D. *La Jalousie Amoureuse*. Bibliotheque de Philosophie Contemporaine. Vols. I & II. Paris: Presses Universitaires de France, 1947.

Langfeldt, G. "The Erotic Jealousy Syndrome: A Clinical Study." *Acta Psychiatrica et Neurologica Scandinavica*. Supplementum 151(1961): 36, 7-68.

La Rochefoucauld, F. *Maximes*. No. 324. 1665.

Lazarus, R. S., Averill, J. R., and Opton, E. M. Jr. "Towards a Cognitive Theory of Emotion." In Magda Arnold, ed. *Feelings and Emotions*. New York: Academic Press, 1970, 207-232.

Lévi-Strauss, Claude. *Elementary Structures of Kinship*. Boston: Beacon Press, 1969.

Lewin, Kurt. "The Background of Conflict in Marriage" (1940). In his *Resolving Social Conflicts: Selected Papers on Group Dynamics*. New York: Harper & Row, 1948.

Libby, Roger, and Whitehurst, Robert N., eds. *Marriage and Alternatives*. Glenview, IL: Scott, Foresman, 1977.

Lifton, Robert J. *History and Human Survival*. New York: Random House, 1969.

Lindsley, D. B. "Emotions and the Electroencephalogram." In M. R. Reymert, ed. *Feelings and Emotions: The Mooseheart Symposium*. New York: McGraw-Hill, 1950.

Lott, A., and Lott, B. "The Power of Liking: Consequences of Interpersonal Attitudes Derived from a Liberalized View of Secondary Reinforcement." In Leonard Berkowitz, ed. *Advances in Experimental Social Psychology* 6 (1972): 109-148.

Lyman, Stanford M. *The Seven Deadly Sins: Society and Evil*. New York: St. Martin's Press, 1978.

Mace, David R. "Two Faces of Jealousy." *McCall's* (May 1962).

Mairet, A., *La Jalousie: Etude Psychophysiologique, Clinique et Medico Legale*. Montpelier, 1908.

Malinowski, Bronislaw. *The Sexual Life of Savages*. New York: Harcourt, Brace, 1929.

_____. *Crime and Custom in Savage Society*. London: Paul, Trench, Trubner, 1932.

Margolin, Gayla. "A Behavioral-Systems Approach to the Treatment of Jealousy." *Clinical Psychology Review* 1(1981): 469-487.

Maslow, Abraham H. *Toward a Psychology of Being*. 2nd ed. New York: Van Nostrand Reinhold, 1968.

_____. *Motivation and Personality*. New York: Harper & Row, 1954 (2nd ed. 1970).

Maynard, Joyce. "The Liberation of Total Woman." *New York Times Magazine* 28 September, 1975: 9ff.

McCarthy, John D., and Hoge, Dean R. "The Dynamics of Self-esteem and Delinquency." *American Journal of Sociology* 90(1984): 2, 396-410.

Mead, Margaret. "Jealousy: Primitive and Civilised." In Samuel Schmalhausen and V. F. Calverton, eds., *Woman's Coming of Age.* New York: Liveright, 1931: 35-48. (In this book, Chapter 10.)

Mendelsohn R. "Can the American Family Survive?" *St. Paul Pioneer Press* 8 December, 1975: 9.

Mills, C. Wright. *The Sociological Imagination.* New York: Grove Press, 1959.

Mitchell, Juliet. *Psychoanalysis and Feminism.* New York: Pantheon, 1974.

Mowat, R. R. *Morbid Jealousy and Murder: A Psychiatric Study of Morbidly Jealous Murderers at Broadmoor.* London: Tavistock Publications, 1966.

Myers, Lonny, and Leggitt, Hunter. *Adultery and Other Private Matters: Your Right to Personal Freedom in Marriage.* Chicago: Nelson-Hall, 1975.

O'Neill, Nena, and O'Neill, George. *Open Marriage: A New Lifestyle for Couples.* New York: M. Evans, 1972.

Orage, Alfred R. *On Love.* New York: Weiser, n.d.

Paige, Paul, and others. "Open Relationships: Process and Problems in Counseling and Workshops." Presentation to the California Association of Marriage and Family Counselors, Anaheim, California, October 1975.

Pines, Ayala M. *Romantic Jealousy: Understanding and Conquering the Shadow of Love.* New York: St. Martin's Press, 1992.

Plutchik, R. "Emotions, Evolution, and Adaptive Processes." In Magda Arnold, ed. *Feelings and Emotions.* New York: Academic Press, 1970, 3-24.

Podolsky, Edward. *The Jealous Child.* New York: Philosophical Library, 1954.

Ramey, James W. *Intimate Friendships.* Englewood Cliffs, NJ: Prentice-Hall, 1975.

Reik, Theodor. *A Psychologist Looks at Love.* New York: Lancer Books, 1944.

_____. *Psychology of Sex Relations.* New York: Rinehart, 1946 (c. 1945).

_____. *Of Love and Lust.* New York: Farrar, Straus and Co., 1949.

Rimmer, Robert H. *The Harrad Experiment.* New York: Bantam, 1966.

_____. *Proposition 31.* New York: New American Library, 1968.

_____. *Adventures in Loving.* New York: New American Library, 1973.

Riviere, Joan. "Jealousy as a Mechanism of Defense." *International Journal of Psychoanalysis* 13 (1932): 414-424.

Rosmarin, D. M., Chambless, D. L., and LaPointe, K. "The Survey of Interpersonal Relations: An Inventory for the Measurement of Jealousy." Unpublished manuscript, University of Georgia, 1979.

Ross, B. M. "Some Traits Associated with Sibling Jealousy in Problem Children." *Smith College Studies in Social Work* 1(1931): 364-376.

Rubin, Zick. "Measurement of Romantic Love." *Journal of Personality and Social Psychology* 16(1970): 2, 265-273.

Russell, Bertrand. *On Education.* London: George Allen & Unwin, 1926.

_____. *Marriage and Morals.* London: George Allen & Unwin, 1929.

Sapirstein, M. R. *Emotional Security.* New York: Crown Press, 1948.

Schachter, Stanley. "The Interaction of Cognitive and Physiological Determinants of Emotional State." In Leonard Berkowitz, ed. *Advances in Experimental Social Psychology.* Vol. 1. New York: Academic Press, 1964, 49-80.

_____, and Wheeler, L. "Epinephrine, Chlorpromazine, and Amusement." *Journal of Abnormal and Social Psychology* 65 (1962): 121-128.

Schapera, I. *Married Life in an African Tribe.* London: Faber and Faber, 1939.

Schmideberg, M. "Some Aspects of Jealousy and Feeling Hurt." *Psychoanalytic Review* 40(1953): 1-16.

Schoeck, Helmut. *Envy: A Theory of Social Behavior.* New York: Harcourt, Brace and World, 1970 (German edition, 1966).

Schoenfeld, Eugene. *Jealousy: Taming the Green-Eyed Monster.* New York: Holt, Rinehart and Winston, 1979.

Secades, Eladio. "Green-eyed Monster." In *Américas* 9 (February 1957).

Seidenberg, Robert. "Fidelity and Jealousy: Socio-Cultural Considerations." *Psychoanalytic Review* 54 (Winter 1967): 583-608. (In this book, Chapter 7.)

Sewall, M. "Some Causes of Jealousy in Young Children." *Smith College Studies in Social Work* 1(1930): 6-22.

Sheehy, Gail. *Passages: Predictable Crises of Adult Life.* New York: Dutton, 1976.

Shettel-Neuber, Joyce, Bryson, Jeff B., and Young, Leanne E. "Physical Attractiveness of the 'Other Person' and Jealousy." *Personality and Social Psychology Bulletin* 4(1978): 612-615.

Simmel, Georg. *Conflict* and *The Web of Group-Affiliations.* Tr. by Kurt H. Wolff and Reinhard Bendix. Glencoe, IL: Free Press, 1955.

Simpson, George. *People in Families: Sociology, Psychoanalysis, and the American Family.* New York: World, 1966 (c. 1960).

Skolnick, Arlene. *The Intimate Environment.* Boston: Little, Brown, 1973.

Slater, Philip E. *The Pursuit of Loneliness.* Boston: Beacon Press, 1970.
_____. *Earthwalk.* New York: Bantam, 1975 (c. 1974).

Smith, James R. and Smith, Lynn G., eds. *Beyond Monogamy: Recent Studies of Sexual Alternatives in Marriage.* Baltimore: Johns Hopkins University Press, 1974.

Smith, Lynn G. "Jealousy and its Alternatives." In Anne Kent Rush, *Getting Clear: Body Work for Women.* New York: Random House, 1973: 189-203.

Sokoloff, Boris, *Jealousy: A Psychiatric Study.* New York: Howell, Soskin, 1947.

Stein, Peter. *Single.* Englewood Cliffs, NJ: Prentice-Hall, 1976.

Stekel, Wilhelm. "Jealousy." In A. Forbath, ed. *Love and Marriage.* New York: Liveright, 1938.

Stephens, William N. *The Family in Cross-Cultural Perspective.* New York: Holt, 1963.

Swidler, Ann. "Love and Adulthood in American Culture." In Neil J. Smelser and Erik H. Erikson, eds. *Themes of Work and Love in Adulthood.* Cambridge, MA: Harvard University Press, 1980.

Thibaut, J.W., and Kelley, H. *The Social Psychology of Groups.* New York: John Wiley and Sons, 1959.

Thoits, Peggy A. "Coping, Social Support, and Psychological Outcomes: The Central Role of Emotion." In Phillip Shaver, ed. *Review of Personality and Social Psychology,* Vol. 5. Beverly Hills, CA: Sage, 1984.

Walster, Elaine. "Passionate Love." In B. Murstein, ed. *Theories of Attraction and Love.* New York: Springer, 1971, 85-99.
_____, and Berscheid, Ellen. "Adrenaline Makes the Heart Grow Fonder." *Psychology Today* (June 1971): 46-62.

Watson, John B. *Behaviorism.* Chicago: University of Chicago Press, 1924.

Watson, Jane Werner, Switzer, Robert E., and Hirschberg, J. Cotter. *Sometimes I'm Jealous.* New York: Golden Press, 1972.

Webster, M. *Webster's Seventh New Collegiate Dictionary.* Springfield, MA: G. and C. Merriam, 1963.

Weissman, Myrna M., and Klerman, Gerald L. "Sex Differences and the Epidemiology of Depression," forthcoming.

Westermarck, Edward. *The History of Human Marriage*, Vol. 1. New York: Allerton, 1922.

White, Gregory L., and Mullen, Paul E. *Jealousy: Theory, Research, and Clinical Strategies*. New York: Guilford Press, 1989.

Whitehurst, Robert N. "Violently Jealous Husbands," *Sexual Behavior* (July 1971).

_____, "Violence Potential in Extramarital Sexual Responses," *Journal of Marriage and the Family* 33 (1971): 4.

Winter, Sara. "Fighting Jealousy," *Issues in Radical Therapy* 3(1975): 4, 2-23.

Young, Michael, and Wilmot, Peter. *The Symmetrical Family*. New York: Pantheon, 1974.

Yorburg, Betty. *The Changing American Family*. New York: Columbia University Press, 1973.

Ziman, Edmund Allan. *Jealousy in Children: A Guide for Parents*. New York: A. A. Wyn, 1949.

Gordon Clanton, Ph.D., teaches sociology at San Diego State University. He previously taught at Rutgers University. He received his graduate education at the University of California at Berkeley. A pioneer in the sociology of emotions, he teaches a popular course on Love, Jealousy, and Envy. He also teaches Minority Group Relations, Social Organization, Classical Sociological Theory, Sociology of Religion, and Business Ethics. Dr. Clanton lectures and consults in a wide range of settings. He writes opinion pieces for newspapers. He has appeared on "Donahue," on the ABC-TV program "20/20," and on dozens of other radio and television programs.

Lynn G. Smith, Ph.D., is a social psychologist who began her research on jealousy while still a graduate student at the University of California at Berkeley. She has been a research associate at the Institute for Sex Research (the "Kinsey Institute") at Indiana University and co-director of the Self-Actualization Laboratory in Berkeley. She is co-editor of *Beyond Monogamy: Recent Studies of Sexual Alternatives in Marriage* (Johns Hopkins University Press, 1974). Her articles have appeared in scholarly journals and encyclopedias. Currently, she specializes in corporate planning and evaluation for non-profit organizations in San Francisco.